MICROSOFT AZURE FUNDAMENTALS AZ-900 - DUMPS - 5 PRACTICE EXAM WITH Q&A DETAILED EXPLANATION - A GUARANTEE FOR YOUR EXAM

100% PASSING RATE

Abstract

It contains 5 section of 55 questions and answers each with detailed explanation. Most of the questions are from real exam question from previous exams. Kindly practice all the Q&A and pass the exam in the first attempt. 100% Guarantee for your exam

G NXT

Question 1:

A company currently has the following unused resources as part of their subscription

- 10 user accounts in Azure AD

- 5 user groups in Azure AD

- 10 public IP address

- 10 network Interfaces

They want to reduce the costs for resources hosted in Azure

They decide to remove the user accounts from Azure AD

Would this fulfil the requirement?

- ○ Yes
- ○ **No** (Correct)

Explanation

Correct Answer – B

When you look at the pricing for Azure Active Directory, you can create 5,00,000 objects as part of the free version. These objects include both users and groups.

The Microsoft documentation mentions the following

	FREE	OFFICE 365 APPS	PREMIUM P1	PREMIUM P2
Core Identity and Access Management				
Directory Objects[1]	5,00,000 Object Limit	No Object Limit	No Object Limit	No Object Limit

For more information on the pricing for Azure Active Directory, please visit the below URL

https://azure.microsoft.com/en-in/pricing/details/active-directory/

Question 2:

A company currently has the following unused resources as part of their subscription

- 10 user accounts in Azure AD

- 5 user groups in Azure AD

- 10 public IP address

- 10 network Interfaces

They want to reduce the costs for resources hosted in Azure

They decide to remove the user groups from Azure AD

Would this fulfil the requirement?

- ○ Yes
- ○ No (Correct)

Explanation

Correct Answer – B

When you look at the pricing for Azure Active Directory, you can create 5,00,000 objects as part of the free version. These objects include both users and groups.

The Microsoft documentation mentions the following

	FREE	OFFICE 365 APPS	PREMIUM P1	PREMIUM P2
Core Identity and Access Management				
Directory Objects[1]	5,00,000 Object Limit	No Object Limit	No Object Limit	No Object Limit

For more information on the pricing for Azure Active Directory, please visit the below URL

https://azure.microsoft.com/en-in/pricing/details/active-directory/

Question 3:
Your company plans to purchase Azure.

The company's support policy states that the Azure environment must provide an option to access support engineers by phone or email.

You need to recommend which support plan meets the support policy requirement.

Solution: Recommend a Standard support plan.

Does this meet the goal

- ○ Yes (Correct)
- ○ No

Explanation

Correct Answer - A

The Standard plan comes with phone and email technical support.

	Basic Request support	DEVELOPER Purchase support	STANDARD Purchase support	PROFESSIONAL DIRECT Purchase support
Price	Included for all Azure customers	$29 per month	$100 per month	$1,000 per month
Scope	Included for all Azure customers	Trial and non-production environments	Production workload environments	Business-critical dependence
Billing and subscription management support	✔	✔	✔	✔
24/7 self-help resources, including Microsoft Learn, Azure portal how-to videos, documentation, and community support	✔	✔	✔	✔
Ability to submit as many support tickets as you need	✔	✔	✔	✔
Azure Advisor—your free, personalized guide to Azure best practices	✔	✔	✔	✔
Azure health status and notifications	✔	✔	✔	✔
24/7 access to technical support by email and phone		Available during business hours by email only.	✔	✔
Case severity and response time		Minimal business impact (Sev C): Within eight business hours[1]	Minimal business impact (Sev C): Within eight business hours[1] Moderate business impact (Sev B): Within four hours Critical business impact (Sev A): Within one hour	Minimal business impact (Sev C): Within four business hours[1] Moderate business impact (Sev B): Within two hours Critical business impact (Sev A): Within one hour
Third-party software support with interoperability and configuration guidance and troubleshooting		✔	✔	✔
Architecture Support		General guidance	General guidance	Guidance from a pool of ProDirect delivery managers
Operations Support				Service reviews and advisory consultation from a pool of ProDirect delivery managers
Training				Webinars led by Azure engineers
Proactive Guidance				From a pool of ProDirect delivery managers

Reference Link:

https://azure.microsoft.com/en-us/support/plans/

Question 4:
A company currently has the following unused resources as part of their subscription

- 10 user accounts in Azure AD

- 5 user groups in Azure AD

- 10 public IP address

- 10 network Interfaces

They want to reduce the costs for resources hosted in Azure

They decide to remove the network interfaces from Azure AD

Would this fulfil the requirement?

- ◉ Yes

- ○ **No** (Correct)

Explanation

Correct Answer – B

There is no price for network interfaces, so this would not help reduce the cost.

For more information on the pricing for the virtual network in Azure, please visit the below URL

https://azure.microsoft.com/en-us/pricing/details/virtual-network/

Question 5:
A company is planning on moving some of their on-premise resources to Azure. They have to provide a business justification for moving to Azure. They have to classify expenses as part of the business justification. Which category would the following expense come under?

"Software Licensing"

- ○ Primary Expenditure
- ○ Capital Expenditure
- ○ Secondary Expenditure
- ○ Operating Expenditure (Correct)

Explanation

Correct Answer – D

This expense comes under the operating expense category.

The Microsoft documentation gives examples of operating expenses

Operational cost reductions

Recurring expenses required to operate a business are often called operating expenses. This is a broad category. In most accounting models, it includes:

- Software licensing.
- Hosting expenses.
- Electric bills.
- Real estate rentals.
- Cooling expenses.
- Temporary staff required for operations.
- Equipment rentals.
- Replacement parts.
- Maintenance contracts.
- Repair services.
- Business continuity and disaster recovery (BCDR) services.
- Other expenses that don't require capital expense approvals.

Since this is clearly mentioned in the documentation, all other options are incorrect

For more information on financial models, please visit the below URL

https://docs.microsoft.com/en-us/azure/architecture/cloud-adoption/business-strategy/financial-models

Question 6:
A company is planning on moving some of their on-premise resources to Azure. They have to provide a business justification for moving to Azure. They have to classify expenses as part of the business justification. Which category would the following expense come under?

"Cooling expenses"

- Primary Expenditure
- Capital Expenditure
- Secondary Expenditure
- Operating Expenditure (Correct)

Explanation

Correct Answer - D

This expense comes under the operating expense category.

The Microsoft documentation gives examples of operating expenses

Operational cost reductions

Recurring expenses required to operate a business are often called operating expenses. This is a broad category. In most accounting models, it includes:

- Software licensing.
- Hosting expenses.
- Electric bills.
- Real estate rentals.
- Cooling expenses.
- Temporary staff required for operations.
- Equipment rentals.
- Replacement parts.
- Maintenance contracts.
- Repair services.
- Business continuity and disaster recovery (BCDR) services.
- Other expenses that don't require capital expense approvals.

Since this is clearly mentioned in the documentation, all other options are incorrect

For more information on financial models, please visit the below URL

https://docs.microsoft.com/en-us/azure/architecture/cloud-adoption/business-strategy/financial-models

Question 7:
A company is planning on moving some of their on-premise resources to Azure. They have to provide a business justification for moving to Azure. They have to classify expenses as part of the business justification. Which category would the following expense come under?

"New On-premise performance cluster to host a Big Data solution"

- Primary Expenditure
- Capital Expenditure (Correct)
- Secondary Expenditure
- Operating Expenditure

Explanation

Correct Answer – B

This expense comes under the capital expense category.

The Microsoft documentation gives examples of capital expenses

Capital expense reductions or avoidance

Capital expenses are slightly different from operating expenses. Generally, this category is driven by refresh cycles or datacenter expansion. An example of a datacenter expansion would be a new high-performance cluster to host a big data solution or data warehouse. This expense would generally fit into a capital expense category. More common are the basic refresh cycles. Some companies have rigid hardware refresh cycles, meaning assets are retired and replaced on a regular cycle (usually every three, five, or eight years). These cycles often coincide with asset lease cycles or the forecasted life span of equipment. When a refresh cycle hits, IT draws capital expense to acquire new equipment.

If a refresh cycle is approved and budgeted, the cloud transformation could help eliminate that cost. If a refresh cycle is planned but not yet approved, the cloud transformation could avoid a capital expenditure. Both reductions would be added to the cost delta.

Since this is clearly mentioned in the documentation, all other options are incorrect

For more information on financial models, please visit the below URL

https://docs.microsoft.com/en-us/azure/architecture/cloud-adoption/business-strategy/financial-models

Question 8:
A company has just setup an Azure subscription and an Azure tenant. They want to start deploying resources on the Azure platform. They want to implement a way to logically group the resources. Which of the following could be used for this requirement?

- **Availability Zones**
- **Azure Resource Groups** (Correct)
- **Azure Resource Manager**
- **Azure Regions**

Explanation

Correct Answer – B

This can be done with the help of resources groups.

The Microsoft documentation mentions the following

What is an Azure resource group?

Each resource in Azure must belong to a resource group. A resource group is simply a logical construct that groups multiple resources together so they can be managed as a single entity. For example, resources that share a similar lifecycle, such as the resources for an n-tier application may be created or deleted as a group.

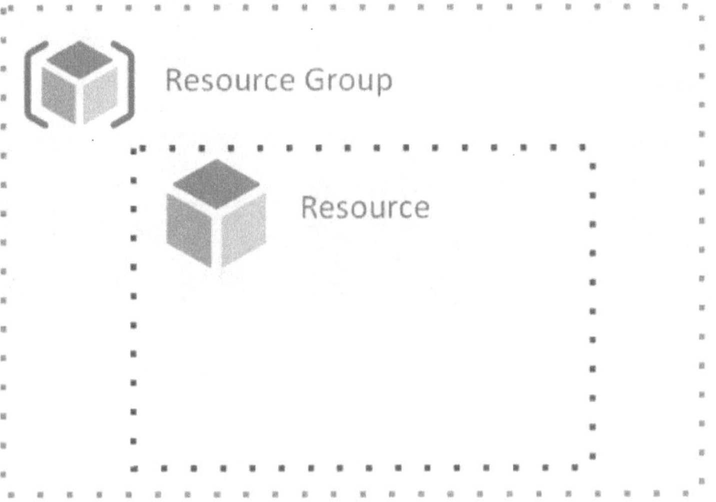

Since this is clearly mentioned in the documentation, all other options are incorrect

For more information on resources and resource group, please visit the below URL

https://docs.microsoft.com/en-us/azure/architecture/cloud-adoption/governance/resource-consistency/azure-resource-access

Question 9:
A company has just setup an Azure subscription and an Azure tenant. They want to start deploying resources on the Azure platform. They want to implement a way to deploy the resources so that they would be located closest to the users accessing those resources. Which of the following could be used for this requirement?

- ○ Availability Zones
- ○ Azure Resource Groups
- ○ Azure Resource Manager

- ○ **Azure Regions** (Correct)

Explanation

Correct Answer – D

You can make use of Azure Regions and deploy the resources to the region that is closest to the user.

The Microsoft documentation mentions the following

Since this is clearly mentioned in the documentation, all other options are incorrect

For more information on Azure Regions, please visit the below URL

https://azure.microsoft.com/en-us/global-infrastructure/regions/

Question 10:
A company has just setup an Azure subscription and an Azure tenant. They want to start deploying resources on the Azure platform. They want to use a platform that could be used to create and update the resources within the Azure subscription.

Which of the following could be used for this requirement?

- ○ Availability Zones
- ○ Azure Resource Groups
- ○ Azure Resource Manager (Correct)
- ○ Azure Regions

Explanation

Correct Answer – C

This can be done with the help of the Azure Resource Manager

The Microsoft documentation mentions the following

Azure Resource Manager overview

08/29/2019 • 5 minutes to read • +7

Azure Resource Manager is the deployment and management service for Azure. It provides a management layer that enables you to create, update, and delete resources in your Azure subscription. You use management features, like access control, locks, and tags, to secure and organize your resources after deployment.

Since this is clearly mentioned in the documentation, all other options are incorrect

For more information on Azure Resource Manager, please visit the below URL

https://docs.microsoft.com/en-us/azure/azure-resource-manager/resource-group-overview

Question 11:
A company is planning on setting up an Azure SQL database. Would the company administrative team have full control over the underlying server hosting the Azure SQL database?

- Yes
- **No** (Correct)

Explanation

Correct Answer – B

The Azure SQL database service is a Platform as a service. Here the underlying infrastructure is completely managed by Azure.

The Microsoft documentation mentions the following

What is the Azure SQL Database service?

04/08/2019 • 20 minutes to read • 👤 👤 👤 👤 👤 +21

Azure SQL Database is a general-purpose relational database, provided as a managed service. With it, you can create a highly available and high-performance data storage layer for the applications and solutions in Azure. SQL Database can be the right choice for a variety of modern cloud applications because it enables you to process both relational data and non-relational structures, such as graphs, JSON, spatial, and XML.

For more information on Azure SQL database, please visit the below URL

https://docs.microsoft.com/en-us/azure/sql-database/sql-database-technical-overview

Question 12:
You are planning on setting up an Azure Free Account. By setting up an Azure Free Account, would you only get access to a subset of services?

- ○ Yes
- ○ **No** (Correct)

Explanation

Correct Answer – B

The Azure Free Account gives access to all services in Azure. This is also mentioned in the FAQ section for the Azure Free Account

Can the Azure free account be used for production or only for development?

The Azure free account provides access to all Azure products and does not block customers from building their ideas into production. The Azure free account includes certain products—and specific quantities of those products—for free. To enable your production scenarios, you may need to use resources beyond the free amounts. You'll be billed for those additional resources at the pay-as-you-go rates.

For more information on the common asked questions for the Azure Free account, please visit the below URL

https://azure.microsoft.com/en-us/free/free-account-faq/

Question 13:
You are planning on setting up an Azure Free Account. Would the Azure Free Account expire after a specific period of time?

- ○ **Yes** (Correct)
- ○ No

Explanation

Correct Answer – A

After a duration of 30 days or if the 200 USD credit gets over, then you have to convert your Free subscription to a Pay-As-You-Go subscription.

This is also mentioned in the FAQ section for the Azure Free Account

What does it mean to upgrade my account?

When you sign up for an Azure free account, you get a $200 credit that acts as a spending limit—that is, in the first 30 days, any usage of resources beyond the free products and quantities will be deducted from the $200 credit. When you've used up the $200 credit or 30 days have expired (whichever happens first), you'll have to upgrade to a pay-as-you-go account. This automatically removes the spending limit so you can continue to get access to all the free products included in the free account. With the spending limit removed, you pay for what you use beyond the free amounts and this is charged to the card you provided.

For more information on the common asked questions for the Azure Free account, please visit the below URL

https://azure.microsoft.com/en-us/free/free-account-faq/

Question 14:
A company wants to deploy a set of Azure Windows virtual machines. They want to ensure that the services on the virtual machines are still accessible even if a single data center goes down.

They decide to deploy the set of virtual machines using scale sets.

Would this fulfill the requirement?

- ○ Yes
- ○ No (Correct)

Explanation

Correct Answer – B

Virtual machine scale sets consist of identical VMs and is load balanced. As the name implies the VMs in a scale set may grow or shrink based on demand. Deploying VMs using scale sets does not guarantee that a VM or VMs would be available when a single data center goes down.

Reference: https://docs.microsoft.com/en-us/azure/virtual-machine-scale-sets/overview

What are virtual machine scale sets?

05/21/2018 • 3 minutes to read •

Azure virtual machine scale sets let you create and manage a group of identical, load balanced VMs. The number of VM instances can automatically increase or decrease in response to demand or a defined schedule. Scale sets provide high availability to your applications, and allow you to centrally manage, configure, and update a large number of VMs. With virtual machine scale sets, you can build large-scale services for areas such as compute, big data, and container workloads.

To avoid a single data center failure and to make your VMs highly available, you need to deploy VMs across multiple availability zones.

Reference: https://docs.microsoft.com/en-us/azure/availability-zones/az-overview

What are Availability Zones in Azure?

10/17/2019 • 4 minutes to read • +27

Availability Zones is a high-availability offering that protects your applications and data from datacenter failures. Availability Zones are unique physical locations within an Azure region. Each zone is made up of one or more datacenters equipped with independent power, cooling, and networking. To ensure resiliency, there's a minimum of three separate zones in all enabled regions. The physical separation of Availability Zones within a region protects applications and data from datacenter failures. Zone-redundant services replicate your applications and data across Availability Zones to protect from single-points-of-failure. With Availability Zones, Azure offers industry best 99.99% VM uptime SLA. The full Azure SLA explains the guaranteed availability of Azure as a whole.

Question 15:
Your company has just set up an Azure subscription and an Azure tenant. They want to use recommendations given by the Azure Advisor tool. If your company starts implementing the recommendations given by the Azure Advisor tool, would the company's security score decrease?

- ○ Yes
- ○ **No** (Correct)

Explanation

Correct Answer – B

If you improve the security stance of your resources, your security score will increase.

The security score is maintained in Azure Security Center.

For more information on the Azure Security Center score, please visit the below URL

https://docs.microsoft.com/en-us/azure/security-center/security-center-secure-score

Question 16:

Your company has just setup an Azure subscription and an Azure tenant. Is it mandatory for the company to implement all Azure security recommendations within a period of 30 days in order to maintain Microsoft support?

- ○ Yes
- ○ **No** (Correct)

Explanation

Correct Answer – B

Microsoft provides the required controls for the customer to implement secure practices for their Azure account. There is no constraint which mentions that you need to implement all security recommendations to maintain Microsoft support

The Microsoft documentation gives a briefing on the Shared responsibility model that needs to be understood by the customer.

Shared responsibility model

It's important to understand the division of responsibility between you and Microsoft. On-premises, you own the whole stack, but as you move to the cloud, some responsibilities transfer to Microsoft. The following graphic illustrates the areas of responsibility, according to the type of deployment of your stack (software as a service [SaaS], platform as a service [PaaS], infrastructure as a service [IaaS], and on-premises).

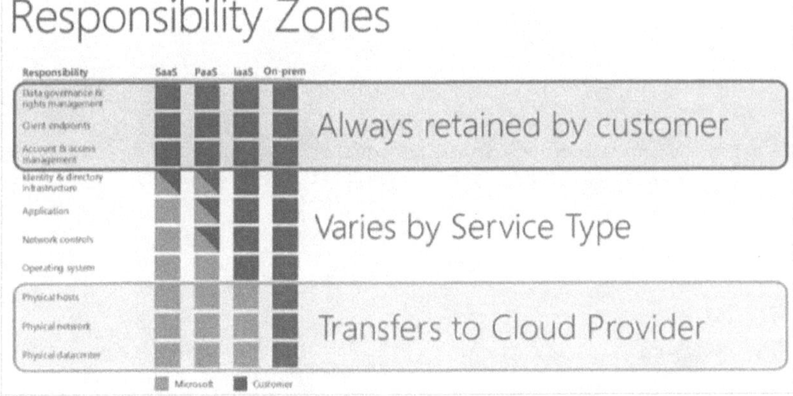

For more information on the fundamentals on Azure Infrastructure security, please visit the below URL

https://docs.microsoft.com/en-us/azure/security/fundamentals/infrastructure

Question 17:
Your company is planning on setting up an Azure subscription and an Azure tenant using Azure Active Directory. Would the company need to implement domain controllers on Azure virtual machines to use the Azure AD service?

- ○ Yes
- ○ **No** (Correct)

Explanation

Correct Answer - B

Azure Active Directory is a completely managed service. You don't need to provision any infrastructure to implement Azure Active Directory

For more information on Azure Active Directory, please visit the below URL

https://docs.microsoft.com/en-us/azure/active-directory/fundamentals/active-directory-whatis

Question 18:
Your company is planning on setting up an Azure subscription and an Azure tenant using Azure Active Directory. Does Azure Active Directory provide authentication services for services hosted in Azure and Microsoft Office 365?

- ○ **Yes** (Correct)
- ○ No

Explanation

Correct Answer - A

You can use Azure Active Directory to authenticate to both Azure based resources and also to Microsoft office 365

The Microsoft documentation mentions the following

What is Azure Active Directory?

07/31/2019 • 9 minutes to read • 🔵 🔵 ⚫ 🔲 🔲 +8

Azure Active Directory (Azure AD) is Microsoft's cloud-based identity and access management service, which helps your employees sign in and access resources in:

- External resources, such as Microsoft Office 365, the Azure portal, and thousands of other SaaS applications.

- Internal resources, such as apps on your corporate network and intranet, along with any cloud apps developed by your own organization.

You can use the various Microsoft Cloud for Enterprise Architects Series posters to better understand the core identity services in Azure, Azure AD, and Office 365.

For more information on Azure Active Directory, please visit the below URL

https://docs.microsoft.com/en-us/azure/active-directory/fundamentals/active-directory-whatis

Question 19:
Your company is planning on setting up an Azure subscription and an Azure tenant using Azure Active Directory. Is it true that multiple licenses cannot be assigned to a single user in Azure Active Directory ?

- ○ Yes
- ○ **No** (Correct)

Explanation

Correct Answer – B

You can assign multiple licences for a user in Azure Active Directory.

As shown below for each user, you can assign a license depending on what licences have been purchased

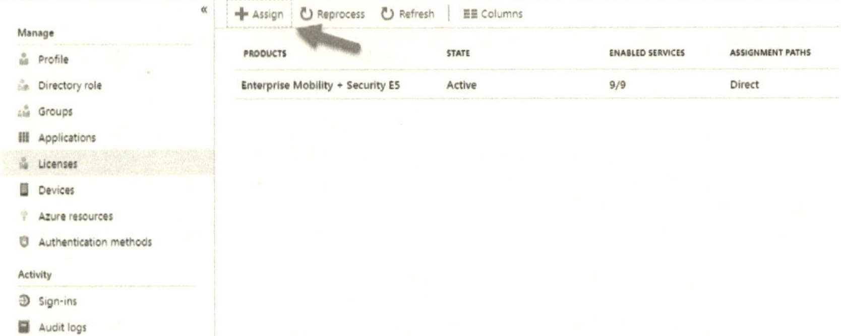

For more information on adding licences in Azure Active Directory, please visit the below URL

https://docs.microsoft.com/en-us/azure/active-directory/fundamentals/license-users-groups

Question 20:

A company is planning on storing 1 TB of data in Azure BLOB storage. Would the cost of data storage be the same regardless of the region the data is stored in?

- ○ Yes
- ○ **No** (Correct)

Explanation

Correct Answer – B

When you look at the pricing for Azure BLOB storage, there is a selector for the region. The cost depends on the region the BLOB is located in.

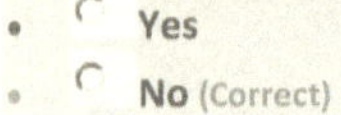

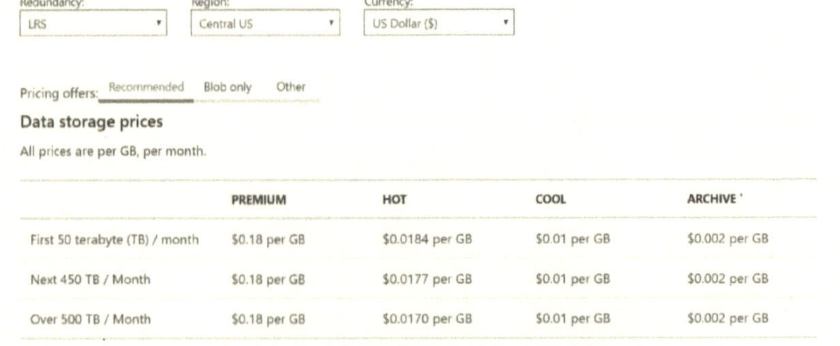

	PREMIUM	HOT	COOL	ARCHIVE
First 50 terabyte (TB) / month	$0.18 per GB	$0.0184 per GB	$0.01 per GB	$0.002 per GB
Next 450 TB / Month	$0.18 per GB	$0.0177 per GB	$0.01 per GB	$0.002 per GB
Over 500 TB / Month	$0.18 per GB	$0.0170 per GB	$0.01 per GB	$0.002 per GB

For more information on Azure BLOB pricing, please visit the below URL

https://azure.microsoft.com/en-us/pricing/details/storage/blobs/

Question 21:

A company is planning on using an Azure storage account. They are planning on provisioning an Azure storage account of the kind "General Purpose v2". Would the company be charged only for the amount of data stored and not for the amount of read and write operations?

- ○ Yes
- ○ **No** (Correct)

Explanation

Correct Answer – B

The cost of Azure storage depends on several factors, and one of them includes the number of read and write operations.

The Microsoft documentation mentions the following when it comes to an example of pricing for Block Blob storage.

Block blob storage is used for streaming and storing documents, videos, pictures, backups, and other unstructured text or binary data.

Total cost of block blob storage depends on:

- Volume of data stored per month.
- Quantity and types of operations performed, along with any data transfer costs.
- Data redundancy option selected.

For more information on Azure BLOB pricing, please visit the below URL

https://azure.microsoft.com/en-us/pricing/details/storage/blobs/

Question 22:
A company is planning on setting up a string of Azure Storage Accounts. Is the transfer of data between Azure storage accounts in different Azure regions free of cost?

- ○ Yes
- ○ **No** (Correct)

Explanation

Correct Answer – B

All services that do cross regional data transfers are subjected to a cost.

A snippet of the cost from the Microsoft documentation is given below

Pricing details

Inbound data transfers

(i.e. data going into Azure data centers): **Free**

Outbound data transfers

(i.e. data going out of Azure data centers; zones refer to source region):

OUTBOUND DATA TRANSFERS	ZONE 1*
First 5 GB /Month [1]	Free
5 GB - 10 TB [2] /Month	$0.087 per GB
Next 40 TB (10 - 50 TB) /Month	$0.083 per GB
Next 100 TB (50 - 150 TB) /Month	$0.07 per GB

For more information on Azure bandwidth pricing details, please visit the below URL

https://azure.microsoft.com/en-us/pricing/details/bandwidth/

Question 23:
A company wants to start using Azure services. They have several departments that would need to make use of Azure services. They want to give the ability for each department to use a different payment option for the amount of Azure services they consume. Which of the following should each department use to fulfill this requirement?

- A resource group
- A subscription (Correct)
- An Azure policy
- A reservation

Explanation

Correct Answer – B

The billing for Azure resources is tagged to a subscription. Hence to segregate the billing for each department, each of them can have a different subscription.

For more information on subscriptions, please visit the below URL which refers to a blog article on the benefits of a Windows subscription

https://blogs.msdn.microsoft.com/arunrakwal/2012/04/09/create-windows-azure-subscription/

Question 24:
A company has just setup an Azure subscription and an Azure tenant. Which of the following can the company use to create an Azure support request?

- The Knowledge Center

- C The Azure Portal (Correct)
- C Support.microsoft.com
- C The Security and Compliance admin center

Explanation

Correct Answer – B

You can create a support request in the Azure portal itself.

You just have to go to "Help + support" and then click on "New support request"

Since this is clear from the implementation, all other options are incorrect

For more information on creating a support request, please visit the below URL

https://docs.microsoft.com/en-us/azure/azure-supportability/how-to-create-azure-support-request

Question 25:
Your company wants to provision a set of Azure virtual machines. An application will be installed on these virtual machines. The company wants to ensure that the user traffic is distributed across the virtual machines.

You decide to use the Azure VPN Gateway service for traffic distribution.

Would this fulfil the requirement?

- C Yes
- C No (Correct)

Explanation

Correct Answer – B

This service is used to help connect an on-premise data center to an Azure virtual Network

The Microsoft documentation mentions the following

What is VPN Gateway?

05/22/2019 • 13 minutes to read • 👤👤👤👤👤 +3

A VPN gateway is a specific type of virtual network gateway that is used to send encrypted traffic between an Azure virtual network and an on-premises location over the public Internet. You can also use a VPN gateway to send encrypted traffic between Azure virtual networks over the Microsoft network. Each virtual network can have only one VPN gateway. However, you can create multiple connections to the same VPN gateway. When you create multiple connections to the same VPN gateway, all VPN tunnels share the available gateway bandwidth.

For more information on the Azure VPN gateway, please visit the below URL

https://docs.microsoft.com/en-us/azure/vpn-gateway/vpn-gateway-about-vpngateways

Question 26:
Your company wants to provision a set of Azure virtual machines. An application will be installed on these virtual machines. The company wants to ensure that the user traffic is distributed across the virtual machines.

You decide to use the Azure Load Balancer service for traffic distribution.

Would this fulfil the requirement?

- ○ **Yes** (Correct)
- ○ **No**

Explanation

Correct Answer – A

The Azure Load Balancer is the ideal service to use for this scenario. It can be used to distribute traffic to the backend virtual machines.

The Microsoft documentation mentions the following

Why use Load Balancer? ↄ

You can use Azure Load Balancer to:

- Load-balance incoming internet traffic to your VMs. This configuration is known as a Public Load Balancer.
- Load-balance traffic across VMs inside a virtual network. You can also reach a Load Balancer front end from an on-premises network in a hybrid scenario. Both scenarios use a configuration that is known as an Internal Load Balancer.
- Port forward traffic to a specific port on specific VMs with inbound network address translation (NAT) rules.
- Provide outbound connectivity for VMs inside your virtual network by using a public Load Balancer.

For more information on the Azure Load Balancer, please visit the below URL

https://docs.microsoft.com/en-us/azure/load-balancer/load-balancer-overview

Question 27:
Your company wants to provision a set of Azure virtual machines. An application will be installed on these virtual machines. The company wants to ensure that the user traffic is distributed across the virtual machines.

You decide to use the Azure HDInsight service for traffic distribution.

Would this fulfil the requirement?

- ○ Yes
- ○ **No** (Correct)

Explanation

Correct Answer – B

The Azure HDInsight service is used for implementing Big Data related open source frameworks.

The Microsoft documentation mentions the following

What is Azure HDInsight?

06/11/2019 • 6 minutes to read •

Azure HDInsight is a managed, full-spectrum, open-source analytics service in the cloud for enterprises. You can use open-source frameworks such as Hadoop, Apache Spark, Apache Hive, LLAP, Apache Kafka, Apache Storm, R, and more.

For more information on the Azure HDInsight, please visit the below URL

https://docs.microsoft.com/en-us/azure/hdinsight/hdinsight-overview

Question 28:
A company is planning on setting up a solution on the Azure platform. The solution has the following main key requirement

- Provide a managed toolset that could be used to manage and scale container-based applications

Which of the following would be best suited for this requirement?

- ○ **Azure Event Grid**
- ○ **Azure DevOps**
- ○ **Azure Kubernetes** (Correct)
- ○ **Azure DevTest Labs**

Explanation

Correct Answer – C

This can be achieved with the Azure Kubernetes service.

The Microsoft documentation mentions the following

Ship faster, operate with ease, and scale confidently

The fully managed Azure Kubernetes Service (AKS) makes deploying and managing containerized applications easy. It offers serverless Kubernetes, an integrated continuous integration and continuous delivery (CI/CD) experience, and enterprise-grade security and governance. Unite your development and operations teams on a single platform to rapidly build, deliver, and scale applications with confidence.

Since this is clearly mentioned in the documentation, all other options are incorrect

For more information on the Azure Kubernetes service, please visit the below URL

https://azure.microsoft.com/en-us/services/kubernetes-service/

Question 29:
A company is planning on setting up a solution on the Azure platform. The solution has the following key requirement:

- Provide a continuous Integration and Delivery toolset that could work with a variety of languages

Which of the following would be best suited for this requirement?

- ○ Azure Event Grid
- ○ **Azure DevOps** (Correct)
- ○ Azure Kubernetes
- ○ Azure DevTest Labs

Explanation

Correct Answer – B

This can be achieved with the Azure DevOps service.

The Microsoft documentation mentions the following

Use all the DevOps services or choose just what you need to complement your existing workflows

Azure Boards

Deliver value to your users faster using proven agile tools to plan, track, and discuss work across your teams.

Learn more >

Azure Pipelines

Build, test, and deploy with CI/CD that works with any language, platform, and cloud. Connect to GitHub or any other Git provider and deploy continuously.

Learn more >

Azure Repos

Get unlimited, cloud-hosted private Git repos and collaborate to build better code with pull requests and advanced file management.

Learn more >

Since this is clearly mentioned in the documentation, all other options are incorrect

For more information on the Azure DevOps service, please visit the below URL

https://azure.microsoft.com/en-us/services/devops/

Question 30:
A company is planning on setting up a solution on the Azure platform. The solution has the following key requirement:

- Provide a service that could be used to quickly provision development and test environments

- Minimize waste on resources with the help of quotas and policies

Which of the following would be best suited for this requirement?

- ○ Azure Event Grid
- ○ Azure DevOps

- ◦ Azure Kubernetes
- ◦ Azure DevTest Labs (Correct)

Explanation

Correct Answer – D

This can be achieved with the Azure DevTest Labs service.

The Microsoft documentation mentions the following

Azure DevTest Labs

Fast, easy, and lean dev-test environments

- ✔ Quickly provision development and test environments
- ✔ Minimize waste with quotas and policies
- ✔ Set automated shutdowns to minimize costs
- ✔ Build Windows and Linux environments

Since this is clearly mentioned in the documentation, all other options are incorrect

For more information on the Azure DevTest Labs service, please visit the below URL

https://azure.microsoft.com/en-us/services/devtest-lab/

Question 31:
A company is planning on setting up a solution on the Azure platform. The solution has the following key requirement:

- Be able to collect events from multiple sources and then relay them to an application

Which of the following would be best suited for this requirement?

- ◦ Azure Event Grid (Correct)
- ◦ Azure DevOps
- ◦ Azure Kubernetes
- ◦ Azure DevTest Labs

Explanation

Correct Answer – A

This can be achieved with the Azure Event Grid service.

The Microsoft documentation mentions the following

Use Event Grid to power your event-driven and serverless apps

Simplify your event-based apps with Event Grid, a single service for managing routing of all events from any source to any destination. Designed for high availability, consistent performance, and dynamic scale, Event Grid lets you focus on your app logic rather than infrastructure.

Since this is clearly mentioned in the documentation, all other options are incorrect

For more information on the Azure Event Grid service, please visit the below URL

https://azure.microsoft.com/en-us/services/event-grid/

Question 32:
A company is planning on using the Azure Firewall service. Would the Azure firewall service encrypt all network traffic sent from Azure to the Internet?

- ○ Yes
- ○ No (Correct)

Explanation

Correct Answer – B

The Azure Firewall service is primarily used to protect your network infrastructure.

The Microsoft documentation mentions the following

What is Azure Firewall?

09/04/2019 • 8 minutes to read • 👤 🔊 ⚫ ⚫ ༀ

Azure Firewall is a managed, cloud-based network security service that protects your Azure Virtual Network resources. It's a fully stateful firewall as a service with built-in high availability and unrestricted cloud scalability.

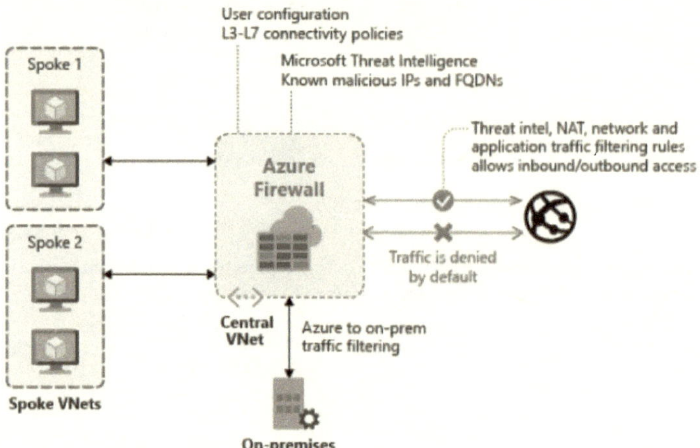

You can centrally create, enforce, and log application and network connectivity policies across subscriptions and virtual networks. Azure Firewall uses a static public IP address for your virtual network resources allowing outside firewalls to identify traffic originating from your virtual network. The service is fully integrated with Azure Monitor for logging and analytics.

For more information on the Azure Firewall service, please visit the below URL

https://docs.microsoft.com/en-us/azure/firewall/overview

Question 33:
A company is planning on using Network Security Groups. Could network security groups be used to encrypt all network traffic sent from Azure to the Internet?

- ○ Yes
- ○ No (Correct)

Explanation

Correct Answer – B

Network Security Groups are used to restrict Inbound and Outbound traffic. It can't be used to encrypt traffic.

The Microsoft documentation mentions the following

Security groups

07/26/2018 • 25 minutes to read • +11

You can filter network traffic to and from Azure resources in an Azure virtual network with a network security group. A network security group contains security rules that allow or deny inbound network traffic to, or outbound network traffic from, several types of Azure resources. To learn about which Azure resources can be deployed into a virtual network and have network security groups associated to them, see Virtual network integration for Azure services. For each rule, you can specify source and destination, port, and protocol.

For more information on the Azure network security, please visit the below URL

https://docs.microsoft.com/en-us/azure/virtual-network/security-overview

Question 34:
A company is planning on deploying an Azure Windows Server 2016 virtual machine. Could the virtual machine be used to encrypt all traffic from the virtual machine itself to a host on the Internet?

- ○ **Yes** (Correct)
- ○ **No**

Explanation

Correct Answer – A

You can install roles such as the Remote Access Server for VPN to ensure traffic is encrypted when it flows out of the server.

An example in the Microsoft documentation is given via the below URL

https://docs.microsoft.com/en-us/windows-server/remote/remote-access/vpn/always-on-vpn/deploy/vpn-deploy-ras

Question 35:
You are planning on deploying an Azure virtual machine. Of the following storage services, which is used to store the data disks for the virtual machine?

- ○ **Blob** (Correct)
- ○ **Files**
- ○ **Tables**

- $\quad$ ○ Queues

Explanation

Correct Answer – A

The data disks are stored in the Blob service of Azure storage accounts.

The Microsoft documentation mentions the following

Blobs

Azure Storage supports three types of blobs:

- **Block blobs** store text and binary data, up to about 4.7 TB. Block blobs are made up of blocks of data that can be managed individually.
- **Append blobs** are made up of blocks like block blobs, but are optimized for append operations. Append blobs are ideal for scenarios such as logging data from virtual machines.
- **Page blobs** store random access files up to 8 TB in size. Page blobs store virtual hard drive (VHD) files and serve as disks for Azure virtual machines. For more information about page blobs, see Overview of Azure page blobs

Since this is clearly mentioned in the documentation, all other options are incorrect

For more information on the Azure Blob storage, please visit the below URL

https://docs.microsoft.com/en-us/azure/storage/blobs/storage-blobs-introduction

https://docs.microsoft.com/en-us/azure/virtual-machines/windows/managed-disks-overview

Question 36:
A company is planning on setting up an Azure Virtual machine. Would the company administrative team have full control over the underlying virtual machine to install an application?

- ○ Yes (Correct)
- ○ No

Explanation

Correct Answer – A

The Azure virtual machine service is an Infrastructure as a service. Here you can install applications on the underlying virtual machine.

The Microsoft documentation mentions the following

Overview of Windows virtual machines in Azure

10/04/2018 • 7 minutes to read • 👥👥👥👥👥 +7

Azure Virtual Machines (VM) is one of several types of <u>on-demand, scalable computing resources</u> that Azure offers. Typically, you choose a VM when you need more control over the computing environment than the other choices offer. This article gives you information about what you should consider before you create a VM, how you create it, and how you manage it.

An Azure VM gives you the flexibility of virtualization without having to buy and maintain the physical hardware that runs it. However, you still need to maintain the VM by performing tasks, such as configuring, patching, and installing the software that runs on it.

For more information on Azure virtual machines, please visit the below URL

<u>https://docs.microsoft.com/en-us/azure/virtual-machines/windows/overview</u>

Question 37:
A company is planning on deploying a web application to the Azure Web App service. Would the company administrative team have full control over the underlying machine hosting the web application?

- ○ Yes
- ○ **No** (Correct)

Explanation

Correct Answer – B

The Azure Web App service is Platform as a service. Here the underlying infrastructure is completely managed by Azure.

The Microsoft documentation mentions the following

App Service overview

01/04/2017 • 2 minutes to read •

Azure App Service is an HTTP-based service for hosting web applications, REST APIs, and mobile back ends. You can develop in your favorite language, be it .NET, .NET Core, Java, Ruby, Node.js, PHP, or Python. Applications run and scale with ease on both Windows and Linux-based environments. For Linux-based environments, see App Service on Linux.

App Service not only adds the power of Microsoft Azure to your application, such as security, load balancing, autoscaling, and automated management. You can also take advantage of its DevOps capabilities, such as continuous deployment from Azure DevOps, GitHub, Docker Hub, and other sources, package management, staging environments, custom domain, and SSL certificates.

For more information on Azure App Service, please visit the below URL

https://docs.microsoft.com/en-us/azure/app-service/overview

Question 38:
A company has just setup an Azure subscription and an Azure tenant. They want to implement strict policies when it comes to the security of Azure resources. They want to implement the following requirements:

"Ensure that the Virtual Machine Administrator team can only deploy virtual machines of a particular size"

Which of the following could be used to fulfill the below requirement?

- ○ Azure Role-Based Access Control
- ○ Azure Identity Protection
- ○ Azure Policies (Correct)
- ○ Azure Locks

Explanation

Correct Answer – C

You can accomplish this with the help of policies. There is an in-built policy also available for this purpose

Allowed virtual machine SKUs
Policy definition

☐→ Assign   ✎ Edit definition   ☐ Duplicate definition   🗑 Delete definition

Name	: Allowed virtual machine SKUs ☐	Definition location	: --
Description	: This policy enables you to specify a set of virtual machine SKUs t...	Definition ID	: /providers/Microsoft.Authorization/policyDefinitions/cccc...
Effect	: Deny	Type	: Built-in
Category	: Compute	Mode	: Indexed

Definition   Assignments (0)   Parameters

Option A is incorrect since this is used to given authorization to use Azure resources

Option B is incorrect since this is used to protect Azure AD identities

Option D is incorrect since this is used to protect Azure resources from users accidentally updating or deleting Azure resources

For more information on Azure policies, please visit the below URL

https://docs.microsoft.com/en-us/azure/governance/policy/overview

Question 39:
A company has just setup an Azure subscription and an Azure tenant. They want to implement strict policies when it comes to the security of Azure resources. They want to implement the following requirements:

"Ensure that the Virtual Machine Administrator team can only deploy virtual machines and their dependent resources."

Which of the following could be used to fulfill the below requirement?

- ○ Azure Role-Based Access Control (Correct)
- ○ Azure Identity Protection
- ○ Azure Policies
- ○ Azure Locks

Explanation

Correct Answer – A

You can achieve this with Role-Based Access Control. You can deploy the Administrators to one group and just provide the role for virtual machine access.

The Microsoft documentation mentions the following

What is role-based access control (RBAC) for Azure resources?

09/11/2019 • 7 minutes to read •

Access management for cloud resources is a critical function for any organization that is using the cloud. Role-based access control (RBAC) helps you manage who has access to Azure resources, what they can do with those resources, and what areas they have access to.

RBAC is an authorization system built on Azure Resource Manager that provides fine-grained access management of Azure resources.

What can I do with RBAC?

Here are some examples of what you can do with RBAC:

- Allow one user to manage virtual machines in a subscription and another user to manage virtual networks
- Allow a DBA group to manage SQL databases in a subscription
- Allow a user to manage all resources in a resource group, such as virtual machines, websites, and subnets
- Allow an application to access all resources in a resource group

Option B is incorrect since this is used to protect Azure AD identities

Option C is incorrect since this is used to govern the resources in Azure

Option D is incorrect since this is used to protect Azure resources from users accidentally updating or deleting Azure resources

For more information on Azure Role based access control, please visit the below URL

https://docs.microsoft.com/en-us/azure/role-based-access-control/overview

Question 40:
A company has just setup an Azure subscription and an Azure tenant. They want to implement strict policies when it comes to the security of Azure resources. They want to implement the following requirements:

"Ensure that no one can accidentally delete the virtual machines deployed by the Virtual Machine Administrator team"

Which of the following could be used to fulfill the below requirement?

- ○ Azure Role-Based Access Control
- ○ Azure Identity Protection
- ○ Azure Policies
- ○ Azure Locks (Correct)

Explanation

Correct Answer – D

This can be achieved with the help of Azure Locks.

The Microsoft documentation mentions the following

Lock resources to prevent unexpected changes

05/14/2019 • 6 minutes to read • +4

As an administrator, you may need to lock a subscription, resource group, or resource to prevent other users in your organization from accidentally deleting or modifying critical resources. You can set the lock level to **CanNotDelete** or **ReadOnly**. In the portal, the locks are called **Delete** and **Read-only** respectively.

- **CanNotDelete** means authorized users can still read and modify a resource, but they can't delete the resource.
- **ReadOnly** means authorized users can read a resource, but they can't delete or update the resource. Applying this lock is similar to restricting all authorized users to the permissions granted by the **Reader** role.

Option A is incorrect since this is used to given authorization to use Azure resources

Option B is incorrect since this is used to protect Azure AD identities

Option C is incorrect since this is used to govern the resources in Azure

For more information on Azure Locks, please visit the below URL

https://docs.microsoft.com/en-us/azure/azure-resource-manager/resource-group-lock-resources

Question 41:
A company has just started using Azure. They have setup resources as part of their subscription. They want to get the current costs being incurred.

They decide to use Azure Cost Management to get this information.

Would this fulfil the requirement?

- ○ **Yes** (Correct)
- ○ **No**

Explanation

Correct Answer – A

Yes, this would give a cost breakdown for the resources being used in Azure.

An example is given below where you go to the Cost Analysis section in Cost Management.

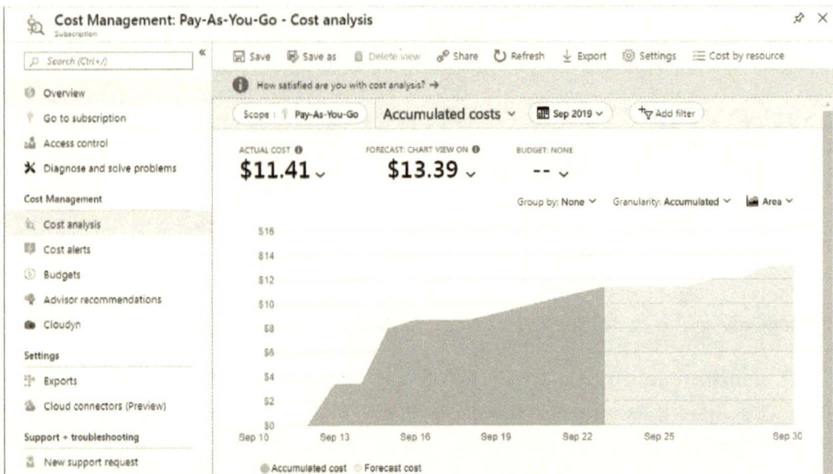

For more information on Azure Cost Management, please visit the below URL

https://docs.microsoft.com/en-us/azure/cost-management/overview

Question 42:
A company has just started using Azure. They have setup resources as part of their subscription. They want to get the current costs being incurred.

They decide to use the Pricing Calculator to get this information.

Would this fulfill the requirement?

- ○ Yes

- ○ **No** (Correct)

Explanation

B, No.

The question says "They want to get the current costs being incurred"

Obviously the answer is NO , because the "Current costs" of the resources can be got from the "Cost Management" in the Azure Portal.

"Pricing Calculator" is only used to get the "estimated cost" of using an Azure resource

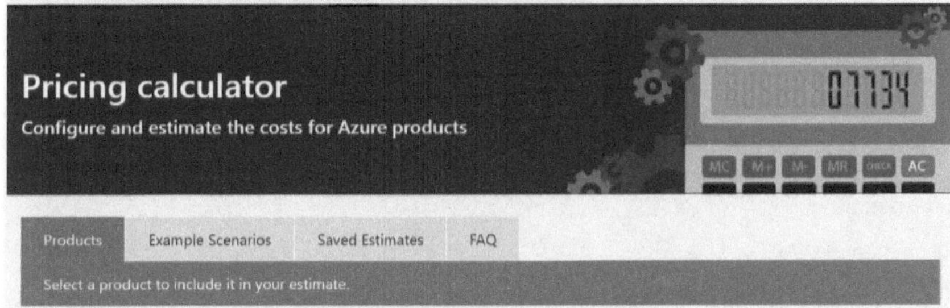

For more information on the pricing calculator, please visit the below URL

https://azure.microsoft.com/en-us/pricing/calculator/

Question 43:
A company has just started using Azure. They have setup resources as part of their subscription. They want to get the current costs being incurred.

They decide to use the TCO calculator to get this information.

Would this fulfill the requirement?

- ○ Yes
- ○ **No** (Correct)

Explanation

Correct Answer - B

This is used to realize the costs when you move your current infrastructure to Azure.

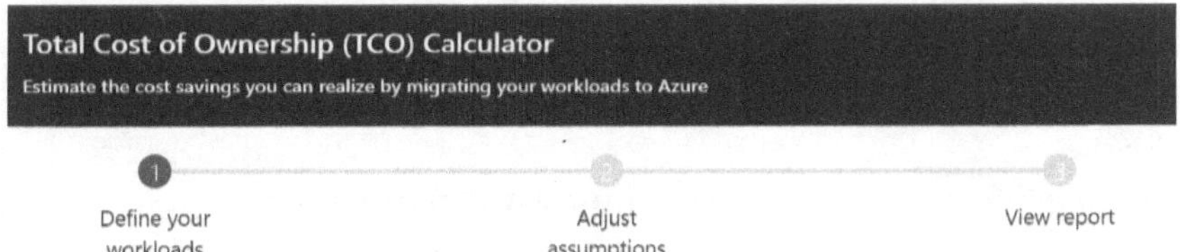

For more information on the TCO calculator, please visit the below URL

https://azure.microsoft.com/en-us/pricing/tco/calculator/

Question 44:
A company is currently planning on setting up resources as part of their Azure subscription. They are looking at different security options that can be used to secure their Azure environment.

Which of the following could be used for the following requirement?

"Provide the ability to restrict traffic into Azure virtual machines"

- ○ Azure Key Vault
- ○ Azure Network Security Groups (Correct)
- ○ Azure Multi-Factor Authentication
- ○ Azure DDoS Protection

Explanation

Correct Answer - B

This can be accomplished with the help of Network Security Groups

The Microsoft documentation mentions the following

Security groups

07/26/2018 • 25 minutes to read • 🧑🧑🧑🧑🧑 +11

You can filter network traffic to and from Azure resources in an Azure virtual network with a network security group. A network security group contains security rules that allow or deny inbound network traffic to, or outbound network traffic from, several types of Azure resources. To learn about which Azure resources can be deployed into a virtual network and have network security groups associated to them, see Virtual network integration for Azure services. For each rule, you can specify source and destination, port, and protocol.

Option A is incorrect since this is used to store secrets, certificates and keys

Option C is incorrect since this is used to provide an extra level of security during user authentication

Option D is incorrect since this is used to protect against Distributed denial of service (DDoS) attacks

For more information on network security, please visit the below URL

https://docs.microsoft.com/en-us/azure/virtual-network/security-overview

Question 45:

A company is currently planning on setting up resources as part of their Azure subscription. They are looking at different security options that can be used to secure their Azure environment.

Which of the following could be used for the following requirement?

"Provide an extra level of security when users log into the Azure Portal"

- ○ Azure Key Vault
- ○ Azure Network Security Groups
- ○ Azure Multi-Factor Authentication (Correct)
- ○ Azure DDoS Protection

Explanation

Correct Answer – C

The extra level of security can be accomplished by providing a facility of Multi-Factor Authentication

The Microsoft documentation mentions the following

How it works: Azure Multi-Factor Authentication

06/03/2018 • 2 minutes to read • 👥👥👥👥👥 +2

The security of two-step verification lies in its layered approach. Compromising multiple authentication factors presents a significant challenge for attackers. Even if an attacker manages to learn the user's password, it is useless without also having possession of the additional authentication method. It works by requiring two or more of the following authentication methods:

- Something you know (typically a password)
- Something you have (a trusted device that is not easily duplicated, like a phone)
- Something you are (biometrics)

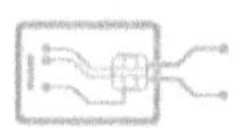

Option A is incorrect since this is used to store secrets, certificates and keys

Option B is incorrect since this is used to restrict traffic into and out of Azure virtual machines

Option D is incorrect since this is used to protect against Distributed denial of service (DDoS) attacks

For more information on multi-factor authentication, please visit the below URL

https://docs.microsoft.com/en-us/azure/active-directory/authentication/concept-mfa-howitworks

Question 46:
A company is currently planning on setting up resources as part of their Azure subscription. They are looking at different security options that can be used to secure their Azure environment.

Which of the following could be used for the following requirement?

"Provide a store that can be used to store secrets."

- ○ **Azure Key Vault** (Correct)
- ○ **Azure Network Security Groups**
- ○ **Azure Multi-Factor Authentication**
- ○ **Azure DDoS Protection**

Explanation

Correct Answer – A

You can store secrets in the Azure Key Vault service.

The Microsoft documentation mentions the following

What is Azure Key Vault?

01/07/2019 • 4 minutes to read • ⬤ ⬤ ⬤ ◕ ◔ +4

Azure Key Vault helps solve the following problems:

- **Secrets Management** - Azure Key Vault can be used to Securely store and tightly control access to tokens, passwords, certificates, API keys, and other secrets
- **Key Management** - Azure Key Vault can also be used as a Key Management solution. Azure Key Vault makes it easy to create and control the encryption keys used to encrypt your data.
- **Certificate Management** - Azure Key Vault is also a service that lets you easily provision, manage, and deploy public and private Secure Sockets Layer/Transport Layer Security (SSL/TLS) certificates for use with Azure and your internal connected resources.
- **Store secrets backed by Hardware Security Modules** - The secrets and keys can be protected either by software or FIPS 140-2 Level 2 validates HSMs

Option B is incorrect since this is used to restrict traffic into and out of Azure virtual machines

Option C is incorrect since this is used to provide an extra level of security during user authentication

Option D is incorrect since this is used to protect against Distributed denial of service (DDoS) attacks

For more information on the Azure Key Vault service, please visit the below URL

https://docs.microsoft.com/en-us/azure/key-vault/key-vault-overview

Question 47:
A company is currently planning on setting up resources as part of their Azure subscription. They are looking at different security options that can be used to secure their Azure environment.

Which of the following could be used for the following requirement?

"Provide Protection against distributed denial of service attacks"

- ○ **Azure Key Vault**
- ○ **Azure Network Security Groups**
- ○ **Azure Multi-Factor Authentication**
- ○ **Azure DDoS Protection** (Correct)

Explanation

Correct Answer – D

You can protect your environment from such attacks by using Azure DDoS Protection

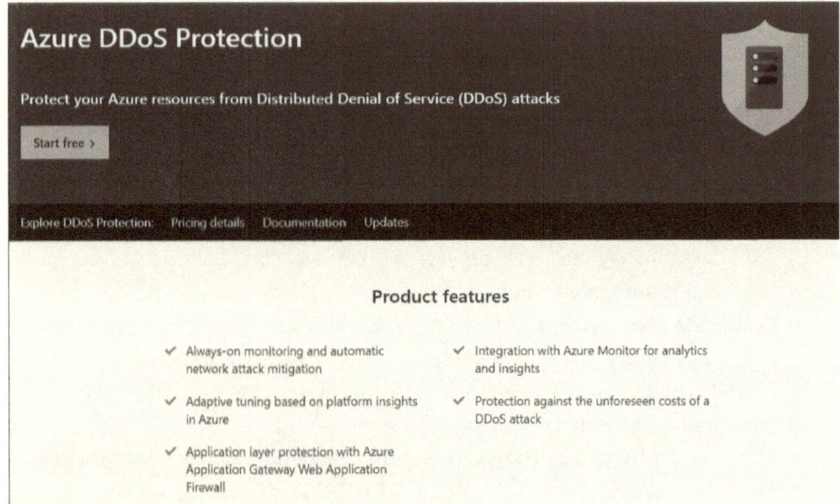

Option A is incorrect since this is used to store secrets, certificates and keys

Option B is incorrect since this is used to restrict traffic into and out of Azure virtual machines

Option C is incorrect since this is used to provide an extra level of security during user authentication

For more information on the Azure DDoS protection service, please visit the below URL

https://azure.microsoft.com/en-us/services/ddos-protection/

Question 48:
You are trying to understand the different cloud models. Which of the following are advantages of using the public cloud? Choose 2 answers from the options give below

- ☐ **Lower costs** (Correct)
- ☐ **Higher maintenance**
- ☐ **High reliability** (Correct)
- ☐ **Higher costs**

Explanation

Correct Answers – A and C

The advantages for using the public cloud is given in the Microsoft documentation

What is a public cloud?

Public clouds are the most common way of deploying cloud computing. The cloud resources (like servers and storage) are owned and operated by a third-party cloud service provider and delivered over the Internet. Microsoft Azure is an example of a public cloud. With a public cloud, all hardware, software, and other supporting infrastructure is owned and managed by the cloud provider. In a public cloud, you share the same hardware, storage, and network devices with other organizations or cloud "tenants." You access services and manage your account using a web browser. Public cloud deployments are frequently used to provide web-based email, online office applications, storage, and testing and development environments.

Advantages of public clouds:

- Lower costs—no need to purchase hardware or software, and you pay only for the service you use.

- No maintenance—your service provider provides the maintenance.

- Near-unlimited scalability—on-demand resources are available to meet your business needs.

- High reliability—a vast network of servers ensures against failure.

Since this is clearly given in the Microsoft documentation, all other options are incorrect

For more information on comparing the different models, please visit the below URL

https://azure.microsoft.com/en-us/overview/what-are-private-public-hybrid-clouds/

Question 49:
You are trying to understand the different cloud models. Which of the following are advantages of using the private cloud? Choose 2 answers from the options give below

- ☐ Less Flexibility
- ☐ Better security (Correct)
- ☐ High scalability (Correct)
- ☐ Less costs

Explanation

Correct Answers – B and C

The advantages for using the private cloud is given in the Microsoft documentation

What is a private cloud?

A private cloud consists of computing resources used exclusively by one business or organization. The private cloud can be physically located at your organization's on-site datacenter, or it can be hosted by a third-party service provider. But in a private cloud, the services and infrastructure are always maintained on a private network and the hardware and software are dedicated solely to your organization. In this way, a private cloud can make it easier for an organization to customize its resources to meet specific IT requirements. Private clouds are often used by government agencies, financial institutions, any other mid- to large-size organizations with business-critical operations seeking enhanced control over their environment.

Advantages of a private clouds:

- More flexibility—your organization can customize its cloud environment to meet specific business needs.

- Improved security—resources are not shared with others, so higher levels of control and security are possible.

- High scalability—private clouds still afford the scalability and efficiency of a public cloud.

Since this is clearly given in the Microsoft documentation, all other options are incorrect

For more information on comparing the different models, please visit the below URL

https://azure.microsoft.com/en-us/overview/what-are-private-public-hybrid-clouds/

Question 50:
You are trying to understand the different cloud models. Which of the following are advantages of using a hybrid cloud model? Choose 2 answers from the options give below

- ☐ Better Control (Correct)
- ☐ Higher costs
- ☐ More Flexibility (Correct)
- ☐ Less Maintenance

Explanation

Correct Answers – A and C

The advantages for using a hybrid cloud model is given in the Microsoft documentation

What is a hybrid cloud?

Often called "the best of both worlds," hybrid clouds combine on-premises infrastructure, or private clouds, with public clouds so organizations can reap the advantages of both. In a hybrid cloud, data and applications can move between private and public clouds for greater flexibility and more deployment options. For instance, you can use the public cloud for high-volume, lower-security needs such as web-based email, and the private cloud (or other on-premises infrastructure) for sensitive, business-critical operations like financial reporting. In a hybrid cloud, "cloud bursting" is also an option. This is when an application or resource runs in the private cloud until there is a spike in demand (such as seasonal event like online shopping or tax filing), at which point the organization can "burst through" to the public cloud to tap into additional computing resources.

Advantages of hybrid clouds:

- Control—your organization can maintain a private infrastructure for sensitive assets.
- Flexibility—you can take advantage of additional resources in the public cloud when you need them.
- Cost-effectiveness—with the ability to scale to the public cloud, you pay for extra computing power only when needed.
- Ease—transitioning to the cloud doesn't have to be overwhelming because you can migrate gradually—phasing in workloads over time.

Since this is clearly given in the Microsoft documentation, all other options are incorrect

For more information on comparing the different models, please visit the below URL

https://azure.microsoft.com/en-us/overview/what-are-private-public-hybrid-clouds/

Question 51:
You are planning on setting up an Azure Free Account. Is there a spending limit when it comes to the spending limit for the free account?

- ○ Yes (Correct)
- ○ No

Explanation

Correct Answer – A

There is a credit of 200 USD which is assigned to the Free account is limited to the first 30 days the account is active. This acts as a spending limit. The Microsoft documentation mentions the following

Do I have to pay something after 30 days?

At the end of your first 30 days, you can continue using your free products after you upgrade your account to a pay-as-you-go pricing and remove the spending limit. If you stay within the service quantities included for free, you won't have to pay anything. The $200 free credit acts as a spending limit.

For more information on the common asked questions for the Azure Free account, please visit the below URL

https://azure.microsoft.com/en-us/free/free-account-faq/

Question 52:

A company has just setup an Azure subscription. The company is planning on creating several resource groups. By creating additional resource groups, would the company incur additional costs?

- ○ Yes
- ○ **No** (Correct)

Explanation

Correct Answer – B

Resource groups have no costs associate with them.

For more information on resource groups, please visit the below URL

https://docs.microsoft.com/en-us/azure/azure-resource-manager/resource-group-overview

Question 53:
A company has just setup an Azure virtual private connection between their on-premise network and an Azure virtual network. Would the company need to pay additional costs if they transfer several gigabits of data from their on-premise network to Azure?

- ○ Yes
- ○ **No** (Correct)

Explanation

Correct Answer – B

Data transfers to the Azure data center are free.

The Microsoft documentation mentions the following

Pricing details

Inbound data transfers

(i.e. data going into Azure data centers): **Free**

For more information on bandwidth pricing, please visit the below URL

https://azure.microsoft.com/en-us/pricing/details/bandwidth/

Question 54:
A company wants to make use of an Azure service that can be used to store certificates. Which of the following could be used for storing certificates?

- ○ Azure Security Center

- ○ **Azure Storage Account**
- ○ **Azure Key Vault** (Correct)
- ○ **Azure Identity Protection**

Explanation

Correct Answer – C

You can store certificates in the Azure Key vault service.

The Microsoft documentation mentions the following

What is Azure Key Vault?

01/07/2019 • 4 minutes to read • ●●● 🔍 ● +4

Azure Key Vault helps solve the following problems:

- **Secrets Management** - Azure Key Vault can be used to Securely store and tightly control access to tokens, passwords, certificates, API keys, and other secrets
- **Key Management** - Azure Key Vault can also be used as a Key Management solution. Azure Key Vault makes it easy to create and control the encryption keys used to encrypt your data.
- **Certificate Management** - Azure Key Vault is also a service that lets you easily provision, manage, and deploy public and private Secure Sockets Layer/Transport Layer Security (SSL/TLS) certificates for use with Azure and your internal connected resources.
- **Store secrets backed by Hardware Security Modules** - The secrets and keys can be protected either by software or FIPS 140-2 Level 2 validates HSMs

Option A is incorrect since this is used to increase the security posture of your resources defined in Azure

Option B is incorrect since this is used for object, file, table and queue storage

Option D is incorrect since this is used to protect Azure AD identities.

For more information on the Azure Key vault service, please visit the below URL

https://docs.microsoft.com/en-us/azure/key-vault/key-vault-overview

Question 55:
Which of the following category does Azure Kubernetes come under?

- ○ Software as a service
- ○ Platform as a service

- ○ **Infrastructure as a service** (Correct)
- ○ **Hardware as a service**

Explanation

Correct Answer – B

Azure Kubernetes comes under the "Infrastructure as a service" category.

The Microsoft documentation mentions the following

Azure services

Here's a big-picture view of the available services and features in Azure.

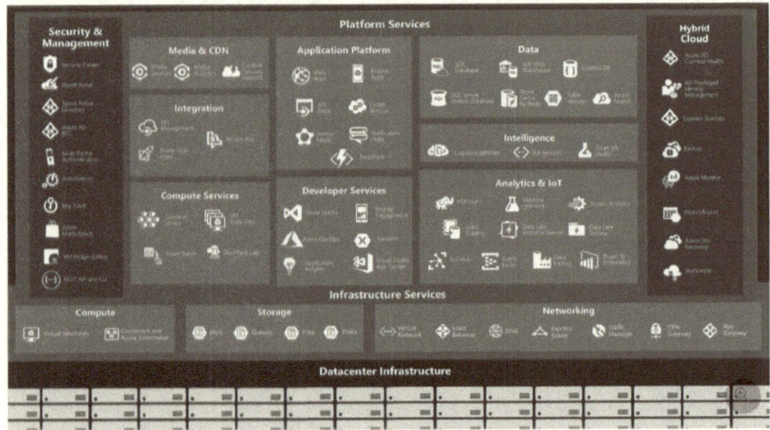

Let's take a closer look at the most commonly-used categories:

- Compute
- Networking
- Storage
- Mobile
- Databases

- Web
- Internet of Things
- Big Data
- Artificial Intelligence
- DevOps

Compute

Compute services are often one of the primary reasons why companies move to the Azure platform. Azure provides a range of options for hosting applications and services. Here are some examples of compute services in Azure:

Service name	Service function
Azure Virtual Machines	Windows or Linux virtual machines (VMs) hosted in Azure
Azure Virtual Machine Scale Sets	Scaling for Windows or Linux VMs hosted in Azure
Azure Kubernetes Service	Enables management of a cluster of VMs that run containerized services

Since this is clearly mentioned in the documentation, all other options are incorrect

For more information on Platform as a service, please visit the below URL:

https://docs.microsoft.com/en-us/learn/modules/welcome-to-azure/3-tour-of-azure-services

Section – 2

Question 1:
You have an Azure environment.

You need to create a new Azure virtual machine from an Android laptop.

Solution: You use Bash in Azure cloud shell.

Does this meet the goal?

- ○ Yes (Correct)
- ○ No

Explanation

Correct Answer - A

When you log in to Azure portal in an Android laptop, you can use "Bash" through "Cloud Shell" as shown below:

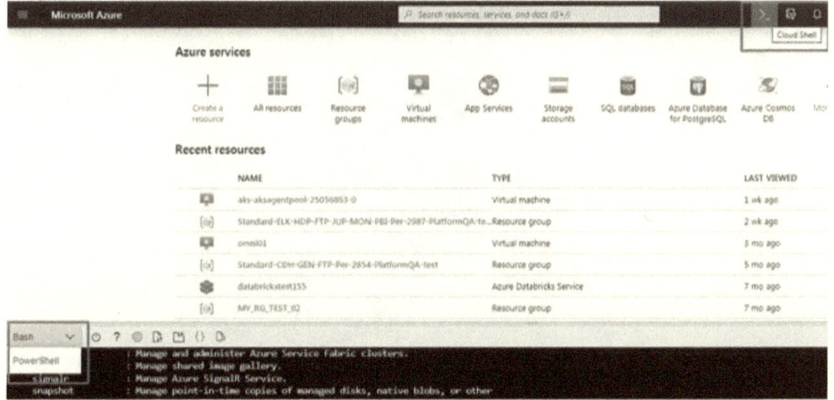

NO cannot be the answer here, because the Azure portal can work with Android OS and the portal by default has "Cloud shell" included as given in the screenshot. Also, the "Cloud Shell" has "Bash" in it. Therefore the answer is YES.

Question 2:
You have an Azure environment.

You need to create a new Azure virtual machine from an Android laptop.

Solution: You use the PowerApps portal.

Does this meet the goal?

- ○ Yes
- ○ **No** (Correct)

Explanation

Correct Answer - B

We use "Azure Portal" to create Virtual Machines from an Android laptop as shown below:

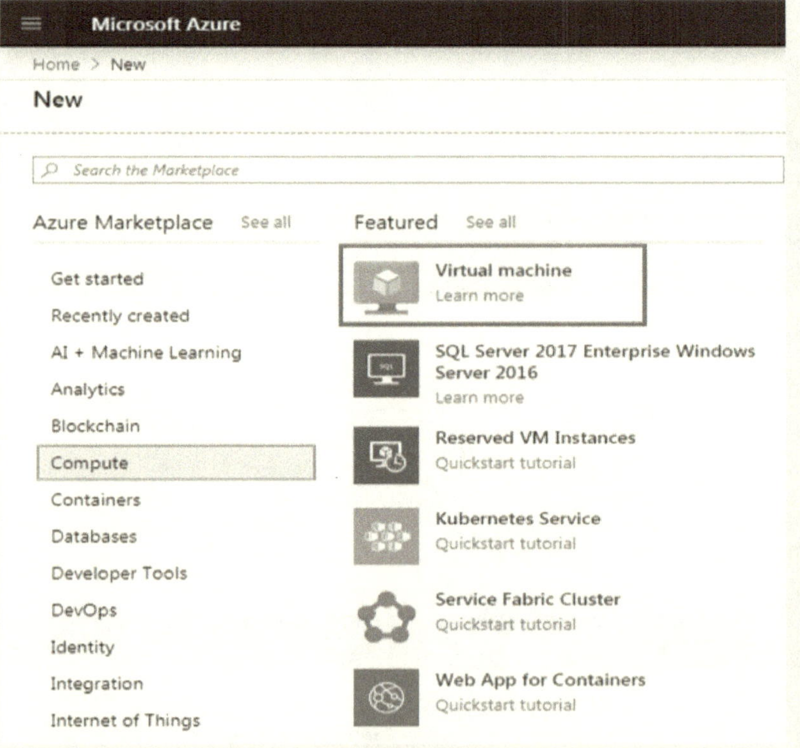

Question 3:
Which two types of customers are eligible to use the Azure Government to develop a cloud solution?

- □ a United States government entity (Correct)
- □ a European government entity
- □ a United States government contractor (Correct)
- □ a European government contractor

Explanation

Correct Answers - A and C

As per the below snapshot, the Azure government document clearly states "US government agencies or their partners" are eligible to use Azure Government to develop a cloud solution.

What is Azure Government?

09/17/2018 • 2 minutes to read • ●●●●

US government agencies or their partners interested in cloud services that meet government security and compliance requirements, can be confident that Microsoft Azure Government provides world-class security, protection, and compliance services. Azure Government delivers a dedicated cloud enabling government agencies and their partners to transform mission-critical workloads to the cloud. Azure Government services handle data that is subject to certain government regulations and requirements, such as FedRAMP, NIST 800.171 (DIB), ITAR, IRS 1075, DoD L4, and CJIS. In order to provide you with the highest level of security and compliance, Azure Government uses physically isolated datacenters and networks (located in U.S. only).

Azure Government customers (US federal, state, and local government or their partners) are subject to validation of eligibility. If there is a question about eligibility for Azure Government, you should consult your account team. To sign up for trial, request your trial subscription.

Reference:

https://docs.microsoft.com/en-us/azure/azure-government/documentation-government-welcome

Question 4:
For each of the following statements, select YES if the statement is true. Otherwise select, NO.

Larger image

	Statement
1	To implement an Azure Multi-Factor Authentication (MFA) solution, you must deploy a federation solution or sync on-premises identities to the cloud.
2	Two valid methods for Azure Multi-Factor Authentication (MFA) are picture identification and passport number
3	Azure Multi-Factor Authentication (MFA) can be required for administrative and non-administrative user accounts

- ○ Statement 1: YES

  Statement 2: YES
  Statement 3: YES

- ● Statement 1: NO

  Statement 2: NO
  Statement 3: NO

- ○ Statement 1: YES

  Statement 2: NO
  Statement 3: YES

- ○ Statement 1: YES

  Statement 2: YES
  Statement 3: NO

- ○ Statement 1: NO

  Statement 2: NO
  Statement 3: YES (Correct)

- ○ Statement 1: NO

  Statement 2: YES
  Statement 3: NO

- ⊙ Statement 1: NO

Statement 2: YES
Statement 3: YES

Explanation

Correct Answer - E

Azure Multi-Factor Authentication (MFA) helps safeguard access to data and applications while maintaining simplicity for users. It provides additional security by requiring a second form of authentication and delivers strong authentication via a range of easy to use authentication methods. **Users may or may not be challenged for MFA based on configuration decisions that an administrator makes.**

Link: https://docs.microsoft.com/en-us/azure/active-directory/authentication/concept-mfa-howitworks

How it works: Azure Multi-Factor Authentication

06/03/2018 • 2 minutes to read • 🧑👤👥👤 +2

The security of two-step verification lies in its layered approach. Compromising multiple authentication factors presents a significant challenge for attackers. Even if an attacker manages to learn the user's password, it is useless without also having possession of the additional authentication method. It works by requiring two or more of the following authentication methods:

- Something you know (typically a password)
- Something you have (a trusted device that is not easily duplicated, like a phone)
- Something you are (biometrics)

Azure Multi-Factor Authentication (MFA) helps safeguard access to data and applications while maintaining simplicity for users. It provides additional security by requiring a second form of authentication and delivers strong authentication via a range of easy to use authentication methods. Users may or may not be challenged for MFA based on configuration decisions that an administrator makes.

To implement MFA a federation solution or sync up on-premises identities to the cloud is not needed.

Picture identification and passport number are not valid methods for MFA.

MFA is required for both the administrative and non-administrative user accounts.

Reference:

https://docs.microsoft.com/en-us/azure/active-directory/authentication/concept-mfa-howitworks

Question 5:
This question requires that you evaluate the italicized text in double quotes to determine if it is correct.

An organization that hosts its infrastructure "*in a private cloud*" can decommission its data center.

Instructions: Review the italicized text in double quotes. If it makes this statement correct, select " No change is needed." If this statement is incorrect, select the answer choice that makes the statement correct.

- ○ No change is needed.
- ○ in a hybrid cloud
- ○ in the public cloud (Correct)
- ○ on a hyper-V host

Explanation

Correct Answer - C

Option c is CORRECT because a public cloud is defined as computing services offered by third-party providers over the public Internet, making them available to anyone who wants to use or purchase them. They may be free or sold on-demand, allowing customers to pay only per usage for the CPU cycles, storage or bandwidth they consume. The public cloud is a shared entity and the general public or institutions are allowed to use a portion of the public cloud as per their requirements. An organization that hosts its infrastructure in a public cloud can decommission its data center.

Option A is INCORRECT because a change is needed in the given statement.

Option B is INCORRECT because in a hybrid cloud usually the data centers are located on-premises and therefore it cannot be decommissioned.

Option D is INCORRECT because a Hyper V host just provides a virtualization environment.

Reference:

https://azure.microsoft.com/en-in/overview/what-is-a-public-cloud/#:~:text=The%20public%20cloud%20is%20defined,storage%2C%20or%20bandwidth%20they%20consume.

Question 6:

You plan to migrate several servers from an on-premises network to Azure

You need to identify the primary benefits of using a public cloud service for the servers

What should you identify?

- ○ The public cloud is a crowd-sourcing solution that provides corporations with the ability to enhance the cloud.
- ○ The public cloud is owned by the public, NOT a private Corporation.
- ○ The public cloud is a shared entity whereby multiple corporations each use a portion of the resources in the cloud. (Correct)
- ○ All public cloud resources can be freely accessed by every member of the public.

Explanation

Correct Answer - C

Option C is CORRECT because a public cloud is a shared entity and the general public or institutions are allowed to use a portion of the public cloud as per their requirements.

Option A is INCORRECT because it is not the benefit of using a public cloud.

Option B is INCORRECT because it is a known fact that a public cloud is not owned by a private entity.

Option D is INCORRECT because it is not the benefit of using a public cloud.

The public cloud is defined as computing services offered by third-party providers over the public Internet, making them available to anyone who wants to use or purchase them. They may be free or sold on-demand, allowing customers to pay only per usage for the CPU cycles, storage or bandwidth they consume.

Unlike private clouds, public clouds can save companies from the expensive costs of having to purchase, manage and maintain on-premises hardware and application infrastructure - the cloud service provider is held responsible for all management and maintenance of the system. Public clouds can also be deployed faster than on-premises infrastructures and with an almost infinitely scalable platform. Every employee of a company can use the same application from any office or branch using their device of choice as long as they can access the Internet. While security concerns have been raised over public cloud environments, when implemented correctly, the public cloud can be as secure as the most effectively managed private cloud implementation if the provider uses proper security methods, such as intrusion detection and prevention systems (IDPS).

Reference:

https://azure.microsoft.com/en-in/overview/what-is-a-public-cloud/#:~:text=The%20public%20cloud%20is%20defined,storage%2C%20or%20bandwidth%2
0they%20consume.

Question 7:

For each of the following statements, select YES if the statement is true. Otherwise select, NO.

Larger image

	Statement
1	Azure provides flexibility between capital expenditure (CapEx) and operational expenditure (OpEx).
2	If you create two Azure virtual machines that use the B2S size, each virtual machine will always generate the same monthly costs
3	When an Azure virtual machine is stopped, you continue to pay storage costs associated to the virtual machine.

- ○ Statement 1: YES

  Statement 2: YES
  Statement 3: YES

- ○ Statement 1: NO

  Statement 2: NO
  Statement 3: NO

- ○ Statement 1: YES

  Statement 2: NO
  Statement 3: YES (Correct)

- ○ Statement 1: YES

  Statement 2: YES
  Statement 3: NO

- ○ Statement 1: NO

  Statement 2: NO
  Statement 3: YES

- ○ Statement 1: NO

  Statement 2: YES
  Statement 3: NO

- ○ Statement 1: NO

Statement 2: YES
Statement 3: YES

Explanation

Correct Answer - C

Azure provides flexibility between capital expenditure (CapEx) and operational expenditure (OpEx).

If you create two Azure virtual machines that use the B2S size, each virtual machine will NOT always generate the same monthly costs. This is because it also depends on the region in which the virtual machines are located and costs differ region-wise

When an Azure virtual machine is stopped, you continue to pay storage costs associated with the virtual machine.

Question 8:
This question requires that you evaluate the italicized text in double quotes to determine if it is correct.

When you are implementing software as a service (SaaS) solution, you are responsible for "_configuring high availability_".

Instructions: Review the italicized text in double quotes. If it makes this statement correct, select " No change is needed". If this statement is incorrect, select the answer choice that makes the statement correct.

- ○ No changes needed
- ○ defining scalability rules
- ○ installing the SaaS solution
- ○ configuring the SaaS solution (Correct)

Explanation

Correct Answer - C

SaaS provides a complete software solution that you purchase on a pay-as-you-go basis from a cloud service provider. You rent the use of an app for your organization, and your users connect to it over the Internet, usually with a web browser. All of the underlying infrastructure, middleware, app software, and app data are located in the service provider's data center. The service provider manages the hardware and software, and with the appropriate service agreement, will ensure the availability and the security of the app and your data as well

To provide SaaS apps to users, you don't need to purchase, install, update, or maintain any hardware, middleware, or software.

You need to configure the SaaS solution as per your requirement.

Option D is CORRECT since you are responsible for configuring the SaaS solution as per your requirement.

Option A is INCORRECT because a change is needed for the given statement.

Option B is INCORRECT because you do not need to define scalability rules.

Option C is INCORRECT because to provide SaaS apps to users, you don't need to purchase, install, update, or maintain any hardware, middleware, or software.

Reference:

https://azure.microsoft.com/en-us/overview/what-is-saas/

Question 9:
Which cloud deployment solution is used for Azure virtual machines?

- ○ Infrastructure as a Service (IaaS) (Correct)
- ○ Platform as a service (PaaS)
- ○ Software as a Service (SaaS)
- ○ None of the above

Explanation

Correct Answer - A

Option A is CORRECT since Infrastructure as a service (IaaS) is an instant computing infrastructure, provisioned and managed over the internet. IaaS quickly scales up and down with demand, letting you pay only for what you use. It helps you avoid the expense and complexity of buying and managing your own physical servers and other datacenter infrastructure. Each resource is offered as a separate service component, and you only need to rent a particular one for as long as you need it.

Four reasons to choose Azure IaaS

Infrastructure for every workload   Hybrid by design   Built-in security and management   Cost-effective

Provision the infrastructure that you need

Scale your compute performance from 1 vCPU to 480 vCPU cores and your memory from 1 GB to 24 TB. Tailor your disk storage capacity from 4 GB to 64 TB and reach up to 160,000 IOPS on a single disk. Rely on networking speeds from 30 Gbps Ethernet to 100 Gbps InfiniBand interconnects.

Choose the SLA that's right for you: from the industry's only 99.9 percent single VM SLA to 99.99 percent VM SLA across two or more Availability Zones.

Learn about Azure Virtual Machines >

Learn about Azure storage >

Learn about Azure networking >

Support the applications that you use

Use Windows or Linux applications and your favorite programming language. Run your enterprise-class applications like SAP, Oracle, IBM, and SharePoint, or choose from thousands of other workloads available in the Azure Marketplace.

Tap into nearly unlimited resources to tackle your most demanding high-performance computing (HPC) or AI challenges, and use purpose-built bare metal infrastructure to scale workloads like SAP HANA to extreme levels.

Run Windows Server on Azure >

Run Linux on Azure >

Run SAP on Azure >

Option B is INCORRECT because Platform as a service (PaaS) is a complete development and deployment environment in the cloud, with resources that enable you to deliver everything from simple cloud-based apps to sophisticated, cloud-enabled enterprise applications.

Option C is INCORRECT because Software as a service (SaaS) allows users to connect to and use cloud-based apps over the Internet. Common examples are email, calendaring, and office tools (such as Microsoft Office 365). SaaS provides a complete software solution that you purchase on a pay-as-you-go basis from a cloud service provider.

Option D is INCORRECT.

Reference:

https://azure.microsoft.com/en-us/overview/what-is-iaas/

Question 10:
Which cloud deployment solution is used for Azure SQL databases?

- ○ Infrastructure as a Service (IaaS)
- ○ Platform as a service (PaaS) (Correct)
- ○ Software as a Service (SaaS)
- ○ None of the above

Explanation

Correct Answer - B

Option B is CORRECT since Azure SQL Database falls under "Platform as a Service (Paas)".

Azure SQL Database - Platform as a Service

Azure SQL Database is a fully managed Platform as a Service (PaaS) Database Engine that handles most of the database management functions such as upgrading, patching, backups, and monitoring without user involvement. Azure SQL Database is always running on the latest stable version of SQL Server Database Engine and patched OS with 99.99% availability. PaaS capabilities that are built-in into Azure SQL database enable you to focus on the domain specific database administration and optimization activities that are critical for your business.

Option A is INCORRECT because Azure SQL Database does not fall under "Infrastructure as a Service (Paas)".

Option C is INCORRECT because Azure SQL Database does not fall under "Software as a Service (Paas)".

Option D is INCORRECT because Azure SQL Database falls under "Platform as a Service (Paas)".

Reference:

https://docs.microsoft.com/en-us/azure/sql-database/sql-database-paas-index

Question 11:

For each of the following statements, select YES if the statement is true. Otherwise select, NO.

STATEMENTS

----

1. A Standard support plan is included in an Azure free account.

2. A Professional Direct support plan can only be purchased by companies that have an Enterprise Agreement (EA)

3. Support from MSDN forums is only provided to companies that have a pay-as-you-go subscription.

- ○ Statement 1: YES

  Statement 2: YES
  Stat ement 3: YES

- ○ Statement 1: NO

  Statement 2: NO
  Statement 3: NO (Correct)

- ○ Statement 1: YES

  Statement 2: NO
  Statement 3: YES

- ○ Statement 1: YES

  Statement 2: YES
  Statement 3: NO

- ○ Statement 1: NO

  Statement 2: NO
  Statement 3: YES

- ○ Statement 1: NO

  Statement 2: YES
  Statement 3: NO

- ○ Statement 1: NO

  Statement 2: YES
  Statement 3: YES

Explanation

Correct Answer - B

	Basic Request support	DEVELOPER Purchase support	STANDARD Purchase support	PROFESSIONAL DIRECT Purchase support
Price	Included for all Azure customers	$29 per month	$100 per month	$1,000 per month
Scope	Included for all Azure customers	Trial and non-production environments	Production workload environments	Business-critical dependence
Billing and subscription management support	✓	✓	✓	✓
24/7 self-help resources, including Microsoft Learn, Azure portal how-to videos, documentation, and community support	✓	✓	✓	✓
Ability to submit as many support tickets as you need	✓	✓	✓	✓
Azure Advisor—your free, personalized guide to Azure best practices	✓	✓	✓	✓
Azure health status and notifications	✓	✓	✓	✓
24/7 access to technical support by email and phone		Available during business hours by email only.	✓	✓
Case severity and response time		Minimal business impact (Sev C): Within eight business hours[1]	Minimal business impact (Sev C): Within eight business hours[1] Moderate business impact (Sev B): Within four hours Critical business impact (Sev A): Within one hour	Minimal business impact (Sev C): Within four business hours[1] Moderate business impact (Sev B): Within two hours Critical business impact (Sev A): Within one hour
Third-party software support with interoperability and configuration guidance and troubleshooting		✓	✓	✓
Architecture Support		Géneral guidance	General guidance	Guidance from a pool of ProDirect delivery managers
Operations Support				Service reviews and advisory consultation from a pool of ProDirect delivery managers
Training				Webinars led by Azure engineers
Proactive Guidance				From a pool of ProDirect delivery managers

A Standard support plan is NOT included in an Azure free account.

A Professional Direct support plan can be purchased by companies even if they do not have an Enterprise Agreement (EA).

Support from MSDN forums is available to companies even if they do not have a pay-as-you-go subscription.

Reference:

https://azure.microsoft.com/en-us/support/plans/

Question 12:
This question requires that you evaluate the italicized text in double quotes to determine if it is correct.

An Azure service is available to all Azure customers when it is in *"public preview"*.

Instructions: Review the italicized text in double quotes. If it makes this statement correct, select " No change is needed". If this statement is incorrect, select the answer choice that makes the statement correct.

- ○ No change is needed (Correct)
- ○ private preview
- ○ development
- ○ an Enterprise Agreement (EA) subscription

Explanation

Correct Answer - A

Option A is CORRECT since no change is needed for the given statement. Public preview is available to all customers.

Option B is INCORRECT since the private preview is available only for select customers.

Option C is INCORRECT since the Azure service is not available to all when it is in development mode.

Option D is INCORRECT since an Enterprise Agreement (EA) subscription is available only for select customers.

Question 13:
You plan to create an Azure virtual machine.

You need to identify which storage service must be used to store the data disks of the virtual machine.

Larger image

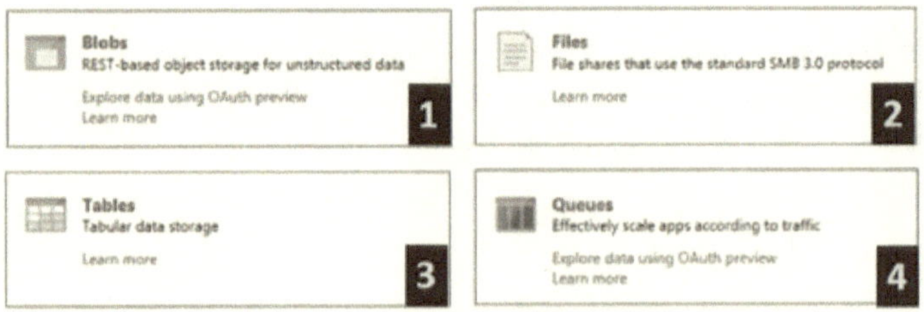

What should you identify?

- ○ 1 (Correct)
- ○ 2

- ○ 3
- ○ 4

Explanation

Correct Answer : A

Option A. is CORRECT since Azure Page Blob storage is used to store random access files up to 8 TB in size. Page blobs store virtual hard drive (VHD) files and serve as disks for Azure virtual machines.

Reference: https://docs.microsoft.com/en-us/azure/storage/blobs/storage-blobs-introduction

Option B. is INCORRECT since Azure Files are not used to store the data disks of the VM.

https://docs.microsoft.com/en-us/azure/storage/files/storage-files-introduction

Option C. is INCORRECT since Azure Table storage is a service that stores structured NoSQL data in the cloud, providing a key/attribute store with a schemaless design.

Reference: https://docs.microsoft.com/en-us/azure/cosmos-db/table-storage-overview

Option D. is INCORRECT since Azure Queue Storage is a service for storing large numbers of messages.

Question 14:
This question requires that you evaluate the italicized text in double quotes to determine if it is correct.

"*Azure policies provide*" a command platform for deploying objects to cloud infrastructure and for implementing consistency across the Azure environment."

Instructions: Review the italicized text in double quotes. If it makes this statement correct, select " No change is needed". If this statement is incorrect, select the answer choice that makes the statement correct.

- ○ No change is needed
- ○ Resource groups provide
- ○ Azure Resource Manager provides (Correct)
- ○ Management groups provide

Explanation

Correct Answer: C

Option C is CORRECT since Azure Resource Manager provides a management layer that enables you to create, update, and delete resources in your Azure subscription and maintain consistency across environments

What is Azure Resource Manager?

03/25/2020 • 5 minutes to read • 🧑

Azure Resource Manager is the deployment and management service for Azure. It provides a management layer that enables you to create, update, and delete resources in your Azure subscription. You use management features, like access control, locks, and tags, to secure and organize your resources after deployment.

To learn about Azure Resource Manager templates, see Template deployment overview.

Consistent management layer

When a user sends a request from any of the Azure tools, APIs, or SDKs, Resource Manager receives the request. It authenticates and authorizes the request. Resource Manager sends the request to the Azure service, which takes the requested action. Because all requests are handled through the same API, you see consistent results and capabilities in all the different tools.

The following image shows the role Azure Resource Manager plays in handling Azure requests.

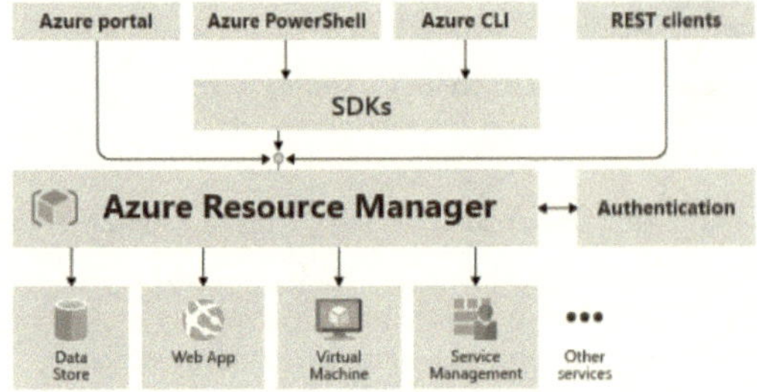

Option A is INCORRECT since the given statement is wrong and change is needed.

Option B is INCORRECT since A resource group is a container that holds related resources for an Azure solution. The resource group can include all the resources for the solution, or only those resources that you want to manage as a group.

Reference: https://docs.microsoft.com/en-us/azure/azure-resource-manager/manage-resource-groups-portal

Option D is INCORRECT since you organize subscriptions into containers called "management groups" and apply your governance conditions to the management groups. All subscriptions within a management group automatically inherit the conditions applied to the management group.

Reference: https://docs.microsoft.com/en-us/azure/governance/management-groups/overview

Question 15:
A team of developers at your company plans to deploy, and then remove, 50 customized virtual machines each week. Thirty of the virtual machines run Windows Server 2016 and 20

of the virtual machines run Ubuntu Linux. You need to recommend which Azure service will minimize the administrative effort required to deploy and remove the virtual machines. What should you recommend?

- ○ Microsoft Virtual Desktop
- ○ Azure Reserved Virtual Machine (VM) Instances
- ○ **Azure DevTest Labs** (Correct)
- ○ Azure virtual machine scale sets

Explanation

Correct Answer - C

Option C is CORRECT since Azure DevTest Labs enables developers on teams to efficiently manage virtual machines (VMs) and PaaS resources without waiting for approvals. DevTest Labs creates labs consisting of pre-configured bases or Azure Resource Manager templates. These have all the necessary tools and software that you can use to create environments. You can create environments in a few minutes, as opposed to hours or days.

Reference: https://docs.microsoft.com/en-us/azure/lab-services/devtest-lab-overview

About Azure DevTest Labs

03/21/2019 • 3 minutes to read • 👤

Azure DevTest Labs enables developers on teams to efficiently self-manage virtual machines (VMs) and PaaS resources without waiting for approvals.

DevTest Labs creates labs consisting of pre-configured bases or Azure Resource Manager templates. These have all the necessary tools and software that you can use to create environments. You can create environments in a few minutes, as opposed to hours or days.

By using DevTest Labs, you can test the latest versions of your applications by doing the following tasks:

- Quickly provision Windows and Linux environments by using reusable templates and artifacts.
- Easily integrate your deployment pipeline with DevTest Labs to provision on-demand environments.
- Scale up your load testing by provisioning multiple test agents and create pre-provisioned environments for training and demos.

Option A is INCORRECT since Windows Virtual Desktop is a desktop and app virtualization service that runs on the cloud.

Reference: https://docs.microsoft.com/en-us/azure/virtual-desktop/overview

Option B is INCORRECT since Azure Reserved VM instances are optimized for instance size flexibility and the reservation you buy can apply to the virtual machines (VMs) sizes in the same instance size flexibility group.

Reference: https://docs.microsoft.com/en-us/azure/virtual-machines/windows/reserved-vm-instance-size-flexibility

Option D is INCORRECT since Azure virtual machine scale sets let you create and manage a group of identical, load-balanced VMs.Scale sets provide high availability to your applications and allow you to centrally manage, configure, and update a large number of VMs. With virtual machine scale sets, you can build large-scale services for areas such as compute, big data, and container workloads.

Reference: https://docs.microsoft.com/en-us/azure/virtual-machine-scale-sets/overview

Question 16:
Fill in the blank with the correct Azure service to correctly complete the statement below:

______________ is a big data analysis service for machine learning.

- ○ Azure Databricks (Correct)
- ○ Azure Function
- ○ Azure App Service
- ○ Azure Application Insights

Explanation

Correct Answer - A

Option A is CORRECT since Azure Databricks has "MLib": Machine Learning library consisting of common learning algorithms and utilities, including classification, regression, clustering, collaborative filtering, dimensionality reduction, as well as underlying optimization primitives.

Reference: https://docs.microsoft.com/en-us/azure/azure-databricks/what-is-azure-databricks

- **MLib**: Machine Learning library consisting of common learning algorithms and utilities, including classification, regression, clustering, collaborative filtering, dimensionality reduction, as well as underlying optimization primitives.

Option B is INCORRECT since Azure Functions is a solution for easily running small pieces of code, or "functions," in the cloud.

Reference: https://docs.microsoft.com/en-us/azure/azure-functions/functions-overview

Option C is INCORRECT since Azure App Service enables you to build and host web apps, mobile back ends, and RESTful APIs in the programming language of your choice without managing infrastructure.

Reference: https://docs.microsoft.com/en-us/azure/app-service/

Option D is INCORRECT since Application Insights, a feature of Azure Monitor is an extensible Application Performance Management (APM) service for web developers on multiple platforms.

Question 17:

Fill in the blank with the correct Azure service to correctly complete the statement below:

___________ detects and diagnoses anomalies in web apps.

- ○ Azure Databricks
- ○ Azure Functions
- ○ Azure App Service
- ○ Azure Application Insights (Correct)

Explanation

Correct Answer - D

Option D is CORRECT since Application Insights, a feature of Azure Monitor is an extensible Application Performance Management (APM) service for web developers on multiple platforms. Use it to monitor your live web application. It will automatically detect performance anomalies.

Reference: https://docs.microsoft.com/en-us/azure/azure-monitor/app/app-insights-overview

What is Application Insights?

06/03/2019 • 5 minutes to read •

Application Insights, a feature of Azure Monitor, is an extensible Application Performance Management (APM) service for web developers on multiple platforms. Use it to monitor your live web application. It will automatically detect performance anomalies. It includes powerful analytics tools to help you diagnose issues and to understand what users actually do with your app. It's designed to help you continuously improve performance and usability. It works for apps on a wide variety of platforms including .NET, Node.js and Java EE, hosted on-premises, hybrid, or any public cloud. It integrates with your DevOps process, and has connection points to a variety of development tools. It can monitor and analyze telemetry from mobile apps by integrating with Visual Studio App Center.

Option A is INCORRECT since Azure Databricks is an Apache Spark-based analytics platform optimized for the Microsoft Azure cloud services platform.

Reference: https://docs.microsoft.com/en-us/azure/azure-databricks/what-is-azure-databricks

Option B is INCORRECT since Azure Functions is a solution for easily running small pieces of code, or "functions," in the cloud.

Reference: https://docs.microsoft.com/en-us/azure/azure-functions/functions-overview

Option C is INCORRECT since Azure App Service enables you to build and host web apps, mobile back ends, and RESTful APIs in the programming language of your choice without managing infrastructure.

Reference: https://docs.microsoft.com/en-us/azure/app-service/

Question 18:
Fill in the blank with the correct Azure service to correctly complete the statement below:

_____________ is a tool that provides guidance and recommendations to improve an Azure environment.

- ○ **Azure Advisor** (Correct)
- ○ **Azure Cognitive Services**
- ○ **Azure DevOps**
- ○ **Azure Application Insights**

Explanation

Correct Answer - A

Option A is CORRECT since Azure Advisor is a tool that provides guidance and recommendations to improve an Azure environment.

Reference: https://docs.microsoft.com/en-us/azure/advisor/advisor-overview

Introduction to Azure Advisor

02/01/2019 • 2 minutes to read • 👤👤👤👤👤 +6

Learn about the key capabilities of Azure Advisor and get answers to frequently asked questions.

What is Advisor?

Advisor is a personalized cloud consultant that helps you follow best practices to optimize your Azure deployments. It analyzes your resource configuration and usage telemetry and then recommends solutions that can help you improve the cost effectiveness, performance, high availability, and security of your Azure resources.

With Advisor, you can:

- Get proactive, actionable, and personalized best practices recommendations.
- Improve the performance, security, and high availability of your resources, as you identify opportunities to reduce your overall Azure spend.
- Get recommendations with proposed actions inline.

Option B is INCORRECT since Azure Cognitive Services are APIs, SDKs, and services available to help developers build intelligent applications without having direct AI or data science skills or knowledge. Azure Cognitive Services enable developers to easily add cognitive features into their applications.

Reference: https://docs.microsoft.com/en-us/azure/cognitive-services/welcome

Option C is INCORRECT since Azure DevOps enables teams located anywhere in the world to communicate effectively during daily development activities as well as to integrate with software development tools for monitoring activities such as deployments.

Reference: https://docs.microsoft.com/en-us/azure/devops/learn/what-is-devops

Option D is INCORRECT since Application Insights, a feature of Azure Monitor is an extensible Application Performance Management (APM) service for web developers on multiple platforms. Use it to monitor your live web application. It will automatically detect performance anomalies.

Reference: https://docs.microsoft.com/en-us/azure/azure-monitor/app/app-insights-overview

Question 19:
This question requires that you evaluate the italicized text in double quotes to determine if it is correct.

You have an Azure virtual network named VNET1 in a resource group named RG1.

You assign an Azure policy specifying that virtual networks are not allowed resource type in RG1. VNET1 "*is deleted automatically*".

Instructions: Review the italicized text in double quotes. If it makes this statement correct, select " No change is needed". If this statement is incorrect, select the answer choice that makes the statement correct.

- ○ No change is needed
- ○ is moved automatically to another resource group
- ○ continues to function normally (Correct)
- ○ is now a read-only object

Explanation

Correct Answer - C

Azure Policy is a service in Azure that you use to create, assign, and manage policies. These policies enforce different rules and effects over your resources, so those resources stay compliant with your corporate standards and service level agreements. Azure Policy meets this need by evaluating your resources for non-compliance with assigned policies. For example, you can have the policy to allow only a certain SKU size of virtual machines in your environment. Once this policy is implemented, new and existing resources are evaluated for compliance.

Azure Policy focuses on resource properties during deployment and for already existing resources.

Overview of the Azure Policy service

12/06/2018 • 9 minutes to read • 👤👤👤 👥 👥

Governance validates that your organization can achieve its goals through effective and efficient use of IT. It meets this need by creating clarity between business goals and IT projects.

Does your company experience a significant number of IT issues that never seem to get resolved? Good IT governance involves planning your initiatives and setting priorities on a strategic level to help manage and prevent issues. This strategic need is where Azure Policy comes in.

Azure Policy is a service in Azure that you use to create, assign, and manage policies. These policies enforce different rules and effects over your resources, so those resources stay compliant with your corporate standards and service level agreements. Azure Policy meets this need by evaluating your resources for non-compliance with assigned policies. For example, you can have a policy to allow only a certain SKU size of virtual machines in your environment. Once this policy is implemented, new and existing resources are evaluated for compliance. With the right type of policy, existing resources can be brought into compliance. Later in this documentation, we'll go over more details on how to create and implement policies with Azure Policy.

Since VNET1 was already created in RG1 before the Azure policy was created, it would function normally. However creation of further VNETs would not be allowed in RG1.

Option C is CORRECT since Azure Policies are evaluated for both the new and existing resources for the compliance, the already created VNET in RG1 would function normally.

Options A, B, and D are therefore INCORRECT.

Reference:

https://docs.microsoft.com/en-us/azure/governance/policy/overview

Question 20:
What can Azure Information Protection encrypt?

- ○ an Azure SQL database
- ○ documents and email messages (Correct)
- ○ an Azure Storage account
- ○ network traffic

Explanation

Correct Answer - B

Option B is CORRECT since Azure Information Protection (sometimes referred to as AIP) is a cloud-based solution that helps an organization to classify and optionally, protect its documents and emails by applying labels.

Reference: https://docs.microsoft.com/en-us/azure/information-protection/what-is-information-protection

What is Azure Information Protection?

10/18/2019 • 8 minutes to read •

Applies to: *Azure Information Protection*

Azure Information Protection (sometimes referred to as AIP) is a cloud-based solution that helps an organization to classify and optionally, protect its documents and emails by applying labels. Labels can be applied automatically by administrators who define rules and conditions, manually by users, or a combination where users are given recommendations.

Option A is INCORRECT since Azure SQL Database handles most of the database management functions

Azure SQL Database - Platform as a Service

Azure SQL Database is a fully managed Platform as a Service (PaaS) Database Engine that handles most of the database management functions such as upgrading, patching, backups, and monitoring without user involvement. Azure SQL Database is always running on the latest stable version of SQL Server Database Engine and patched OS with 99.99% availability. PaaS capabilities that are built-in into Azure SQL database enable you to focus on the domain specific database administration and optimization activities that are critical for your business.

Reference: https://docs.microsoft.com/en-us/azure/sql-database/sql-database-paas-index

Option C is INCORRECT since An Azure storage account contains all of your Azure Storage data objects: blobs, files, queues, tables, and disks.

Reference: https://docs.microsoft.com/en-us/azure/storage/common/storage-account-overview

Option D is INCORRECT since network traffic cannot be encrypted by the Azure Information Protection.

Question 41:
You have an Azure subscription named Subscription1. Subscription1 contains the resource groups in the following table.

***

Name: RG1,··················Azure region: West Europe,····Policy: Policy1

Name: RG2,··················Azure region: North Europe,···Policy: Policy2

Name: RG3,··················Azure region: France Central,·Policy: Policy3

***

RG1 has a web app named WebApp1. WebApp1 is located in West Europe.

You move WebApp1 to RG2.

What is the effect of the move?

- The App Service plan for WebApp1 moves to North Europe. Policy2 applies to WebApp1.
- The App Service plan for WebApp1 remains in West Europe. Policy2 applies to WebApp1. (Correct)
- The App Service plan for WebApp1 moves to North Europe. Policy1 applies to WebApp1.
- The App Service plan for WebApp1 remains in West Europe. Policy1 applies to WebApp1.

Explanation

Correct Answer - B

You can move an app to another App Service plan, as long as the source plan and the target plan are in the same resource group and geographical region.

The region in which your app runs is the region of the App Service plan it's in. However, you cannot change an App Service plan's region.

Question 42:
Your Azure environment contains multiple Azure virtual machines.

You need to ensure that a virtual machine named VM1 is accessible from the Internet over HTTP.

Solution: You modify a DDoS protection plan.

Does this meet the goal?

- Yes
- No (Correct)

Explanation

Correct Answer - B

You open a port, or create an endpoint, to a virtual machine (VM) in Azure by creating a network filter on a subnet or a VM network interface. You place these filters, which control both inbound and outbound traffic, on a network security group attached to the resource that receives the traffic.

The example in this article demonstrates how to create a network filter that uses the standard TCP port 80 (it's assumed you've already started the appropriate services and opened any OS firewall rules on the VM).

After you've created a VM that's configured to serve web requests on the standard TCP port 80, you can:

1. Create a network security group.

2. Create an inbound security rule allowing traffic and assign values to the following settings:

a. Destination port ranges: 80.

b. Source port ranges: * (allows any source port).

c. Priority value: Enter a value that is less than 65,500 and higher in priority than the default catch-all deny inbound rule.

Associate the network security group with the VM network interface or subnet.

Question 43:
You plan to store 20 TB of data in Azure. The data will be accessed infrequently and visualized by using Microsoft Power BI.

You need to recommend a storage solution for the data. Which two solutions should you recommend?

- ☐ Azure Data Lake (Correct)
- ☐ Azure SQL Data Warehouse (Correct)
- ☐ Azure SQL Database
- ☐ Azure Cosmos DB
- ☐ Azure Database for PostgreSQL

Explanation

Correct Answers - A and B

Option A is CORRECT since A data lake is a storage repository that holds a large amount of data in its native, raw format. Data lake stores are optimized for scaling to terabytes and petabytes of data.

Link: https://docs.microsoft.com/en-us/azure/architecture/data-guide/scenarios/data-lake

Data lakes

02/12/2018 · 2 minutes to read ·

A data lake is a storage repository that holds a large amount of data in its native, raw format. Data lake stores are optimized for scaling to terabytes and petabytes of data. The data typically comes from multiple heterogeneous sources, and may be structured, semi-structured, or unstructured. The idea with a data lake is to store everything in its original, untransformed state. This approach differs from a traditional data warehouse, which transforms and processes the data at the time of ingestion.

Option B is CORRECT since the data warehouse is a centralized repository of integrated data from one or more disparate sources. Data warehouses store current and historical data and are used for reporting and analysis of the data. The data warehouse becomes a permanent data store for reporting, analysis, and business intelligence (BI).

Reference: https://docs.microsoft.com/en-us/azure/architecture/data-guide/relational-data/data-warehousing

Data warehousing

04/20/2019 · 11 minutes to read · ·5

A data warehouse is a centralized repository of integrated data from one or more disparate sources. Data warehouses store current and historical data and are used for reporting and analysis of the data.

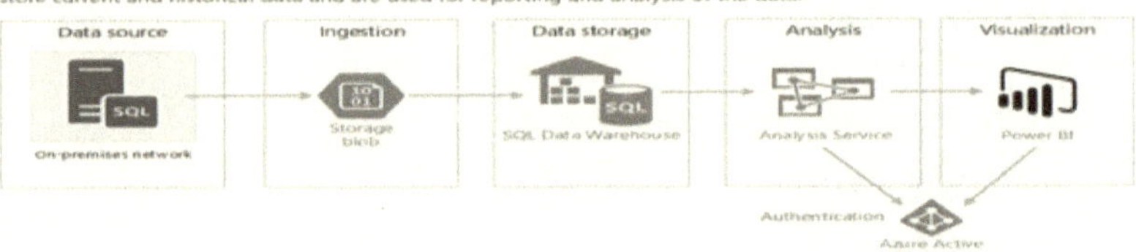

To move data into a data warehouse, data is periodically extracted from various sources that contain important business information. As the data is moved, it can be formatted, cleaned, validated, summarized, and reorganized. Alternatively, the data can be stored in the lowest level of detail, with aggregated views provided in the warehouse for reporting. In either case, the data warehouse becomes a permanent data store for reporting, analysis, and business intelligence (BI).

Option C is INCORRECT since Azure SQL Database is a general-purpose relational database, provided as a managed service. With it, you can create a highly available and high-performance data storage layer for the applications and solutions in Azure. SQL Database can be the right choice for a variety of modern cloud applications because it enables you to process both relational data and non-relational structures, such as graphs, JSON, spatial, and XML.

Reference: https://docs.microsoft.com/en-us/azure/sql-database/sql-database-technical-overview

Option D is INCORRECT since Azure Cosmos DB is Microsoft's globally distributed, multi-model database service. With a click of a button, Cosmos DB enables you to elastically and independently scale throughput and storage across any number of Azure regions worldwide. You can elastically scale throughput and storage, and take advantage of fast, single-digit-millisecond data access using your favorite API including SQL, MongoDB, Cassandra, Tables, or Gremlin. Cosmos DB provides comprehensive service level

agreements **(SLAs)** for throughput, latency, availability, and consistency guarantees, something no other database service offers.

Reference: https://docs.microsoft.com/en-us/azure/cosmos-db/introduction

Option e is INCORRECT since Azure Database for PostgreSQL is a relational database service in the Microsoft cloud built for developers. It is based on the community version of the open-source PostgreSQL database engine and is available in two deployment options: Single Server and Hyperscale (Citus).

Reference: https://docs.microsoft.com/en-us/azure/postgresql/overview

Question 44:
This question requires that you evaluate the italicized text in double quotes to determine if it is correct.

When you need to delegate permissions to several Azure virtual machines simultaneously, you must deploy the Azure virtual machines "*to the same Azure region*".

Instructions: Review the italicized text in double quotes. If it makes this statement correct, select " No change is needed". If this statement is incorrect, select the answer choice that makes the statement correct.

- ○ No change is needed
- ○ by using the same Azure Resource Manager template
- ○ to the same resource group (Correct)
- ○ to the same availability zone

Explanation

Correct Answer - C

Option C is CORRECT since A resource group is a container that holds related resources for an Azure solution. The resource group can include all the resources for the solution, or only those resources that you want to manage as a group.

Reference: https://docs.microsoft.com/en-us/azure/azure-resource-manager/manage-resource-groups-portal

What is a resource group

A resource group is a container that holds related resources for an Azure solution. The resource group can include all the resources for the solution, or only those resources that you want to manage as a group. You decide how you want to allocate resources to resource groups based on what makes the most sense for your organization. Generally, add resources that share the same lifecycle to the same resource group so you can easily deploy, update, and delete them as a group.

The resource group stores metadata about the resources. Therefore, when you specify a location for the resource group, you are specifying where that metadata is stored. For compliance reasons, you may need to ensure that your data is stored in a particular region.

The resource group stores metadata about the resources. When you specify a location for the resource group, you're specifying where that metadata is stored.

Option A is INCORRECT since the given statement is wrong and change is needed.

Option B is INCORRECT since To implement infrastructure as code for your Azure solutions, use Azure Resource Manager templates. The template is a JavaScript Object Notation (JSON) file that defines the infrastructure and configuration for your project.

Reference: https://docs.microsoft.com/en-us/azure/azure-resource-manager/template-deployment-overview

Option D is INCORRECT since Availability Zones is a high-availability offering that protects your applications and data from datacenter failures. Availability Zones are unique physical locations within an Azure region. Each zone is made up of one or more data centers equipped with independent power, cooling, and networking.

Reference: https://docs.microsoft.com/en-us/azure/availability-zones/az-overview

Question 45:
You have an Azure subscription that contains a policy-based virtual network gateway named GW1 and a virtual network named VNet1.

You need to ensure that you can configure a point-to-site connection from VNet1 to an on-premises computer.

Which two actions should you perform?

- [ ] Reset GW1.
- [ ] Create a route-based virtual network gateway. (Correct)
- [ ] Delete GW1. (Correct)
- [ ] Add a public IP address space to VNet1.
- [ ] Add a connection to GW1.
- [ ] Add a service endpoint to VNet1.

Explanation

Correct Answers - B and C

A VPN gateway is used when creating a VPN connection to your on-premises network.

Route-based VPN devices use any-to-any (wildcard) traffic selectors, and let routing/forwarding tables direct traffic to different IPsec tunnels. It is typically built on router platforms where each IPsec tunnel is modeled as a network interface or VTI (virtual tunnel interface).

Policy-based VPN devices use the combinations of prefixes from both networks to define how traffic is encrypted/decrypted through IPsec tunnels. It is typically built on firewall devices that perform packet filtering. IPsec tunnel encryption and decryption are added to the packet filtering and processing engine.

Point-to-Site connections do not require a VPN device or a public-facing IP address.

References

https://docs.microsoft.com/en-us/azure/vpn-gateway/create-routebased-vpn-gateway-portal

https://docs.microsoft.com/en-us/azure/vpn-gateway/vpn-gateway-connect-multiple-policybased-rm-ps

Question 46:
Fill in the blank with the correct Azure service to correctly complete the statement below:

____________ provides the platform for serverless code.

- ○ Azure Databricks
- ○ Azure Functions (Correct)
- ○ Azure App Service
- ○ Azure Application Insights

Explanation

Correct Answer - B

Option B is CORRECT since Azure Functions is a solution for easily running small pieces of code, or "functions," in the cloud.

Reference: https://docs.microsoft.com/en-us/azure/azure-functions/functions-overview

An introduction to Azure Functions

10/03/2017 · 4 minutes to read · ● ● ● ● ● ~15

Azure Functions is a solution for easily running small pieces of code, or "functions," in the cloud. You can write just the code you need for the problem at hand, without worrying about a whole application or the infrastructure to run it. Functions can make development even more productive, and you can use your development language of choice, such as C#, Java, JavaScript, PowerShell, and Python. Pay only for the time your code runs and trust Azure to scale as needed. Azure Functions lets you develop _serverless_ applications on Microsoft Azure.

This topic provides a high-level overview of Azure Functions. If you want to jump right in and get started with Functions, start with Create your first Azure Function. If you are looking for more technical information about Functions, see the developer reference.

Option A is INCORRECT since Azure Databricks is an Apache Spark-based analytics platform optimized for the Microsoft Azure cloud services platform.

Reference: https://docs.microsoft.com/en-us/azure/azure-databricks/what-is-azure-databricks

Option C is INCORRECT since Azure App Service enables you to build and host web apps, mobile back ends, and RESTful APIs in the programming language of your choice without managing infrastructure.

Reference: https://docs.microsoft.com/en-us/azure/app-service/

Option D is INCORRECT since Application Insights, a feature of Azure Monitor, is an extensible Application Performance Management (APM) service for web developers on multiple platforms.

Reference: https://docs.microsoft.com/en-us/azure/azure-monitor/app/app-insights-overview

Question 47:
Fill in the blank with the correct Azure service to correctly complete the statement below:

______________ hosts web apps.

- ○ Azure Databricks
- ○ Azure Functions
- ○ **Azure App Service** (Correct)
- ○ Azure Application Insights

Explanation

Correct Answer - C

Option C is CORRECT since Azure App Service enables you to build and host web apps, mobile back ends, and RESTful APIs in the programming language of your choice without managing infrastructure.

Reference: https://docs.microsoft.com/en-us/azure/app-service/

App Service Documentation

Azure App Service enables you to build and host web apps, mobile back ends, and RESTful APIs in the programming language of your choice without managing infrastructure. It offers auto-scaling and high availability, supports both Windows and Linux, and enables automated deployments from GitHub, Azure DevOps, or any Git repo. Learn how to use Azure App Service with our quickstarts, tutorials, and samples.

Option A is INCORRECT since Azure Databricks is an Apache Spark-based analytics platform optimized for the Microsoft Azure cloud services platform.

Reference: https://docs.microsoft.com/en-us/azure/azure-databricks/what-is-azure-databricks

Option B is INCORRECT since Azure Functions is a solution for easily running small pieces of code, or "functions," in the cloud.

Reference: https://docs.microsoft.com/en-us/azure/azure-functions/functions-overview

Option D is INCORRECT since Application Insights, a feature of Azure Monitor **is an extensible Application Performance Management (APM) service for web developers on multiple platforms.**

Reference: https://docs.microsoft.com/en-us/azure/azure-monitor/app/app-insights-overview

Question 48:
Your company plans to migrate to Azure. The company has several departments. All the Azure resources used by each department will be managed by a department administrator.

You need to recommend an Azure deployment that provides the ability to segment Azure for the departments. The solution must minimize administrative effort.

What should you include in the recommendation?

- ○ Multiple subscriptions (Correct)
- ○ Multiple Azure Active Directory (Azure AD) directories.
- ○ Multiple regions.
- ○ Multiple resource groups.

Explanation

Correct Answer - A

Reference:
https://blogs.msdn.microsoft.com/arunrakwal/2012/04/09/create-windows-azure-subscription/#:~:targetText=A%20Windows%20Azure%20subscription%20grants,reported%20and%20services%20are%20billed.

What is Azure Subscription

A Windows Azure subscription grants you access to Windows Azure services and to the Windows Azure Platform Management Portal.

A Windows Azure subscription has two aspects:

- The Windows Azure account, through which resource usage is reported and services are billed.
- The subscription itself, which governs access to and use of the Windows Azure services that are subscribed to. The subscription holder manages services (Windows Azure , SQL Azure, Storage etc) through the Windows Azure Platform Management Portal

Let's relate this concept with real world. When our decided to move one of the critical application to Azure following is the model we opted for Azure subscription. We created separate subscription for Dev , Test and Production environment. It helps in multiple ways :-

- I can monitor billing and usage for each of this environment separately

- To ensure security I can have different co-admin for each of this Subscription

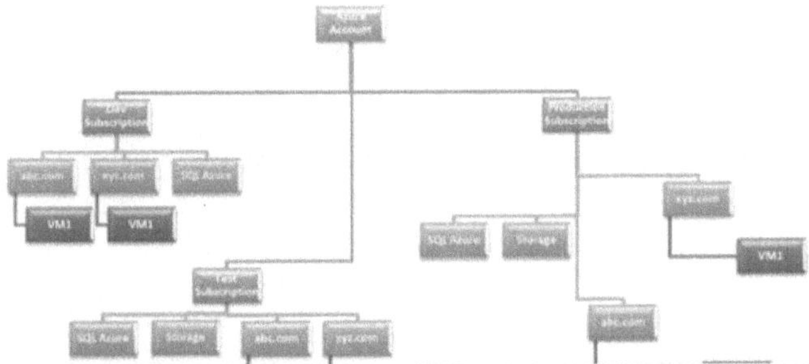

Option B is INCORRECT since Azure AD does not provide segmentation department-wise.

Option C is INCORRECT since deploying Azure resources in multiple regions does not give segmentation based on the department.

Option D is INCORRECT since having multiple resource groups does not prove segmentation department-wise.

Question 49:
You have a public load balancer that balances ports 80 and 443 across three virtual machines.

You need to direct all the Remote Desktop Protocol (RDP) connections to VM3 only.

What should you configure?

- ○ **An inbound NAT rule.** (Correct)
- ○ A load balancing rule.
- ○ A new public load balancer for VM3.
- ○ A frontend IP configuration.

Explanation

Correct Answer: A

Option A is CORRECT since, with Load Balancer, you can create an inbound NAT rule to port forward traffic from a specific port of a specific frontend IP address to a specific port of a specific backend instance inside the virtual network. This is also accomplished by the same hash-based distribution as load balancing. Common scenarios for this capability are Remote Desktop Protocol (RDP) or Secure Shell (SSH) sessions to individual VM instances inside the Azure Virtual Network.

- **Port forwarding**

  With Load Balancer, you can create an inbound NAT rule. This NAT rule forwards traffic from a specific port of a specific front-end IP address to a specific port of a specific back-end instance inside the virtual network. This forwarding is done by the same hash-based distribution as load balancing. Common scenarios for this capability are Remote Desktop Protocol (RDP) or Secure Shell (SSH) sessions to individual VM instances inside an Azure Virtual Network.

  You can map multiple internal endpoints to ports on the same front-end IP address. You can use the front-end IP addresses to remotely administer your VMs without an additional jump box.

Options B, C, and D are incorrect since the question states that a public load balancer is already available and therefore with the help of the load balancer we create an Inbound NAT rule to meet the requirements given in the question.

Reference: https://docs.microsoft.com/en-us/azure/load-balancer/load-balancer-overview

Question 50:
Fill in the blank with the correct Azure service to correctly complete the statement below:

___________ monitors web applications.

- ○ Azure Advisor
- ○ Azure Cognitive Services
- ○ Azure DevOps
- ○ Azure Application Insights (Correct)

Explanation

Correct Answer - D

What is Application Insights?

06/03/2019 • 5 minutes to read •

Application Insights, a feature of Azure Monitor, is an extensible Application Performance Management (APM) service for web developers on multiple platforms. Use it to monitor your live web application. It will automatically detect performance anomalies. It includes powerful analytics tools to help you diagnose issues and to understand what users actually do with your app. It's designed to help you continuously improve performance and usability. It works for apps on a wide variety of platforms including .NET, Node.js and Java EE, hosted on-premises, hybrid, or any public cloud. It integrates with your DevOps process, and has connection points to a variety of development tools. It can monitor and analyze telemetry from mobile apps by integrating with Visual Studio App Center.

Option A is INCORRECT since Azure Advisor is a tool that provides guidance and recommendations to improve an Azure environment.

Reference: https://docs.microsoft.com/en-us/azure/advisor/advisor-overview

Option B is INCORRECT since Azure Cognitive Services are APIs, SDKs, and services available to help developers build intelligent applications without having direct AI or data science skills or knowledge.

Reference: https://docs.microsoft.com/en-us/azure/cognitive-services/welcome

Option C is INCORRECT since Azure DevOps enables teams located anywhere in the world to communicate effectively during daily development activities as well as to integrate with software development tools for monitoring activities such as deployments.

Reference: https://docs.microsoft.com/en-us/azure/devops/learn/what-is-devops

Question 51:
What are the two characteristics of the public cloud?

- ☐ Dedicated hardware.
- ☐ Unsecured connections.
- ☐ Limited storage.
- ☐ Metered pricing. (Correct)
- ☐ Self-service management. (Correct)

Explanation

Correct Answers - D and E

Option A is INCORRECT since dedicated hardware is not available in a Public cloud.

Option B is INCORRECT because connections are secured to a public cloud.

Option C is INCORRECT since a public cloud has unlimited storage.

Option D is CORRECT because the public cloud is metered.

Option E is CORRECT since Self-service Management is a feature of the public cloud.

Reference:

https://azure.microsoft.com/en-in/overview/what-is-a-public-cloud/#:~:text=The%20public%20cloud%20is%20defined,storage%2C%20or%20bandwidth%20they%20consume.

Question 52:
You plan to use the Azure Import/Export service to copy files to a storage account.

Which two files should you create before you prepare the drives for the import job?

- ☐ A driveset CSV file. (Correct)
- ☐ A JSON configuration file.
- ☐ A PowerShell PS1 file.
- ☐ An XML manifest file.
- ☐ A dataset CSV file. (Correct)

Explanation

Correct Answers - A and E

Security considerations

The data on the drive is encrypted using BitLocker Drive Encryption. This encryption protects your data while it is in transit.

For import jobs, drives are encrypted in two ways.

- Specify the option when using *dataset.csv* file while running the WAImportExport tool during drive preparation.

- Enable BitLocker encryption manually on the drive. Specify the encryption key in the *driveset.csv* when running WAImportExport tool command line during drive preparation.

For export jobs, after your data is copied to the drives, the service encrypts the drive using BitLocker before shipping it back to you. The encryption key is provided to you via the Azure portal.

Options B, C, and D are INCORRECT since a CSV file needs to be used here and it should be only "driveset.csv" and "dataset.csv" as per the illustration given above.

Reference:
https://docs.microsoft.com/en-us/azure/storage/common/storage-import-export-service

Question 53:

Your company plans to purchase Azure.

The company's support policy states that the Azure environment must provide an option to access engineers by phone or email.

You need to recommend which support plan meets the support policy requirement.

Solution: Recommend a Basic support plan.

Does this mean the goal

- ○ Yes
- ○ No (Correct)

Explanation

Correct Answer - B

The Basic plan does not provide phone and email support, as evident from the table below:

	Basic	DEVELOPER	STANDARD	PROFESSIONAL DIRECT
	Request support	Purchase support	Purchase support	Purchase support
Price	Included for all Azure customers	$29 per month	$100 per month	$1,000 per month
Scope	Included for all Azure customers	Trial and non-production environments	Production workload environments	Business-critical dependence
Billing and subscription management support	✓	✓	✓	✓
24/7 self-help resources, including Microsoft Learn, Azure portal how-to videos, documentation, and community support	✓	✓	✓	✓
Ability to submit as many support tickets as you need	✓	✓	✓	✓
Azure Advisor—your free, personalized guide to Azure best practices	✓	✓	✓	✓
Azure health status and notifications	✓	✓	✓	✓
24/7 access to technical support by email and phone		Available during business hours by email only.	✓	✓
Case severity and response time		Minimal business impact (Sev C): Within eight business hours[1]	Minimal business impact (Sev C): Within eight business hours[1] Moderate business impact (Sev B): Within four hours Critical business impact (Sev A): Within one hour	Minimal business impact (Sev C): Within four business hours[1] Moderate business impact (Sev B): Within two hours Critical business impact (Sev A): Within one hour
Third-party software support with interoperability and configuration guidance and troubleshooting		✓	✓	✓
Architecture Support		General guidance	General guidance	Guidance from a pool of ProDirect delivery managers
Operations Support				Service reviews and advisory consultation from a pool of ProDirect delivery managers
Training				Webinars led by Azure engineers
Proactive Guidance				From a pool of ProDirect delivery managers

Reference Link:

https://azure.microsoft.com/en-us/support/plans/

Question 54:
What is guaranteed in an Azure Service Level Agreement (SLA)?

- ○ **Uptime** (Correct)
- ○ **Performance**
- ○ **Feature availability**
- ○ **Bandwidth**

Explanation

Correct Answer - A

Option A is CORRECT because an SLA describes Microsoft's commitments for uptime and connectivity.

Understand service-level agreements

In Azure, the Service Level Agreement describes Microsoft's commitments for uptime and connectivity. If the SLA for a particular service is 99.9%, you should expect the service to be available 99.9% of the time. Different services have different SLAs.

The Azure SLA also includes provisions for obtaining a service credit if the SLA is not met, along with specific definitions of *availability* for each service. That aspect of the SLA acts as an enforcement policy.

Option B is INCORRECT because SLA does not define performance.

Option C is INCORRECT because SLA does not define feature availability (it depends on the service availed in specific).

Option D is INCORRECT because SLA does not bandwidth.

Reference:
https://docs.microsoft.com/en-us/azure/architecture/reliability/requirements

Question 55:
Your company plans to automate the deployment of servers to Azure.

Your manager is concerned that you may expose administrative credentials during the deployment. You need to recommend an Azure solution that encrypts the administrative credentials during the deployment. What should you include in the recommendation?

- Azure Information Protection
- Azure Key Vault (Correct)
- Azure Multi-Factor Authentication (MFA)
- Azure Security Center

Explanation

Correct Answer - B

Option B is CORRECT since an Azure Key Vault enables Microsoft Azure applications and users to store and use several types of secret/key data.

Reference: https://docs.microsoft.com/en-us/azure/key-vault/about-keys-secrets-and-certificates

About keys, secrets, and certificates

09/04/2019 • 26 minutes to read • 😊 🦊 🐻 🅰 😀 +9

Azure Key Vault enables Microsoft Azure applications and users to store and use several types of secret/key data:

- Cryptographic keys: Supports multiple key types and algorithms, and enables the use of Hardware Security Modules (HSM) for high value keys.
- Secrets: Provides secure storage of secrets, such as passwords and database connection strings.
- Certificates: Supports certificates, which are built on top of keys and secrets and add an automated renewal feature.
- Azure Storage: Can manage keys of an Azure Storage account for you. Internally, Key Vault can list (sync) keys with an Azure Storage Account, and regenerate (rotate) the keys periodically.

For more general information about Key Vault, see What is Azure Key Vault?

Option A is INCORRECT since Azure Information Protection (sometimes referred to as AIP) is a cloud-based solution that helps an organization to classify and optionally, protect its documents and emails by applying labels.

Reference: https://docs.microsoft.com/en-us/azure/information-protection/what-is-information-protection

Option C is INCORRECT since Azure Multi-Factor Authentication (MFA) helps safeguard access to data and applications while maintaining simplicity for users. It provides additional security by requiring a second form of authentication and delivers strong authentication via a range of easy to use authentication methods.

Reference: https://docs.microsoft.com/en-us/azure/active-directory/authentication/concept-mfa-howitworks

Option D is INCORRECT since Security Center gives you defence in depth with its ability to both detect and help protect against threats. Using machine learning to process trillions of signals across Microsoft services and systems, Security Center alerts you of threats to your environments, such as remote desktop protocol (RDP) brute-force attacks and SQL injections. And it provides actionable recommendations for mitigating these threats.

Reference: https://azure.microsoft.com/en-us/services/security-center/

Question 1:

A company is planning on hosting their resources within Microsoft Azure.

Management wants to know the Capital Expenditure (CapEx) and Operational Expenditure (OpEx) costs that would be incurred if they migrated their entire IT infrastructure to Microsoft Azure.

Does Microsoft Azure provide flexibility to companies when it comes to Capital Expenditures (CapEx) and Operational Expenditures (OpEx)?

- Yes (Correct)
- No

Explanation

Yes, Microsoft Azure provides flexibility for cost, control, and operational management.

You must know the definition of each term to under the differences, they are defined below:

Capital Expenditures (CapEx) *generate benefits over a long period. These expenditures are generally nonrecurring and result in the acquisition of permanent assets. Some examples include physical buildings, office equipment, computers, servers, software, essentially any asset that is expected to provide utility to a business.*

Operational Expenditures (OpEx) *is your operating costs, the expenses to run day-to-day business operations, like services and consumable items that get used up and are paid for according to use. This includes rent/utilities, wages/salaries, legal fees, website hosting fees, software licensing fees, essentially any costs a company incurs for running their day-to-day operations.*

	CapEx	OpEx
Purpose	Assets intended to benefit the organization for more than one year	Ongoing expenses to run day-to-day business
When paid	One-time purchase	Pay-as-you-go approach
Accounting treatment	CapEx can't be fully deducted in the incurry period. They are depreciated or amortized over time.	OpEx are fully deducted in the incurry period.
Listed as	Property or equipment	Operating cost
Tax treatment	Deducted over time as asset cost is depreciated or amortized	OpEx items are fully tax-deductible in the year they are made
Examples	Purchasing office buildings, equipment, vehicles, intellectual property assets	Consumables, wages, rent, maintenance and repair of machinery

For more information, please download Microsoft's PDF here:

http://download.microsoft.com/documents/australia/insightsquarterly/iq_report_capx.pdf

Question 2:
A company is planning on setting up a Pay-as-You-Go subscription within Microsoft Azure.

Would the company have access to the support forums?

- ○ **Yes**(Correct)
- ○ **No**

Explanation

Yes, *because community support is available for all plans as shown in the visual below. You can find specific forum topics and questions other Azure users have or post your own for guidance on a subject to get answers from Microsoft engineers and members within the Azure community.*

	Basic Request support	DEVELOPER Purchase support	STANDARD Purchase support	PROFESSIONAL DIRECT Purchase support
Price	Included for all Azure customers	$29 per month	$100 per month	$1,000 per month
Scope	Included for all Azure customers	Trial and non-production environments	Production workload environments	Business-critical dependence
Billing and subscription management support	✔	✔	✔	✔
24/7 self-help resources, including Microsoft Learn, Azure portal how-to videos, documentation and community support	✔	✔	✔	✔
Ability to submit as many support tickets as you need	✔	✔	✔	✔
Azure Advisor—your free, personalized guide to Azure best practices	✔	✔	✔	✔
Azure health status and notifications	✔	✔	✔	✔
24/7 access to technical support by email and phone		Available during business hours by email only.	✔	✔
Case severity and response time		Minimal business impact (Sev C): Within eight business hours[1]	Minimal business impact (Sev C): Within eight business hours[1] Moderate business impact (Sev B): Within four hours Critical business impact (Sev A): Within one hour	Minimal business impact (Sev C): Within four business hours[1] Moderate business impact (Sev B): Within two hours Critical business impact (Sev A): Within one hour
Third-party software support with interoperability and configuration guidance and troubleshooting		✔	✔	✔
Architecture Support		General guidance	General guidance	Guidance from a pool of ProDirect delivery managers
Operations Support				Service reviews and advisory consultation from a pool of ProDirect delivery managers
Training			.	Webinars led by Azure engineers
Proactive Guidance				From a pool of ProDirect delivery managers

For for more information on each support plan, visit https://azure.microsoft.com/en-us/support/plans/

Question 3:

A company is planning on using an Azure App Service to host their set of web applications utilizing the Platform-as-a-Service (PaaS) cloud computing model.

In the PaaS model, does Microsoft Azure provide to the customer, full control over the operating system that hosts the web applications?

- ○ Yes
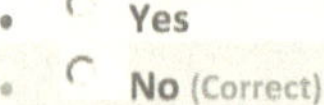
- ○ **No** (Correct)

Explanation

No, *because in a Platform-as-a-Service (PaaS) cloud computing model, Microsoft Azure has full control over the physical data center, networking, firewalls/security, servers, storage, operating systems, development tools, database management tools and business analytics.*

In an Infrastructure -as-a-Service (IaaS) cloud computing model, Microsoft Azure only has full control over the physical data center, networking, firewalls/security, servers, and storage, but not the operating systems, development tools, databases, or applications. The below visual illustrates this concept, as you can see with SaaS (Software-as-a-Service), Microsoft Azure has full control over everything, you would need to simply choose or provide the application solution.

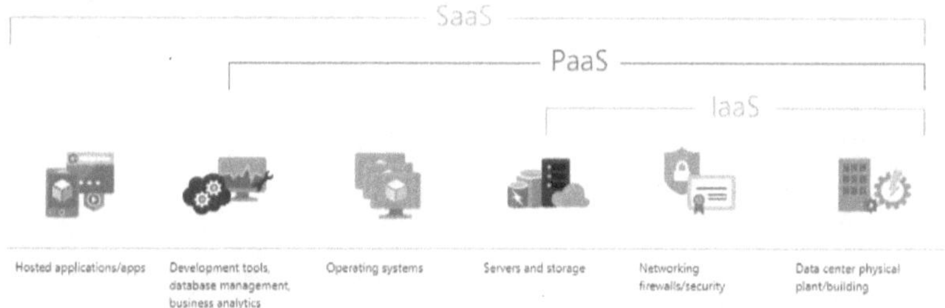

For more information on IaaS, please visit:

https://azure.microsoft.com/en-us/overview/what-is-iaas/

For more information on PaaS, please visit:
https://azure.microsoft.com/en-us/overview/what-is-paas/

For more information on SaaS, please visit:

https://azure.microsoft.com/en-us/overview/what-is-saas/

Question 4:
Your company plans to purchase Azure.

The company's support policy states that the Azure environment must provide an option to access support engineers by phone or email.

You need to recommend a support plan that meets the support policy requirement.

Solution: Recommend a Professional Direct support plan.

Does this meet the goal?

- ○ **Yes** (Correct)
- ○ **No**

Explanation

Correct Answer - A

The below snapshot clearly identifies with the solution.

	Basic	DEVELOPER	STANDARD	PROFESSIONAL DIRECT
	Request support	Purchase support	Purchase support	Purchase support
Price	Included for all Azure customers	$29 per month	$100 per month	$1,000 per month
Scope	Included for all Azure customers	Trial and non-production environments	Production workload environments	Business-critical dependence
Billing and subscription management support	✓	✓	✓	✓
24/7 self-help resources, including Microsoft Learn, Azure portal how to videos, documentation, and community support	✓	✓	✓	✓
Ability to submit as many support tickets as you need	✓	✓	✓	✓
Azure Advisor—your free, personalized guide to Azure best practices	✓	✓	✓	✓
Azure health status and notifications	✓	✓	✓	✓
24/7 access to technical support by email and phone		Available during business hours by email only.	✓	✓
Case severity and response time		Minimal business impact (Sev C): Within eight business hours[1]	Minimal business impact (Sev C): Within eight business hours[1] Moderate business impact (Sev B): Within four hours Critical business impact (Sev A): Within one hour	Minimal business impact (Sev C): Within four business hours[1] Moderate business impact (Sev B): Within two hours Critical business impact (Sev A): Within one hour
Third-party software support with interoperability and configuration guidance and troubleshooting		✓	✓	✓
Architecture Support		General guidance	General guidance	Guidance from a pool of ProDirect delivery managers
Operations Support				Service reviews and advisory consultation from a pool of ProDirect delivery managers
Training				Webinars led by Azure engineers
Proactive Guidance				From a pool of ProDirect delivery managers

Reference Link:

https://azure.microsoft.com/en-us/support/plans/

Question 5:
A company is planning on using an Azure App Service to host it set of web applications.

The company has the Basic tier service plan.

Does Microsoft automatically provide professional technical support services with the Basic support plan?

- ○ Yes
- ○ **No** (Correct)

Explanation

No, Microsoft does not automatically provide professional services with the Basic plan. You must be familiar and aware that there are 4 tiers of support plans available, Basic, Developer, Standard, and Professional Direct. In order to obtain additional support outside the scope of Basic (which is free), you would need to purchase one of the other 3 support plans (Developer, Standard, or Professional Direct).

	Basic	DEVELOPER	STANDARD	PROFESSIONAL DIRECT
	Request support	Purchase support	Purchase support	Purchase support
Price	Included for all Azure customers	$29 per month	$100 per month	$1,000 per month
Scope	Included for all Azure customers	Trial and non-production environments	Production workload environments	Business-critical dependence
Billing and subscription management support	✓	✓	✓	✓
24/7 self-help resources, including Microsoft Learn, Azure portal how-to videos, documentation, and community support	✓	✓	✓	✓
Ability to submit as many support tickets as you need	✓	✓	✓	✓
Azure Advisor—your free, personalized guide to Azure best practices	✓	✓	✓	✓
Azure health status and notifications	✓	✓	✓	✓
24/7 access to technical support by email and phone		Available during business hours by email only.	✓	✓
Case severity and response time		Minimal business impact (Sev C): Within eight business hours[1]	Minimal business impact (Sev C): Within eight business hours[1] Moderate business impact (Sev B): Within four hours Critical business impact (Sev A): Within one hour	Minimal business impact (Sev C): Within four business hours[1] Moderate business impact (Sev B): Within two hours Critical business impact (Sev A): Within one hour
Third party software support with interoperability and configuration guidance and troubleshooting		✓	✓	✓
Architecture Support		General guidance	General guidance	Guidance from a pool of ProDirect delivery managers
Operations Support				Service reviews and advisory consultation from a pool of ProDirect delivery managers
Training				Webinars led by Azure engineers
Proactive Guidance				From a pool of ProDirect delivery managers

For more information, please visit:

https://azure.microsoft.com/en-us/support/plans/

Question 6:

A company wants to migrate their current on-premise servers to the cloud utilizing Microsoft Azure.

They require that their servers are running even in the event that a single Data Center goes down.

Which of the following terms best refers to the concept that needs to be implemented to fulfill this requirement?

- ○ **Fault tolerance** (Correct)
- ○ Elasticity
- ○ Scalability
- ○ Low Latency

Explanation

Correct Answer: A. Fault tolerance

A context clue is given in the question itself that helps identify which term best describes the concept the company wants, "They want to ensure that their servers are running even in the event that a single Data Center goes down".

Fault Tolerance is a concept in IT in which a computer system or set of infrastructure is designed in such a way that when one component fails (be it hardware , software, or network) a backup component takes over operations immediately so that there is no loss of service. So if the company hosted servers at two Data Centers, even if one Data Center went down the other Data Center would "turn on" and continue running those servers without any loss in service.

It is also good to know why options B,C,D are incorrect and the easiest way is to simply remember their definitions:

Elasticity is a term related to scaling. Elastic computing is the ability to quickly expand or decrease computer processing, memory, or storage resources to meet changing demands.

Scalability is a term related to the adaptability of the system to the changed amount of workload or traffic to the web application. You can "Scale-up" (Upgrade the capacity of the host where the app is hosted by increasing RAM size for example) and you can "Scale-out" (Upgrade the capacity of the hosted application by increasing the number of host instances such as having a 'Load Balancer' where your application is hosted on multiple instances).

Low Latency is a term that describes a computer network that is optimized to process a very high volume of data with minimal delay (latency).

For more information on the concept of Fault Tolerance, please visit:

https://docs.microsoft.com/en-us/archive/msdn-magazine/2015/september/microsoft-azure-fault-tolerance-pitfalls-and-resolutions-in-the-cloud

Question 7:
A (fill in the blank) cloud is a computing environment that combines a public cloud and a private cloud by allowing data and applications to be shared between them.

- ○ **Hybrid** (Correct)
- ○ Private
- ○ Public

Explanation

A. Hybrid, *A hybrid cloud is a computing environment that combines a public cloud and a private cloud by allowing data and applications to be shared between them. When computing and processing demand fluctuates, hybrid cloud computing gives businesses the ability to seamlessly scale their on-premises infrastructure up to the public cloud to handle any overflow—without giving third-party datacenters access to the entirety of their data. Organizations gain the flexibility and computing power of the public cloud for basic and non-sensitive computing tasks, while keeping business-critical applications and data on-premises, safely behind a company firewall.*

For more information, please visit:

https://azure.microsoft.com/en-us/overview/what-is-hybrid-cloud-computing/

Private *clouds consists of computing resources used exclusively by one business or organization. The private cloud can be physically located at your organization's on-site datacenter, or it can be hosted by a third-party service provider. But in a private cloud, the services and infrastructure are always maintained on a private network and the hardware and software are dedicated solely to your organization. In this way, a private cloud can make it easier for an organization to customize its resources to meet specific IT requirements. Private clouds are often used by government agencies, financial institutions, any other mid- to large-size organizations with business-critical operations seeking enhanced control over their environment.*

For more information, please visit:

https://azure.microsoft.com/en-us/overview/what-are-private-public-hybrid-clouds/

Public *clouds are the most common way of deploying cloud computing. The cloud resources (like servers and storage) are owned and operated by a third-party cloud service provider and delivered over the Internet. Microsoft Azure is an example of a public cloud. With a public cloud, all hardware, software, and other supporting infrastructure is owned and managed by the cloud provider. In a public cloud, you share the same hardware, storage, and network devices with other organizations or cloud "tenants." You access services and manage your account using a web browser. Public cloud deployments are frequently used to provide web-based email, online office applications, storage, and testing and development environments.*

For more information, please visit:

https://azure.microsoft.com/en-us/overview/what-are-private-public-hybrid-clouds/

Question 8:
A company is planning on migrating their public web site to Microsoft Azure.

Which of the following should the company consider when it comes to hosting their public web site within Microsoft Azure?

- ○ They would need to consider the level of traffic their website gets.
- ○ They would need to consider deploying a VPN connection from their on-premise site to Microsoft Azure.
- ○ They would need to consider paying a monthly cost for their solution of choice.(Correct)
- ○ They would need to consider paying for the user data to be transferred onto the site.

Explanation

C. They would need to consider paying a monthly cost for their chosen solution.

Through Microsoft Azure Web Sites, a PaaS platform, you choose the plan you want with specifics to meet your needs.

If you need to host a web application in Azure, there are a couple of options. But for each option, you have to pay a monthly fee. An example is the pricing model available for Azure Web apps. If you are planning on deploying a public web site, then you would need to consider using a Basic App service plan or higher.

	FREE Try for free	SHARED Environment for dev/test	BASIC Dedicated environment for dev/test	STANDARD Run production workloads	PREMIUM Enhanced performance and scale	ISOLATED High-Performance, Security and Isolation
Web, mobile, or API apps	10	100	Unlimited	Unlimited	Unlimited	Unlimited
Disk space	1 GB	1 GB	10 GB	50 GB	250 GB	1 TB
Maximum instances	–	–	Up to 3	Up to 10	Up to 30**	Up to 100*
Custom domain	–	Supported	Supported	Supported	Supported	Supported
Auto Scale	–	–	–	Supported	Supported	Supported
VPN hybrid connectivity	–	–	–	Supported	Supported	Supported
Network Isolation						Supported
Price	Free	$0.013/hour	$0.075/hour	$0.10/hour	$0.20/hour	$0.40/hour

Option A is incorrect because Azure can support a high number of connections.

Option B is incorrect since only if you need to connect your web application to a resource in your on-premise data center then maybe you need to consider this.

Option D is incorrect since you don't need to pay for the data transfer.

Visit the following resource to get a better understanding of Azure App Service pricing:

https://azure.microsoft.com/en-us/pricing/details/app-service/windows/

Question 9:
A company needs a list of planned maintenance events that could possibly affect the availability of their Microsoft Azure subscription.

Which of the following would help them achieve this requirement?

Larger image

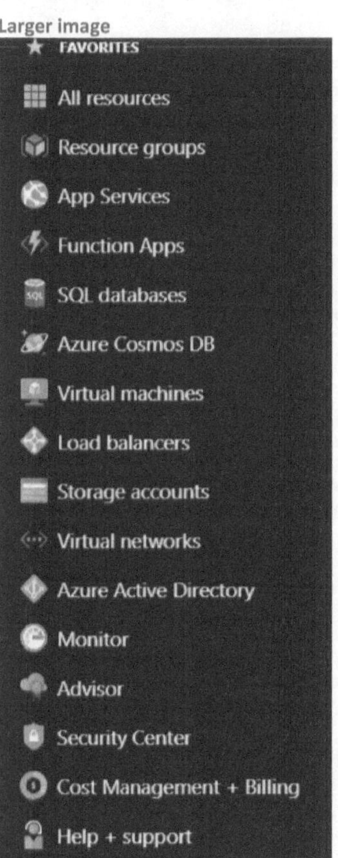

- ○ Azure App Service
- ○ Resource Groups
- ○ Azure Virtual Machines
- ○ Microsoft Azure Active Directory
- ○ **Help + Support** (Correct)

Explanation

E. Help + Support *is the correct answer as it will showcase maintenance events that can affect the availability of a Microsoft Azure subscription.*

For more information, please visit:

https://azure.microsoft.com/en-us/support/faq/

Azure App Service *would be incorrect because an Azure App Service is a fully managed "Platform-as-a-Service" (PaaS) that integrates Microsoft Azure Websites, Mobile Services, and BizTalk Services into a single service, adding new capabilities that enable integration with on-premises or cloud systems.*

For more information, please visit:

https://docs.microsoft.com/en-us/azure/app-service/

Resource Groups *would be incorrect because in Microsoft Azure, Resource Groups provide a new approach to grouping a collection of assets in logical groups for easy or even automatic provisioning, monitoring, and access control, and for more effective management of their costs.*

For more information, please visit:

https://docs.microsoft.com/en-us/azure/azure-resource-manager/resource-group-overview

Azure Virtual Machines *would be incorrect because Azure Virtual Machines are one of several types of on-demand, scalable computing resources that Azure offers. Typically, you choose a VM when you need more control over the computing environment than the other choices offer.*

For more information, please visit:

https://docs.microsoft.com/en-us/azure/virtual-machines/windows/overview

Microsoft Azure Active Directory *is incorrect because Microsoft Azure Active Directory is a comprehensive identity and access management cloud solution that combines core directory services, application access management, and advanced identity protection.*

For more information, please visit:

https://docs.microsoft.com/en-us/azure/active-directory/fundamentals/active-directory-whatis

Question 10:
A company has several on-premise computers that run Windows 10.

They want to map a network drive from these machines onto Microsoft Azure Storage.

Which of the following solutions would best fulfill this requirement?

- ○ Azure SQL Database
- ○ Azure SQL Datawarehouse
- ○ Azure Storage account – BLOB service
- ○ Azure Storage account – File service (Correct)

Explanation

D. Azure Storage account – File service is the correct answer as Microsoft's Azure Storage accounts are a cloud storage solution for modern data storage scenarios. Azure Storage offers a massively scalable object store for data objects, a file system service for the cloud, a messaging store for reliable messaging, and a NoSQL store. Azure Storage is durable and highly available, secure, scalable, managed, and accessible.

For more information, please visit:

https://docs.microsoft.com/en-us/azure/storage/common/storage-account-overview

Azure SQL Database *is incorrect because it is a general-purpose relational database, provided as a managed service. With it, you can create a highly available and high-performance data storage layer for the applications and solutions within Azure. SQL Database can be the right choice for a variety of modern cloud applications because it enables you to process both relational data and non-relational structures, such as graphs, JSON, spatial, and XML.*

For more information, please visit:

https://docs.microsoft.com/en-us/azure/sql-database/

Azure SQL Data Warehouse (now known as Azure Synapse) *is incorrect because it is a limitless analytics service that brings together enterprise data warehousing and Big Data analytics. It gives you the freedom to query data on your terms, using either server-less on-demand or provisioned resources—at scale.*

For more information, please visit:

https://docs.microsoft.com/en-us/azure/sql-data-warehouse/sql-data-warehouse-overview-what-is

Azure Storage account – BLOB service *is incorrect because Blob storage is Microsoft's object storage solution for the cloud. Blob storage is optimized for storing massive amounts of unstructured data, such as text or binary data. This solution is ideal for serving images or documents directly to a browser, storing files for distributed access, streaming video and audio, storing data for backup and restore, disaster recovery, archiving, and lastly storing data for analysis by an on-premises or Azure-hosted service.*

For more information, please visit:

https://azure.microsoft.com/en-us/services/storage/blobs/

Question 11:
A company has a VPN device that will be used as Site-to-Site connection from Microsoft Azure to their on-premise location.

Which of the following would be used to represent the VPN device?

Larger image

DNS zone	Microsoft	Recommended
App Service Domain	Microsoft	Recommended
Application Gateway	Microsoft	Recommended
Connection	Microsoft	Recommended
DDoS protection plan	Microsoft	Recommended
ExpressRoute	Microsoft	Recommended
Local network gateway	Microsoft	Recommended
Reserved IP Address	Microsoft	Recommended
Route filter	Microsoft	Recommended
Virtual network gateway	Microsoft	Recommended

- ○ DNS Zone
- ○ Application Gateway
- ○ Local Network Gateway (Correct)
- ○ Virtual Network gateway

Explanation

C. Local Network Gateway *is the correct answer because a Local Network Gateway represents the hardware or software VPN device in your local network. Use this with a connection to set up a Site-to-Site VPN connection between an Azure virtual network and your local network. There are no additional charges for creating local network gateways in Microsoft Azure.*

For more information, please visit:

https://docs.microsoft.com/en-us/azure/vpn-gateway/vpn-gateway-howto-site-to-site-resource-manager-portal

DNS Zone *is incorrect because a DNS zone is a data resource that contains the DNS records for a domain name. You can use Microsoft Azure DNS to host a DNS zone and manage the DNS records for a domain within Microsoft Azure.*

For more information, please visit:

https://docs.microsoft.com/en-us/azure/dns/dns-zones-records

Azure Application Gateway *is incorrect because an Azure Application Gateway is a web traffic load balancer that enables you to manage traffic to your web applications. Traditional load balancers operate at the transport layer (OSI layer 4 - TCP and UDP) and route traffic based on source IP address and port, to a destination IP address and port. With Azure Application Gateway, you can make routing decisions based on additional attributes of an HTTP request, such as URI path or host headers.*

For more information, please visit:

https://docs.microsoft.com/en-us/azure/application-gateway/overview

Azure Virtual Network Gateway is incorrect because an Azure Virtual Network Gateway is a specific type of virtual network gateway that is used to send encrypted traffic between an Azure virtual network and an on-premises location over the public Internet. You can also use a VPN gateway to send encrypted traffic between Azure virtual networks over the Microsoft network. Each virtual network can have only one VPN gateway. However, you can create multiple connections to the same VPN gateway. When you create multiple connections to the same VPN gateway, all VPN tunnels share the available gateway bandwidth.

For more information, please visit:

https://docs.microsoft.com/en-us/azure/vpn-gateway/vpn-gateway-about-vpngateways

Question 12:
A company wants to deploy an Artificial Intelligence solution in Microsoft Azure.

The development team wants to have a solution in place that can be used to build, test, and deploy predictive analytics solutions.

Which of the following solutions would satisfy this purpose?

- ○ Azure Logic Apps
- ○ Azure Machine Learning Studio (Correct)
- ○ Azure Batch
- ○ Azure App service

Explanation

Correct Answer: B. Azure Machine Learning Studio

There are 2 context clues in this question that should be noted, the first being, "deploy an Artificial Intelligence solution…" and the second clue being "…wants to have a tool in place that can be used to build, test, and deploy predictive analytics solutions."

Azure Machine Learning Studio is a collaborative, drag-and-drop tool you can use to build, test, and deploy predictive analytics solutions on your data. Machine Learning Studio publishes models as web services that can easily be consumed by custom applications or BI tools.

For more information, please visit:
https://docs.microsoft.com/en-us/azure/machine-learning/studio/what-is-ml-studio

As you understand the terms for options A,C,D, you'll better understand why they aren't correct for this question:

Azure Logic Apps is a cloud service that helps you schedule, automate, orchestrate tasks, business processes, and workflows when you need to integrate apps, data, systems, and services across enterprises or organizations.

For more information, please visit:

https://docs.microsoft.com/en-us/azure/logic-apps/

Azure Batch is a cloud based job scheduling and compute management platform that enables running large-scale parallel high performance computing applications efficiently in the cloud. Azure Batch Service provides job scheduling, automatically scaling, and managing virtual machines running those jobs.

For more information, please visit:

https://docs.microsoft.com/en-us/azure/batch/

Azure App Service enables you to build and host web apps, mobile back ends, and RESTful APIs in the programming language of your choice without managing infrastructure. It offers auto-scaling and high availability, supports both Windows and Linux, and enables automated deployments from GitHub, Azure DevOps, or any Git repository, so this option is not correct.

For more information, please visit:

https://docs.microsoft.com/en-us/azure/app-service/

Question 13:
A company has a set of resources deployed to Microsoft Azure.

They want to make use of Microsoft Azure Advisor solution.

Would the Microsoft Azure Advisor solution give recommendations on how to reduce the cost of running Microsoft Azure Virtual Machines?

- ○ **Yes** (Correct)
- ○ No

Explanation

Yes, Microsoft Azure Advisor *would give recommendations on how to reduce the cost of running Microsoft Azure Virtual Machines. Azure Advisor is a personalized cloud consultant that helps you follow best practices to optimize your Azure deployments. It analyzes your resource configuration usage, telemetry, and then recommends solutions that can help you improve the cost effectiveness, performance, high availability, and security of your Azure resources. Azure Advisor provides recommendations for Application Gateway, App Services, availability sets, Azure Cache, Azure Data Factory, Azure Database for MySQL, Azure Database for PostgreSQL, Azure Database for MariaDB, Azure ExpressRoute, Azure Cosmos DB, Azure public IP addresses, SQL Data Warehouse, SQL servers, storage accounts, Traffic Manager profiles, and virtual machines.*

For more information, please visit:

https://docs.microsoft.com/en-us/azure/advisor/advisor-overview

Question 14:
A company has a set of IT engineers that are responsible for implementing and managing the resources in their Microsoft Azure account.

The IT engineers have a set of on-premise workstations that have the following different types of operating systems:

- Windows 10

- MacOS

- Ubuntu

Which of the following user interfaces can you use on the Windows 10 machines?

- ○ The Azure CLI and Azure Portal only
- ○ The Azure CLI and Powershell only
- ○ The Azure Portal and Powershell only
- ○ The Azure CLI, Azure Powershell and Azure Portal (Correct)

Explanation

D. The Azure CLI, Azure Powershell and Azure Portal *are all correct because all three user interfaces work on Windows 10.*

The Azure Command Line Interface (CLI) provides a command line and scripting environment for creating and managing Azure resources. The Azure CLI is available for macOS, Linux, and Windows operating systems.

Azure PowerShell is basically an extension of Windows PowerShell. It lets Windows PowerShell users control Azure's robust functionality. From the command line, Azure PowerShell programmers use preset scripts called cmdlets to perform complex tasks like provisioning virtual machines (VMs) or creating cloud services.

Azure Portal is a platform provided by Microsoft for its Azure clients where they can see, manage and buy the services offered by Azure. To access this user interface, visit https://portal.azure.com/.

Powershell itself is a task automation and configuration management framework from Microsoft, consisting of a command-line shell and associated scripting language.

For more information on Azure CLI please visit:

https://docs.microsoft.com/en-us/cli/azure/get-started-with-azure-cli?view=azure-cli-latest

For more information on Azure Cloud Shell please visit:

https://docs.microsoft.com/en-us/azure/cloud-shell/overview?view=azure-cli-latest

For more information on Azure Portal please visit:

https://azure.microsoft.com/en-us/features/azure-portal/

Question 15:
A company has a set of IT engineers that are responsible for implementing and managing the resources within their Microsoft Azure account.

The IT engineers have a set of on-premise workstations that have the following different types of operating systems:

- Windows 10

- MacOS

- Ubuntu

Which of the following tools can you use on the Ubuntu machines?

- ○ The Azure CLI and Azure Portal only
- ○ The Azure CLI and Powershell only
- ○ The Azure Portal and Powershell only
- ○ The Azure CLI, Azure Powershell and Azure Portal (Correct)

Explanation

D. The Azure CLI, Azure Powershell and Azure Portal *are all correct because all three interfaces can be used on Ubuntu. It is important to know Ubuntu is a flavor of the Linux operating system.*

The Azure Command Line Interface (CLI) *provides a command line and scripting environment for creating and managing Azure resources. The Azure CLI is available for macOS, Linux, and Windows operating systems.*

Azure Powershell *can be installed on any Linux distro through modules using PowerShellGet.*

Azure Portal *can be accessed from Ubuntu's web browser of choice (Chromium, Chrome, Firefox, Midori, Opera, Vivaldi, Qupzilla, and Brave are just a few examples of such browsers).*

For more information on Azure CLI please visit:

https://docs.microsoft.com/en-us/cli/azure/get-started-with-azure-cli?view=azure-cli-latest

For more information on Azure Cloud Shell please visit:

https://docs.microsoft.com/en-us/azure/cloud-shell/overview?view=azure-cli-latest

For more information on Azure Portal please visit:

https://azure.microsoft.com/en-us/features/azure-portal/

Question 16:
A company has a set of IT engineers that are responsible for implementing and managing the resources in their Microsoft Azure account. The IT engineers have a set of on-premise workstations that have the following different types of operating systems:

- Windows 10

- macOS

- Ubuntu

Which of the following tools can you use on the macOS machines?

- ○ The Azure CLI and Azure Portal only
- ○ The Azure CLI and Powershell only
- ○ The Azure Portal and Powershell only
- ○ The Azure CLI, Azure Powershell and Azure Portal (Correct)

Explanation

D. The Azure CLI, Azure Powershell and Azure Portal *is the correct answer.*

The Azure CLI for the macOS platform, can be installed via the Homebrew package manager. Homebrew makes it easy to keep your installation of the CLI update to date.

Azure Powershell can be installed on a macOS machine using PowerShell Core.

Azure Portal can installed on any macOS machcine by installing the proper SDKs.

For more information on Azure CLI please visit:

https://docs.microsoft.com/en-us/cli/azure/get-started-with-azure-cli?view=azure-cli-latest

For more information on Azure Cloud Shell please visit:

https://docs.microsoft.com/en-us/azure/cloud-shell/overview?view=azure-cli-latest

For more information on Azure Portal please visit:

https://azure.microsoft.com/en-us/features/azure-portal/

Question 17:
A company is planning on setting up a solution in Microsoft Azure. The solution would have the following key requirement:

- Provides a platform for creating workflows

Which of the following would be best suited for this requirement?

- ○ Azure Databricks
- ○ Azure Logic Apps (Correct)
- ○ Azure App Service
- ○ Azure Application Insights

Explanation

B. Azure Logic Apps *is correct because Azure Logic Apps are a cloud service that helps you schedule, automate, and orchestrate tasks, business processes, and workflows when you need to integrate apps, data, systems, and services across enterprises or organizations.*

For more information, please visit:

https://docs.microsoft.com/en-us/azure/logic-apps/

Azure Databricks are an Apache Spark-based analytics platform optimized for the Microsoft Azure cloud services platform. Designed with the founders of Apache Spark, Databricks is integrated with Microsoft Azure to provide one-click setup, streamlined workflows, and an interactive workspace that enables collaboration between data scientists, data engineers, and business analysts as well as giving the ability to host and analyze services for machine learning.

For more information, please visit:

https://docs.microsoft.com/en-us/azure/azure-databricks/

Azure App Service is a fully managed "Platform as a Service" (PaaS) that integrates Microsoft Azure Websites (hosting of web-based applications), Mobile Services, and BizTalk Services into a single service, adding new capabilities that enable integration with on-premises or cloud systems.

More for information, please visit:

https://docs.microsoft.com/en-us/azure/app-service/

Azure Application Insights is a feature of Azure Monitor, is an extensible Application Performance Management (APM) service for web developers on multiple platforms. Use it to monitor your live web application. It will automatically detect performance anomalies. It includes powerful analytics tools to help you diagnose issues and to understand what users actually do with your app. It's designed to help you continuously improve performance and usability. It works for apps on a wide variety of platforms including .NET, Node.js and Java EE, hosted on-premises, hybrid, or any public cloud. It integrates with your DevOps process, and has connection points to a variety of development tools. It can monitor and analyze telemetry from mobile apps by integrating with Visual Studio App Center.

For more information, please visit:

https://docs.microsoft.com/en-us/azure/azure-monitor/app/cloudservices

Question 18:
A company is planning on setting up a solution in Microsoft Azure.

The solution would have the following key requirement:

- Gives the ability to host a big data analysis service for machine learning

Which of the following would be best suited for this requirement?

- ○ **Azure Databricks** (Correct)
- ○ **Azure Logic Apps**
- ○ **Azure App Service**
- ○ **Azure Application Insights**

Explanation

A. Azure Databricks *are an Apache Spark-based analytics platform optimized for the Microsoft Azure cloud services platform. Designed with the founders of Apache Spark, Databricks is integrated with Microsoft Azure to provide one-click setup, streamlined workflows, and an interactive workspace that enables collaboration between data scientists, data engineers, and* *business analysts as well as giving the ability to host and analyze services for machine learning.*

For more information, please visit:

https://docs.microsoft.com/en-us/azure/azure-databricks/

Azure Logic Apps *are a cloud service that helps you schedule, automate, and orchestrate tasks, business processes, and workflows when you need to integrate apps, data, systems, and services across enterprises or organizations.*

For more information, please visit:

https://docs.microsoft.com/en-us/azure/logic-apps/

Azure App Service *is a fully managed "Platform as a Service" (PaaS) that integrates Microsoft Azure Websites (hosting of web-based applications), Mobile Services, and BizTalk Services into a single service, adding new capabilities that enable integration with on-premises or cloud systems.*

More for information, please visit:

https://docs.microsoft.com/en-us/azure/app-service/

Azure Application Insights *is a feature of Azure Monitor, is an extensible Application Performance Management (APM) service for web developers on multiple platforms. Use it to monitor your live web application. It will automatically detect performance anomalies. It includes powerful analytics tools to help you diagnose issues and to understand what users actually do with your app. It's designed to help you continuously improve performance and usability. It works for apps on a wide variety of platforms including .NET, Node.js and Java EE, hosted on-premises, hybrid, or any public cloud. It integrates with your DevOps process, and has connection points to a variety of development tools. It can monitor and analyze telemetry from mobile apps by integrating with Visual Studio App Center.*

For more information, please visit:

https://docs.microsoft.com/en-us/azure/azure-monitor/app/cloudservices

Question 19:
A company is planning on setting up a solution within Microsoft Azure.

The solution would have the following key requirement:

- Give the ability to detect and diagnose anomalies in web apps

Which of the following would be best suited for this requirement?

- ○ **Azure Databricks**
- ○ **Azure Logic Apps**
- ○ **Azure App Service**

Explanation

C. Azure Application Insights a feature of Azure Monitor, is an extensible Application Performance Management (APM) service for web developers on multiple platforms. Use it to monitor your live web application. It will automatically detect performance anomalies. It includes powerful analytics tools to help you diagnose issues and to understand what users actually do with your app. It's designed to help you continuously improve performance and usability. It works for apps on a wide variety of platforms including .NET, Node.js and Java EE, hosted on-premises, hybrid, or any public cloud. It integrates with your DevOps process, and has connection points to a variety of development tools. It can monitor and analyze telemetry from mobile apps by integrating with Visual Studio App Center.

For more information, please visit:

https://docs.microsoft.com/en-us/azure/azure-monitor/app/cloudservices

Azure Databricks an Apache Spark-based analytics platform optimized for the Microsoft Azure cloud services platform. Designed with the founders of Apache Spark, Databricks is integrated with Microsoft Azure to provide one-click setup, streamlined workflows, and an interactive workspace that enables collaboration between data scientists, data engineers, and business analysts as well as giving the ability to host and analyze services for machine learning.

For more information, please visit:

https://docs.microsoft.com/en-us/azure/azure-databricks/

Azure Logic Apps are a cloud service that helps you schedule, automate, and orchestrate tasks, business processes, and workflows when you need to integrate apps, data, systems, and services across enterprises or organizations.

For more information, please visit:

https://docs.microsoft.com/en-us/azure/logic-apps/

Azure App Service is a fully managed "Platform as a Service" (PaaS) that integrates Microsoft Azure Websites (hosting of web-based applications), Mobile Services, and BizTalk Services into a single service, adding new capabilities that enable integration with on-premises or cloud systems.

For more information, please visit:

https://docs.microsoft.com/en-us/azure/app-service/

Question 20:
A company is planning on setting up a solution in Microsoft Azure.

The solution would have the following key requirement:

- Allows the hosting of web-based applications

Which of the following would be best suited for this requirement?

- ○

Azure Databricks

- ○

Azure Logic Apps

- ○

Azure App Service

(Correct)

- ○

Azure Application Insights

Explanation

C. Azure App Service *is a fully managed "Platform as a Service" (PaaS) that integrates Microsoft Azure Websites (hosting of web-based applications), Mobile Services, and BizTalk Services into a single service, adding new capabilities that enable integration with on-premises or cloud systems.*

For more information, please visit:

https://docs.microsoft.com/en-us/azure/app-service/

Azure Application Insights is a feature of Azure Monitor, is an extensible Application Performance Management (APM) service for web developers on multiple platforms. Use it to monitor your live web application. It will automatically detect performance anomalies. It includes powerful analytics tools to help you diagnose issues and to understand what users actually do with your app. It's designed to help you continuously improve performance and usability. It works for apps on a wide variety of platforms including .NET, Node.js and Java EE, hosted on-premises, hybrid, or any public cloud. It integrates with your DevOps process, and has connection points to a variety of development tools. It can monitor and analyze telemetry from mobile apps by integrating with Visual Studio App Center.

For more information, please visit:

https://docs.microsoft.com/en-us/azure/azure-monitor/app/cloudservices

Azure Databricks are an Apache Spark-based analytics platform optimized for the Microsoft Azure cloud services platform. Designed with the founders of Apache Spark, Databricks is integrated with Microsoft Azure to provide one-click setup, streamlined workflows, and an interactive workspace that enables collaboration between data scientists, data engineers, and

Question 21:
A company wants to host an application on a set of Virtual Machines.

The application must be made available 99.99% of the time.

In order to comply with the SLA requirement, what is the minimum number of Virtual Machines required to ensure 99.99% up time to host the application?

○

1 Virtual Machine

○

2 Virtual Machines

(Correct)

○

3 Virtual Machines

○

4 Virtual Machines

Explanation

B. 2 Virtual Machines *is the correct answer because Microsoft Azure's SLA for all Virtual Machines that have two or more instances deployed across two or more Availability Zones in the same Azure region, Microsoft guarantees you will have Virtual Machine Connectivity to at least one instance at least 99.99% of the time.*

For more information, please visit:

https://azure.microsoft.com/en-us/support/legal/sla/virtual-machines/v1_8/

Question 22:
A company is planning on hosting solutions within Microsoft Azure Cloud.

They need to implement MFA for identities hosted in Microsoft Azure.

There are only two valid ways of authentications for MFA as listed below:

- Picture Identification

- Passport Number

Is the above true or false?

○

True

○

False

(Correct)

Explanation

B. False *because the security of two-step verification lies in its layered approach. Compromising multiple authentication factors presents a significant challenge for attackers. Even if an attacker manages to learn the user's password, it is useless without also having possession of the additional authentication method. It works by requiring two or more of the following authentication methods:*

Something you know (typically a password)

Something you have (a trusted device that is not easily duplicated, like a phone)

Something you are (biometrics)

For more information, please visit:

https://docs.microsoft.com/en-us/azure/active-directory/authentication/howto-mfa-mfasettings

Question 23:
You are working on understanding all the key terms when it comes to International Standards, data privacy and data protection policies.

Which of the following choices pertains to the following?

"An organization that defines international standards across all industries"

○

Azure Government

- ○

GDPR

- ○

ISO

(Correct)

- ○

NIST

Explanation

C. ISO *is the correct answer because ISO, International Organization for Standardization, is an organization defines international standards across all industries.*

For more information, please visit: https://docs.microsoft.com/en-us/microsoft-365/compliance/offering-iso-27001

NIST *is incorrect because NIST, National Institute of Standards and Technology (is a physical sciences laboratory, and a non-regulatory agency of the United States Department of Commerce. Its mission is to promote innovation and industrial competitiveness. NIST's activities are organized into laboratory programs that include nanoscale science and technology, engineering, information technology, neutron research, material measurement, and physical measurement.*

For more information, please visit:

For more information, please https://docs.microsoft.com/en-us/microsoft-365/compliance/offering-nist-csf

GDPR *is incorrect because GDPR is a new set of rules designed to give EU citizens more control over their personal data. It aims to simplify the regulatory environment for business so both citizens and businesses in the European Union can fully benefit from the digital economy.*

For more information, please visit:

https://azure.microsoft.com/en-us/blog/protecting-privacy-in-microsoft-azure-gdpr-azure-policy-updates/

Question 24:
You are working on understanding all the key terms when it comes to International standards, data privacy and data protection policies.

Which of the following pertains to the following?

"An organization that defines standards used by the United States government"

- ○

Azure Government

- ◌

GDPR

- ◌

ISO

- ◌

NIST

(Correct)

Explanation

C. NIST *is correct because NIST, National Institute of Standards and Technology (is a physical sciences laboratory, and a non-regulatory agency of the United States Department of Commerce. Its mission is to promote innovation and industrial competitiveness. NIST's activities are organized into laboratory programs that include nanoscale science and technology, engineering, information technology, neutron research, material measurement, and physical measurement.*

For more information, please visit:

For more information, please https://docs.microsoft.com/en-us/microsoft-365/compliance/offering-nist-csf

Azure Government *is incorrect because Azure Government delivers a dedicated cloud enabling only US government agencies and their partners to transform mission-critical workloads to the cloud. ... In order to provide you with the highest level of security and compliance, Azure Government uses physically isolated data-centers and networks.*

For more information, please visit:

https://docs.microsoft.com/en-us/azure/azure-government/documentation-government-welcome

ISO *is the incorrect answer because ISO, International Organization for Standardization, is an organization defines international standards across all industries.*

For more information, please visit:

https://docs.microsoft.com/en-us/microsoft-365/compliance/offering-iso-27001

Question 25:
You are working on understanding all the key terms when it comes to International standards, data privacy and data protection policies. Which of the following pertains to the following?

"A European policy that regulates data privacy and data protection"

- ○

  Azure Government

- ○

  GDPR

  (Correct)

- ○

  ISO

- ○

  NIST

Explanation

B. GDPR is correct because GDPR is a new set of rules designed to give EU citizens more control over their personal data. It aims to simplify the regulatory environment for business so both citizens and businesses in the European Union can fully benefit from the digital economy.

For more information, please visit:

https://azure.microsoft.com/en-us/blog/protecting-privacy-in-microsoft-azure-gdpr-azure-policy-updates/

ISO is the incorrect answer because ISO, International Organization for Standardization, is an organization defines international standards across all industries.

For more information, please visit:

https://docs.microsoft.com/en-us/microsoft-365/compliance/offering-iso-27001

Azure Government is incorrect because Azure Government delivers a dedicated cloud enabling only US government agencies and their partners to transform mission-critical workloads to the cloud. In order to provide you with the highest level of security and compliance, Azure Government uses physically isolated data-centers and networks.

For more information, please visit:

https://docs.microsoft.com/en-us/azure/azure-government/documentation-government-welcome

NIST is incorrect because NIST, National Institute of Standards and Technology (is a physical sciences laboratory, and a non-regulatory agency of the United States Department of Commerce. Its mission is to promote innovation and industrial competitiveness. NIST's activities are organized into laboratory programs that include nanoscale science and technology, engineering, information technology, neutron research, material measurement, and physical measurement.

For more information, please visit:

For more information, please https://docs.microsoft.com/en-us/microsoft-365/compliance/offering-nist-csf

Question 26:
You are working on understanding all the key terms when it comes to International standards, data privacy and data protection policies. Which of the following pertains to the following?

"A dedicated public cloud for federal and state agencies in the United States"

- ○

Azure Government

(Correct)

- ○

GDPR

- ○

ISO

- ○

NIST

Explanation

A. Azure Government *is correct because Azure Government delivers a dedicated cloud enabling only US government agencies and their partners to transform mission-critical* *workloads to the cloud. In order to provide you with the highest level of security and compliance, Azure Government uses physically isolated data-centers and networks.*

For more information, please visit:

https://docs.microsoft.com/en-us/azure/azure-government/documentation-government-welcome

NIST is incorrect because NIST, National Institute of Standards and Technology (is a physical sciences laboratory, and a non-regulatory agency of the United States Department of Commerce. Its mission is to promote innovation and industrial competitiveness. NIST's activities are organized into laboratory programs that include nanoscale science and technology, engineering, information technology, neutron research, material measurement, and physical measurement.

For more information, please visit:

https://docs.microsoft.com/en-us/microsoft-365/compliance/offering-nist-csf

GDPR is incorrect because GDPR is a new set of rules designed to give EU citizens more control over their personal data. It aims to simplify the regulatory environment for business so both citizens and businesses in the European Union can fully benefit from the digital economy.

For more information, please visit:

https://azure.microsoft.com/en-us/blog/protecting-privacy-in-microsoft-azure-gdpr-azure-policy-updates/

ISO is the incorrect answer because ISO, International Organization for Standardization, is an organization defines international standards across all industries.

For more information, please visit:

https://docs.microsoft.com/en-us/microsoft-365/compliance/offering-iso-27001

Question 27:
A company plans on purchasing a Microsoft Azure Support plan.

Below is a key requirement for the support plan:

- Provide an option to contact Microsoft support engineers by phone or email during business hours.

A recommendation is made to purchase the Basic Support plan.

Would this recommendation fulfill the requirement

- ⌀

Yes

No

(Correct)

Explanation

B. No *is the correct answer, because being able to contact Microsoft Support Engineers by phone or email during business hours is only available under the 'Developer, Standard, and Professional Direct support plans. The company would not be able to contact Microsoft Support Engineers by phone or email during business hours under the Basic Support plan as "Technical Support" is not included.*

	Basic	DEVELOPER	STANDARD	PROFESSIONAL DIRECT
	Request support	Purchase support	Purchase support	Purchase support
Price	Included for all Azure customers	$29 per month	$100 per month	$1,000 per month
Scope	Included for all Azure customers	Trial and non-production environments	Production workload environments	Business-critical dependence
Billing and subscription management support	✓	✓	✓	✓
24/7 self-help resources, including Microsoft Learn, Azure portal how-to videos, documentation, and community support	✓	✓	✓	✓
Ability to submit as many support tickets as you need	✓	✓	✓	✓
Azure Advisor—your free, personalized guide to Azure best practices	✓	✓	✓	✓
Azure health status and notifications	✓	✓	✓	✓
24/7 access to technical support by email and phone		Available during business hours by email only.	✓	✓

More information can be found here: https://azure.microsoft.com/en-us/support/plans/

Question 28:
A company plans on purchasing a Microsoft Azure Support plan.

Below is a key requirement for the support plan:

- Provide an option to contact Microsoft support engineers by phone or email 24/7.

A recommendation is made to purchase the Standard Support plan.

Would this recommendation fulfill the requirement?

Yes

(Correct)

No

Explanation

A. Yes *is the correct answer as, under the Standard Support plan, the company has the ability to contact support engineers via phone or email 24/7.*

	Basic Request support	DEVELOPER Purchase support	STANDARD Purchase support	PROFESSIONAL DIRECT Purchase support
Price	Included for all Azure customers	$29 per month	$100 per month	$1,000 per month
Scope	Included for all Azure customers	Trial and non-production environments	Production workload environments	Business-critical dependence
Billing and subscription management support	✔	✔	✔	✔
24/7 self-help resources, including Microsoft Learn, Azure portal how-to videos, documentation, and community support	✔	✔	✔	✔
Ability to submit as many support tickets as you need	✔	✔	✔	✔
Azure Advisor—your free, personalized guide to Azure best practices	✔	✔	✔	✔
Azure health status and notifications	✔	✔	✔	✔
24/7 access to technical support by email and phone		Available during business hours by email only.	✔	✔

For more information on all the Support plans offered please visit

https://azure.microsoft.com/en-us/support/plans/

Question 29:
A company plans on purchasing a Microsoft Azure Support plan.

Below is a key requirement for the support plan:

- Provide an option to contact Microsoft Support Engineers by phone or email 24/7.

A recommendation is made to purchase the Professional Direct plan.

Would this recommendation fulfill the requirement?

- ○

Yes

(Correct)

- ○

No

Explanation

A. Yes *, under the* **Professional Direct** *support plan, the company would be able to contact Microsoft Support Engineers by phone or email 24/7.*

	Basic	DEVELOPER	STANDARD	PROFESSIONAL DIRECT
	Request support	Purchase support	Purchase support	Purchase support
Price	Included for all Azure customers	$29 per month	$100 per month	$1,000 per month
Scope	Included for all Azure customers	Trial and non-production environments	Production workload environments	Business-critical dependence
Billing and subscription management support	✓	✓	✓	✓
24/7 self-help resources, including Microsoft Learn, Azure portal how-to videos, documentation, and community support	✓	✓	✓	✓
Ability to submit as many support tickets as you need	✓	✓	✓	✓
Azure Advisor—your free, personalized guide to Azure best practices	✓	✓	✓	✓
Azure health status and notifications	✓	✓	✓	✓
24/7 access to technical support by email and phone		Available during business hours by email only.	✓	✓

More for information on the 5 Support plans offered by Microsoft Azure, please visit:

https://azure.microsoft.com/en-us/support/plans/

Question 30:
A company is currently planning on deploying resources to Microsoft Azure.

They want to have the ability to manage the compliance of resources across multiple subscriptions.

Which of the following can help you achieve this requirement?

- ○ **Resource Groups**

- ○ **Management Groups**

(Correct)

- ○ **Azure Policy**

- ○ **Azure App Service**

Explanation

B. Management Groups is the correct answer because Management Groups are containers that help you manage access, policy, and compliance across multiple subscriptions. You can create these containers to build an effective and efficient hierarchy that can be used with Azure Policy and Azure Role Based Access Controls.

For more information, please visit:

https://docs.microsoft.com/en-us/azure/governance/management-groups/overview

Azure Policy *is incorrect because Azure Policy is a service in Azure that you use to create, assign, and manage policies. These policies enforce different rules and effects over your resources, so those resources stay compliant with your corporate standards and service level agreements. Azure Policy meets this need by evaluating your resources for non-compliance with assigned policies.*

For more information, please visit:

https://docs.microsoft.com/en-us/azure/governance/policy/overview

Azure App Service *is incorrect because this service enables you to build and host web apps, mobile back ends, and RESTful APIs in the programming language of your choice without managing infrastructure. It offers auto-scaling and high availability, supports both Windows and Linux, and enables automated deployments from GitHub, Azure DevOps, or any Git repo.*
For more information, please visit:

https://docs.microsoft.com/en-us/azure/app-service/

Resource Groups *are incorrect because Resources Groups are logical collections of virtual machines, storage accounts, virtual networks, web apps, databases, and/or database servers. Typically, users will group related resources for an application, divided into groups for production and non-production — but you can subdivide further as needed.*

For more information, please visit:

https://docs.microsoft.com/en-us/azure/azure-resource-manager/resource-group-overview

Question 31:
Microsoft Azure services normally follow the below life-cycle:

- 1st they are deployed in private preview

- 2nd they are released in public preview

- finally they are finally released to general availability

Is this an accurate life cycle for an Azure service?

○

Yes

(Correct)

○

No

Explanation

A. Yes, *this is the life-cycle Microsoft Azure services normally follows.*

For more information, please visit:

https://support.microsoft.com/en-us/help/18486/lifecycle-faq-azure

Question 32:
A company wants to try out a couple of Microsoft Azure services which are available in public preview.

Is it true that services in public preview can only be used via the Azure CLI interface?

○

Yes

○

No

(Correct)

Explanation

B. No, *this is incorrect, all public preview services can be used via all user interfaces, not only the Azure CLI. A service in Public Preview means that the service is in public beta and can be tried out by anyone with an Azure subscription. You can often use these services at a discount as long as they are in preview.*

For more information, please visit:

https://azure.microsoft.com/en-us/updates/storage-explorer-preview-now-available-in-azure-portal/

Question 33:
A company is planning on setting up an Azure account and spinning up resources within their purchased subscription.

When it comes to the Service Level Agreement (SLA), does Microsoft ensure a SLA of 99.9% up-time for paid Azure services?

○

Yes

(Correct)

○

No

Explanation

A. Yes, when it comes to paid Azure services, Microsoft Azure ensures a SLA of 99.9% up-time for paid Azure services.

For more information, please visit:

https://azure.microsoft.com/en-us/support/legal/sla/summary/

Question 34:
A company is planning on setting up a solution in Microsoft Azure. The solution would have the following key requirement:

- Provide a service for hosting a web application

Which of the following would be best suited for this requirement?

- ○

Azure Data Lake Analytics

- ○

Azure Virtual Machine Scale Sets

- ○

Azure Virtual Network

- ○

Azure App Service

(Correct)

Explanation

D. Azure App Service *is the correct answer because an Azure App Service enables you to build and host web apps, mobile back ends, and RESTful APIs in the programming language of your choice without managing infrastructure. It offers auto-scaling and high availability, supports both Windows and Linux, and enables automated deployments from GitHub, Azure DevOps, or any Git repo.*

Azure Data Lake Analytics *is incorrect because Azure Data Lake Analytics is a distributed, cloud-based data processing architecture offered by Microsoft in the Azure cloud. It is based on YARN, the same as the open-source Hadoop platform. It pairs with Azure Data Lake Store, a cloud-based storage platform designed for Big Data analytics.*

Azure Virtual Machine Scale Sets *is incorrect because Azure Virtual Machine Scale Sets are identical pools of virtual machines running some application you control. Azure provides tools* *for you to build and configure the VM the way you want it, then create or remove instances of it until you have as many, or as few, as you need at any point in time.*

Azure Virtual Network is incorrect because Azure Virtual Networks are a representation of your own network in the cloud. It is a logical isolation of the Azure cloud dedicated to your subscription. Each VNet you create has its own CIDR block and can be linked to other VNets and on-premises networks as long as the CIDR blocks do not overlap.

Question 35:
A company is planning on setting up a solution in Microsoft Azure.

The solution would have the following key requirement:

- Provide a solution to host and manage a group of identical Virtual Machines

Which of the following would be best suited for this requirement?

- ○

  Azure Data Lake Analytics

- ○

  Azure Virtual Machine Scale Sets

  (Correct)

- ○

  Azure Virtual Network

- ○

  Azure App Service

Explanation

B. Azure Virtual Machine Scale Sets *is correct because Azure Virtual Machine Scale Sets are identical pools of virtual machines running some application you control. Azure provides tools for you to build and configure the VM's the way you want it, then create or remove instances of it until you have as many, or as few, as you need at any point in time.*

For more information, please visit:

https://docs.microsoft.com/en-us/azure/virtual-machine-scale-sets/overview

Azure Virtual Network is incorrect because Azure Virtual Networks are a representation of your own network in the cloud. It is a logical isolation of the Azure cloud dedicated to your subscription. Each VNet you create has its own CIDR block and can be linked to other VNets and on-premises networks as long as the CIDR blocks do not overlap.

For more information, please visit:

https://docs.microsoft.com/en-us/azure/virtual-network/virtual-networks-overview

Azure App Service is the incorrect because an Azure App Service enables you to build and host web apps, mobile back ends, and RESTful APIs in the programming language of your choice without managing infrastructure. It offers auto-scaling and high availability, supports both Windows and Linux, and enables automated deployments from GitHub, Azure DevOps, or any Git repo.

For more information, please visit:

https://docs.microsoft.com/en-us/azure/app-service/

Azure Data Lake Analytics is incorrect because an Azure Data Lake Analytics is a distributed, cloud-based data processing architecture offered by Microsoft in the cloud. It is based on YARN, the same as the open-source Hadoop platform. It pairs with Azure Data Lake Store, a cloud-based storage platform designed for Big Data analytics.

For more information, please visit:

https://docs.microsoft.com/en-us/azure/data-lake-analytics/data-lake-analytics-overview

Question 36:
A company is planning on setting up a solution in Microsoft Azure. The solution would have the following key requirement:

- Provide an isolated environment for hosting of Virtual Machines

Which of the following would be best suited for this requirement?

- ○ Azure Data Lake Analytics

- ○ Azure Virtual Machine Scale Sets

- ○ Azure Virtual Network

  (Correct)

- ○ Azure App Service

Explanation

C. Azure Virtual Network is the correct answer because Azure Virtual Networks are a representation of your own network in the cloud. It is a logical isolation of the Azure cloud dedicated to your subscription where hosting of isolated Virtual Machines is possible. Each VNet you create has its own CIDR block and can be linked to other VNets and on-premises networks as long as the CIDR blocks do not overlap.

Azure App Service is the incorrect because an Azure App Service enables you to build and host web apps, mobile back ends, and RESTful APIs in the programming language of your choice without managing infrastructure. It offers auto-scaling and high availability, supports both Windows and Linux, and enables automated deployments from GitHub, Azure DevOps, or any Git repo.

Azure Data Lake Analytics is incorrect because Azure Data Lake Analytics is a distributed, cloud-based data processing architecture offered by Microsoft in the Azure cloud. It is based on YARN, the same as the open-source Hadoop platform. It pairs with Azure Data Lake Store, a cloud-based storage platform designed for Big Data analytics.

Azure Virtual Machine Scale Sets is incorrect because Azure Virtual Machine Scale Sets are identical pools of virtual machines running some application you control. Azure provides tools for you to build and configure the VM the way you want it, then create or remove instances of it until you have as many, or as few, as you need at any point in time.

Question 37:
A company is planning on setting up a solution in Microsoft Azure.

The solution would have the following key requirement:

- Provide a cloud service that helps to transform data and provide valuable insights on the data itself

Which of the following would be best suited for this requirement?

- ◦

Azure Data Lake Analytics

(Correct)

- ◦

Azure Virtual Machine Scale Sets

- ◦

Azure Virtual Network

- ◦

Azure App Service

Explanation

A. Azure Data Lake Analytics *is correct because Azure Data Lake Analytics is a distributed, cloud-based data processing architecture offered by Microsoft in the Azure cloud. It is based on YARN, the same as the open-source Hadoop platform. It pairs with Azure Data Lake Store, a cloud-based storage platform designed for Big Data analytics.*

For more information, please visit:

https://docs.microsoft.com/en-us/azure/data-lake-analytics/data-lake-analytics-overview

Azure Virtual Machine Scale Sets *is incorrect because Azure Virtual Machine Scale Sets are identical pools of virtual machines running some application you control. Azure provides tools for you to build and configure the VM the way you want it, then create or remove instances of it until you have as many, or as few, as you need at any point in time.*

For more information, please visit:

https://docs.microsoft.com/en-us/azure/virtual-machine-scale-sets/overview

Azure Virtual Network *is incorrect because Azure Virtual Networks are a representation of your own network in the cloud. It is a logical isolation of the Azure cloud dedicated to your subscription where hosting of isolated Virtual Machines is possible. Each VNet you create has its own CIDR block and can be linked to other VNets and on-premises networks as long as the CIDR blocks do not overlap.*

For more information, please visit:

https://docs.microsoft.com/en-us/azure/virtual-network/virtual-networks-overview

Azure App Service *is incorrect because an Azure App Service enables you to build and host web apps, mobile back ends, and RESTful APIs in the programming language of your choice without managing infrastructure. It offers auto-scaling and high availability, supports both Windows and Linux, and enables automated deployments from GitHub, Azure DevOps, or any Git repo.*

For more information, please visit:

https://docs.microsoft.com/en-us/azure/app-service/

Question 38:
A company has setup a Virtual Machine as part of their purchase subscription.

They now want to move the Virtual Machine to another subscription. Is this possible?

○

Yes

(Correct)

○

No

Explanation

A. Yes, you can move a VM and its associated resources to a different subscription by using the Azure Portal simply by selecting the subscription where you want the VM to be moved, or select an existing resource group, or enter a name to have a new resource group created are all possible methods of accomplishing the same thing.

For more information please visit:

https://docs.microsoft.com/en-us/azure/virtual-machines/windows/move-vm

Question 39:
A company has 100 machines in their on-premise environment.

They want to extend their infrastructure without using too much extra capital or increasing their operational expenditures.

Which of the following could they opt to carry out for this requirement?

- ○

  Migrate everything to the public cloud

- ○

  Move everything to the private cloud

- ○

  Implement a hybrid architecture

  (Correct)

- ○

  Move just 50 machines to the public cloud

Explanation

C. Have a hybrid architecture is the correct answer because a hybrid cloud is a computing environment that combines a public cloud and a private cloud by allowing data and applications to be shared between them. When computing and processing demand fluctuates, hybrid cloud computing gives businesses the ability to seamlessly scale their on-premises infrastructure up to the public cloud to handle any overflow—without giving third-party datacenters access to the entirety of their data. Organizations gain the flexibility and computing power of the public cloud for basic and non-sensitive computing tasks, while keeping business-critical applications and data on-premises, safely behind a company firewall. This architecture can also be utilized by companies interested in expanding to the cloud gradually if their heavily invested with on-premise infrastructure.

For more information, please visit:

https://docs.microsoft.com/en-us/azure/architecture/reference-architectures/dmz/secure-vnet-dmz

Question 40:
A company wants to migrate some scripts to Microsoft Azure.

They want to make use of the serverless features available in Azure.

They decide to use the Azure Virtual Machine service.

Would this service meet the requirement?

- ○

Yes

- ○

No

(Correct)

Explanation

B. No this service does not meet the requirement, *Azure Virtual Machine service is incorrect because an Azure Virtual Machine service is one of several types of on-demand, scalable computing resources that Azure offers. Typically, you choose a VM when you need more control over the computing environment than the other choices offer. An Azure VM gives the flexibility of virtualization without having to buy and maintain the physical hardware that runs it. However, you still need to maintain the VM by performing tasks, such as configuring, patching, and installing the software that runs on it.*

For more information, please visit:

https://docs.microsoft.com/en-us/azure/virtual-machines/windows/overview

Question 41:
A company wants to migrate some scripts to Microsoft Azure.

They want to make use of the serverless features available in Azure.

They decide to use the Azure Functions service.

Would this service meet the requirement?

- ○

Yes

(Correct)

- ○

No

Explanation

A. Yes, is the correct answer. Azure Functions is a server-less compute service that lets you run event-triggered code without having to explicitly provision or manage infrastructure. You can write just the code you need for the problem at hand, without worrying about a whole application or the infrastructure to run it. Functions can make development even more productive, and you can use your development language of choice, such as C#, Java, JavaScript, PowerShell, and Python. Pay only for the time your code runs and trust Azure to scale as needed. Azure Functions lets you develop server-less applications on Microsoft Azure.

For more information, please visit:

https://docs.microsoft.com/en-us/azure/azure-functions/

Question 42:
A company wants to migrate some scripts to Microsoft Azure.

They want to make use of the serverless features available in Azure.

They decide to use the Azure Content Delivery Network service.

Would this service meet the requirement?

○

Yes

○

No

(Correct)

Explanation

B. No, is the correct answer because Azure Content Delivery Network (CDN) lets you reduce load times, save bandwidth, and speed responsiveness—whether you're developing or managing websites or mobile apps, or encoding and distributing streaming media, gaming software, firmware updates, or IoT endpoints.

As the name suggests it is used for content distribution to worldwide users using the global infrastructure of Azure. This means that the CDN uses the servers that are distributed throughout the globe for distributing content globally.

For more information, please visit:

https://docs.microsoft.com/en-us/azure/cdn/cdn-overview

Question 43:
A company is planning on using an entire suite of Microsoft products within Microsoft Azure.

Which of the following belongs to the category of Software-as-a-Service (SaaS)?

- ○

  Azure Virtual Machine service

- ○

  Microsoft Office 365

  (Correct)

- ○

  Azure App Service

- ○

  Azure Content Delivery Network Service

Explanation

B. Microsoft Office 365, *is the correct answer because Software as a service (SaaS) is a software distribution model in which a third-party provider hosts applications and makes them available to customers over the Internet. SaaS is one of three main categories of cloud computing, alongside infrastructure as a service (IaaS) and platform as a service (PaaS). Office 365 is SaaS, which provides an online version of MS Office Suite (Office Web Apps) along with SharePoint Server, Exchange Server and Lync Server. Windows Azure is both IaaS and PaaS, which makes the Windows Server operating system and other features available as services.*

For more information, please visit:
https://docs.microsoft.com/en-us/microsoft-365/

Azure App Service *is incorrect because an Azure App Service enables you to build and host web apps, mobile back ends, and RESTful APIs in the programming language of your choice without managing infrastructure. It offers auto-scaling and high availability, supports both Windows and Linux, and enables automated deployments from GitHub, Azure DevOps, or any Git repo.*

For more information, please visit:
https://docs.microsoft.com/en-us/azure/app-service/

Azure Content Delivery Network (CDN) *is incorrect because it lets you reduce load times, save bandwidth, and speed responsiveness—whether you're developing or managing websites or mobile apps, or encoding and distributing streaming media, gaming software, firmware updates, or IoT endpoints.*

Azure Virtual Machine Service *is incorrect because an Azure Virtual Machine service is one of several types of on-demand, scalable computing resources that Azure offers. Typically, you choose a VM when you need more control over the computing environment than the other choices offer. An Azure VM gives you the flexibility of virtualization without having to buy and maintain the physical hardware that runs it. However, you still need to maintain the VM by performing tasks, such as configuring, patching, and installing the software that runs on it. This service is ideal for development and testing, running applications in the cloud, or used as an extension to a data-center.*

For more information, please visit:

https://azure.microsoft.com/en-us/services/virtual-machines/

Question 44:
A company has a Virtual Machine defined in Microsoft Azure as shown below:

Larger image

demovm
Virtual machine

Search (Ctrl+/)

Overview
Activity log
Access control (IAM)
Tags
Diagnose and solve proble...

Settings
Networking
Disks
Size
Security
Extensions
Continuous delivery (Previe...
Availability set
Configuration
Identity
Properties
Locks
Automation script

You want to ensure that no one accidentally deletes the Virtual Machine.

Which of the following would you modify to effectively implement this requirement?

○

Access Control (IAM)

○

Security

○

Configuration

○

Locks

(Correct)

Explanation

D. Locks *is the correct answer because With Azure Locks, an administrator may need to lock a subscription, resource group, or resource to prevent other users in your organization from accidentally deleting or modifying critical resources. You can set the lock level to CanNotDelete or ReadOnly. In the Azure portal, the locks are called Delete and Read-only respectively.*

CanNotDelete means authorized users can still read and modify a resource, but they can't delete the resource.

ReadOnly means authorized users can read a resource, but they can't delete or update the resource. Applying this lock is similar to restricting all authorized users to the permissions granted by the Reader role.

For more information, please visit:

https://docs.microsoft.com/en-us/azure/azure-resource-manager/resource-group-lock-resources

Access Control (IAM) *is incorrect because Access Control (IAM) is the blade that you use to manage access to Azure resources. It's also known as identity and access management and appears in several locations in the Azure portal.*

For more information, please visit:

Security *is incorrect because the Security tab is designed to implement means to protect data, apps, and infrastructure quickly with built-in security services in Microsoft Azure that include unparalleled security intelligence to help identify rapidly evolving threats early—so you can respond quickly. One could implement a layered, defense in-depth strategy across identity, data, hosts, and networks or unify security management and enable advanced threat protection across hybrid cloud environments.*

Configuration *is incorrect because configuration is an Azure service that allows users to manage configuration within the cloud. Users can create App Configuration stores to store key-value settings and consume stored settings from within applications, deployment pipelines, release processes, microservices, and other Azure resources.*

Question 45:
A company wants to provision a solution within Microsoft Azure with the following requirements:

- Provision a WordPress solution

- Host the solution on a Virtual Machine

Which of the following could be used to quickly deploy the above solutions?

- ○

  Virtual Machine Scale sets

- ○

  Azure Resource Groups

- ○

  Azure Marketplace

  (Correct)

- ○

  Azure Web Apps

Explanation

C. Azure Marketplace *is the correct answer because the Azure Marketplace is an online store that offers applications and services either built on or designed to integrate with Microsoft's Azure public cloud. Such solutions include Virtual Machines, developer* *services, API apps, Azure AD applications, web applications (such as WordPress), data services,and Microsoft Dynamics solutions.*

For more information, please visit:

https://azuremarketplace.microsoft.com/en-us

Azure Web Apps *is incorrect because Azure App Service supports applications defined by Azure as "Web Apps", "Mobile Apps", "API Apps", and "Logic Apps". Azure Cloud Services is a platform that allows developers access to the underlying virtual machines and still manages the application container and deployment automatically.*

For more information, please visit:

https://azure.microsoft.com/en-us/services/app-service/web/

Azure Virtual Machine Scale Sets *is incorrect because Azure Virtual Machine Scale Sets are identical pools of virtual machines running some application you control. Azure provides tools for you to build and configure the VM the way you want it, then create or remove instances of it until you have as many, or as few, as you need at any point in time.*

For more information, please visit:

https://azure.microsoft.com/en-us/services/virtual-machine-scale-sets/

Resource Groups *is incorrect because Resource groups (RG) in Azure is a new approach to group a collection of assets in logical groups for easy or even automatic provisioning, monitoring, and access control, and for more effective management of their costs.*

For more information, please visit:

https://docs.microsoft.com/en-us/azure/azure-resource-manager/resource-group-overview

Question 46:
A company wants to host a set of tables in Microsoft Azure.

They want absolutely zero administration of the underlying infrastructure and low latency access to data.

You recommend using the SQL Database service.

Would this meet the requirement?

Yes

(Correct)

- ○

No

Explanation

YES,

It is fully managed by Azure and therefore it does not entail any administration activities from user end

Refer link
https://docs.microsoft.com/en-us/azure/sql-database/sql-database-paas-index

Question 47:
A company wants to host a set of tables within Microsoft Azure.

They want absolutely zero administration of the underlying infrastructure and low latency access to data.

You recommend using the CosmosDB service.

Would this meet the requirement?

- ○

Yes

(Correct)

- ○

No

Explanation

A. Yes is correct because Azure Cosmos DB is Microsoft's globally distributed, multi-model database service. With a click of a button, Cosmos DB enables you to elastically and independently scale throughput and storage across any number of Azure regions worldwide. You can elastically scale throughput and storage, and take advantage of fast, single-digit-millisecond data access using your favorite API including SQL, MongoDB, Cassandra, Tables, or Gremlin. Cosmos DB provides comprehensive service level agreements (SLAs) for throughput, latency, availability, and consistency guarantees, something no other database service offers.

For more information, please visit:

https://docs.microsoft.com/en-us/azure/cosmos-db/introduction

Question 48:

A company wants to host a set of tables within Microsoft Azure.

They want absolutely zero administration of the underlying infrastructure and low latency access to data.

You recommend using the Azure App service.

Would this fulfill this requirement?

○

Yes

○

No

(Correct)

Explanation

B. No *is the correct answer because an Azure App Service enables you to build and host web apps, mobile back ends, and RESTful APIs in the programming language of your choice without managing infrastructure. It offers auto-scaling and high availability, supports both Windows and Linux, and enables automated deployments from GitHub, Azure DevOps, or any Git repo.*

For more information, please visit:

https://docs.microsoft.com/en-us/azure/app-service/

Question 49:
A company wants to implement an IoT solution service available in Microsoft Azure.

Which of the following would meet the below requirement?

"Monitor and control billions of Internet of Things (IoT) assets".

○

IoT Hub

(Correct)

○

IoT Central

○

IoT Edge

Explanation

A. IoT Hub *is correct because an IoT Hub is a managed service, hosted in the cloud, that acts as a central message hub for bi-directional communication between your IoT application and the devices it manages. You can use Azure IoT Hub to build IoT solutions with reliable and secure communications between millions of IoT devices and a cloud-hosted solution back end. You can connect virtually any device to IoT Hub.*

For more information, please visit:

https://docs.microsoft.com/en-us/azure/iot-hub/about-iot-hub

IoT Central *is incorrect because IoT Central is an app platform that reduces the burden and cost associated with developing, managing, and maintaining enterprise-grade IoT solutions. Choosing to build with Azure IoT Central gives you the opportunity to focus your time, money, and energy on transforming your business with IoT data, rather than just maintaining and updating a complex and continually evolving IoT infrastructure. The easy-to-use interface makes it simple to monitor device conditions, create rules, and manage millions of devices and their data throughout their life cycle. Furthermore, it enables you to act on device insights by extending IoT intelligence into line-of-business applications.*

For more information, please visit:

https://docs.microsoft.com/en-us/azure/iot-central/core/overview-iot-central

IoT Edge *is incorrect because it moves cloud analytics and custom business logic to devices so that your organization can focus on business insights instead of data management. Scale out your IoT solution by packaging your business logic into standard containers, then you can deploy those containers to any of your devices and monitor it all from the cloud.*

Analytics drives business value in IoT solutions, but not all analytics needs to be in the cloud. If you want to respond to emergencies as quickly as possible, you can run anomaly detection workloads at the edge. If you want to reduce bandwidth costs and avoid transferring terabytes of raw data, you can clean and aggregate the data locally then only send the insights to the cloud for analysis.

Azure IoT Edge is made up of three components:

IoT Edge modules are containers that run Azure services, third-party services, or your own code. Modules are deployed to IoT Edge devices and execute locally on those devices.

The IoT Edge runtime runs on each IoT Edge device and manages the modules deployed to each device.

A cloud-based interface enables you to remotely monitor and manage IoT Edge devices.

For more information, please see:

https://docs.microsoft.com/en-us/azure/iot-edge/about-iot-edge

Azure Time Series Insights is incorrect because Azure Time Series Insights is a fully managed analytics, storage, and visualization service that makes it simple to explore and analyze billions of IoT events simultaneously. It gives you a global view of your data, which lets you quickly validate your IoT solution and avoid costly downtime to mission-critical devices. For more information, please see:

https://docs.microsoft.com/en-us/azure/time-series-insights/time-series-insights-explorer

Question 50:
A company wants to implement an IoT solution service available in Microsoft Azure.

Which of the following would meet the below requirement?

"Used to analyze data on end user devices".

- ○

IoT Hub

- ○

IoT Central

- ○

IoT Edge

(Correct)

- ○

Azure Time Series Insights

Explanation

C. IoT Edge *is correct because it moves cloud analytics and custom business logic to devices so that your organization can focus on business insights instead of data management. Scale out your IoT solution by packaging your business logic into standard containers, then you can deploy those containers to any of your devices and monitor it all from the cloud. Analytics drives business value in IoT solutions, but not all analytics needs to be in the cloud. If you want to respond to emergencies as quickly as possible, you can run anomaly detection workloads at the edge. If you want to reduce bandwidth costs and avoid transferring terabytes of raw data, you can clean and aggregate the data locally then only send the insights to the cloud for analysis.*

Azure IoT Edge is made up of three components:

IoT Edge modules are containers that run Azure services, third-party services, or your own code. Modules are deployed to IoT Edge devices and execute locally on those devices.

The IoT Edge runtime runs on each IoT Edge device and manages the modules deployed to each device.

A cloud-based interface enables you to remotely monitor and manage IoT Edge devices.

For more information, please see:

https://docs.microsoft.com/en-us/azure/iot-edge/about-iot-edge

Azure Time Series Insights is incorrect because Azure Time Series Insights is a fully managed analytics, storage, and visualization service that makes it simple to explore and analyze billions of IoT events simultaneously. It gives you a global view of your data, which lets you quickly validate your IoT solution and avoid costly downtime to mission-critical devices. For more information, please see:

https://docs.microsoft.com/en-us/azure/time-series-insights/time-series-insights-explorer

IoT Hub is incorrect because an IoT Hub is a managed service, hosted in the cloud, that acts as a central message hub for bi-directional communication between your IoT application and the devices it manages. You can use Azure IoT Hub to build IoT solutions with reliable and secure communications between millions of IoT devices and a cloud-hosted solution back end. You can connect virtually any device to IoT Hub.

For more information, please visit:

https://docs.microsoft.com/en-us/azure/iot-hub/about-iot-hub

IoT Central is incorrect because IoT Central is an app platform that reduces the burden and cost associated with developing, managing, and maintaining enterprise-grade IoT solutions. Choosing to build with Azure IoT Central gives you the opportunity to focus your time, money, and energy on transforming your business with IoT data, rather than just maintaining and updating a complex and continually evolving IoT infrastructure. The easy-to-use interface makes it simple to monitor device conditions, create rules, and manage millions of devices and their data throughout their life cycle. Furthermore, it enables you to act on device insights by extending IoT intelligence into line-of-business applications.

For more information, please visit:

https://docs.microsoft.com/en-us/azure/iot-central/core/overview-iot-central

Question 51:
A company wants to implement an IoT solution service available in Microsoft Azure.

Which of the following would meet the below requirement?

"Provides a fully managed SaaS (software-as-a-service) solution that makes it easy to connect, monitor and manage IoT assets at scale".

- IoT Hub
- IoT Central

  (Correct)
- IoT Edge
- Azure Time Series Insights

Explanation

B. IoT Central *is correct because IoT Central is an app platform that reduces the burden and cost associated with developing, managing, and maintaining enterprise-grade IoT solutions. Choosing to build with Azure IoT Central gives you the opportunity to focus your time, money, and energy on transforming your business with IoT data, rather than just maintaining and updating a complex and continually evolving IoT infrastructure.*

The easy-to-use interface makes it simple to monitor device conditions, create rules, and manage millions of devices and their data throughout their life cycle. Furthermore, it enables you to act on device insights by extending IoT intelligence into line-of-business applications.

For more information, please visit:

https://docs.microsoft.com/en-us/azure/iot-central/core/overview-iot-central

IoT Edge *is incorrect because it moves cloud analytics and custom business logic to devices so that your organization can focus on business insights instead of data management. Scale out your IoT solution by packaging your business logic into standard containers, then you can deploy those containers to any of your devices and monitor it all from the cloud. Analytics drives business value in IoT solutions, but not all analytics needs to be in the cloud. If you want to respond to emergencies as quickly as possible, you can run anomaly detection workloads at the edge. If you want to reduce bandwidth costs and avoid transferring terabytes of raw data, you can clean and aggregate the data locally then only send the insights to the cloud for analysis.*

Azure IoT Edge is made up of three components:

IoT Edge modules are containers that run Azure services, third-party services, or your own code. Modules are deployed to IoT Edge devices and execute locally on those devices.

The IoT Edge runtime runs on each IoT Edge device and manages the modules deployed to each device.

A cloud-based interface enables you to remotely monitor and manage IoT Edge devices.

For more information, please see:

https://docs.microsoft.com/en-us/azure/iot-edge/about-iot-edge

Azure Time Series Insights is incorrect because Azure Time Series Insights is a fully managed analytics, storage, and visualization service that makes it simple to explore and analyze billions of IoT events simultaneously. It gives you a global view of your data, which lets you quickly validate your IoT solution and avoid costly downtime to mission-critical devices.

For more information, please visit:

https://docs.microsoft.com/en-us/azure/time-series-insights/time-series-insights-explorer

IoT Hub is incorrect because an IoT Hub is a managed service, hosted in the cloud, that acts as a central message hub for bi-directional communication between your IoT application and the devices it manages. You can use Azure IoT Hub to build IoT solutions with reliable and secure communications between millions of IoT devices and a cloud-hosted solution back end. You can connect virtually any device to IoT Hub.

For more information, please visit:

https://docs.microsoft.com/en-us/azure/iot-hub/about-iot-hub

Question 52:
A company wants to implement an IoT solution service available in Microsoft Azure.

Which of the following would meet the below requirement?

"Helps provide powerful data exploration and telemetry tools to help refine operational analysis"

- ○
  IoT Hub

- ○
  IoT Central

- ○

Explanation

C. Azure Time Series Insights *is correct because Azure Time Series Insights is a fully managed analytics, storage, and visualization service that makes it simple to explore and analyze billions of IoT events simultaneously. It gives you a global view of your data, which lets you quickly validate your IoT solution and avoid costly downtime to mission-critical devices. For more information,*

For more information, please visit:

https://docs.microsoft.com/en-us/azure/time-series-insights/time-series-insights-explorer

IoT Hub *is incorrect because an IoT Hub is a managed service, hosted in the cloud, that acts as a central message hub for bi-directional communication between your IoT application and the devices it manages. You can use Azure IoT Hub to build IoT solutions with reliable and secure communications between millions of IoT devices and a cloud-hosted solution back end. You can connect virtually any device to IoT Hub.*

For more information, please visit:

https://docs.microsoft.com/en-us/azure/iot-hub/about-iot-hub

IoT Central *is incorrect because IoT Central is an app platform that reduces the burden and cost associated with developing, managing, and maintaining enterprise-grade IoT solutions. Choosing to build with Azure IoT Central gives you the opportunity to focus your time, money, and energy on transforming your business with IoT data, rather than just maintaining and updating a complex and continually evolving IoT infrastructure.*

The easy-to-use interface makes it simple to monitor device conditions, create rules, and manage millions of devices and their data throughout their life cycle. Furthermore, it enables you to act on device insights by extending IoT intelligence into line-of-business applications.

For more information, please visit:

https://docs.microsoft.com/en-us/azure/iot-central/core/overview-iot-central

IoT Edge *is incorrect because it moves cloud analytics and custom business logic to devices so that your organization can focus on business insights instead of data management. Scale out your IoT solution by packaging your business logic into standard containers, then*

Question 53:
A company is planning on hosting a set of resources in Microsoft Azure.

They want to protect their resources against DDoS attacks and also get real time attack metrics.

Which of the following should the company select to meet this requirement?

○

DDoS Protection Basic

○

DDoS Protection Standard

(Correct)

○

DDoS Protection Premium

○

DDoS Protection Isolated

Explanation

B. DDoS Protection Standard *is correct because DDoS Standard Protection provides additional mitigation capabilities over the Basic service tier that are tuned specifically to Azure Virtual Network resources. DDoS Protection Standard is simple to enable, and requires no application changes. Protection policies are tuned through dedicated traffic* *monitoring and machine learning algorithms. Policies are applied to public IP addresses associated to resources deployed in virtual networks, such as Azure Load Balancer, Azure Application Gateway, and Azure Service Fabric instances, but this protection does not apply to App Service Environments. Real-time telemetry is available through Azure Monitor views during an attack, and for history. Rich attack mitigation analytics are available via diagnostic settings. Application layer protection can be added through the Azure Application Gateway Web Application Firewall or by installing a 3rd party firewall from Azure Marketplace. Protection is provided for IPv4 and IPv6 Azure public IP addresses.*

For more information, please visit:

https://docs.microsoft.com/en-us/azure/virtual-network/ddos-protection-overview

DDoS Protection Premium *is incorrect because Microsoft Azure only provides Basic and Standard DDoS Protection.*

For more information, please visit:

https://docs.microsoft.com/en-us/azure/virtual-network/ddos-protection-overview

DDoS Protection Isolated *is incorrect because Microsoft Azure only provides Basic and Standard DDoS Protection.*

For more information, please visit:

https://docs.microsoft.com/en-us/azure/virtual-network/ddos-protection-overview

DDoS Protection Basic *is incorrect because Basic DDos protection is automatically enabled as part of the Azure platform. Always-on traffic monitoring, and real-time mitigation of common network-level attacks, provide the same defenses utilized by Microsoft's online services. The entire scale of Azure's global network can be used to distribute and mitigate attack traffic across regions. Protection is provided for IPv4 and IPv6 Azure public IP addresses.*

For more information, please visit:

https://docs.microsoft.com/en-us/azure/virtual-network/ddos-protection-overview

Question 54:
A company is planning on deploying resources to a Resource Group (RG) within Microsoft Azure.

The company is planning on assigning tags to the Resource Groups.

Would the resources in the Resource Group (RG) also inherit the same tags?

- $\circ$

Yes

- $\circ$

No

(Correct)

Explanation

B. No, *resources in the Resource Group (RG) will not inherit the same tags because you apply tags to your Azure resources giving metadata to logically organize them into a taxonomy. Each tag consists of a name and a value pair. For example, you can apply the name "Environment" and the value "Production" to all the resources in production. After you apply tags, you can retrieve all the resources in your subscription with that tag name and value. Tags enable you to retrieve related resources from different resource groups. This approach is helpful when you need to organize resources for billing or management. It is important to note that Tags applied to the resource group are not inherited by the resources in that resource group.*

For more information, please visit:

https://docs.microsoft.com/en-us/azure/azure-resource-manager/resource-group-using-tags

Question 55:
A company is planning on deploying resources to a Resource Group (RG) within Microsoft Azure.

The company is planning on assigning permissions to the Resource Group (RG).

Would the resources within the Resource Group (RG) also inherit the same permissions?

- $\circ$

Yes

(Correct)

- $\circ$

No

Explanation

A. Yes, *the Resource Group (RG) will inherit the same permissions because permissions in the top level scope are automatically inherited to the level below – meaning subscription level users have the same permissions to the resource groups and the resource group level users have the same permission to the individual resources within the resource group.*

Section – 4

Question 1:
This question requires that you evaluate the bold-italicized text to determine if it is correct.

"***Authorization*** is the process of verifying a user's credentials."

Instructions: Review the bold-italicized text. If it makes this statement correct, select " No change is needed". If this statement is incorrect, select the answer choice that makes the statement correct.

- ○ No change is needed
- ○ **Authentication** (Correct)
- ○ Federation
- ○ Ticketing

Explanation

Correct Answer - B

Option B is CORRECT since Authentication is the process of proving you are who you say you are.

Reference: https://docs.microsoft.com/en-us/azure/active-directory/develop/authentication-scenarios

Authentication is the process of proving you are who you say you are. Authentication is sometimes shortened to AuthN.

Authorization is the act of granting an authenticated party permission to do something. It specifies what data you're allowed to access and what you can do with that data. Authorization is sometimes shortened to AuthZ.

Option A is INCORRECT since a change is needed in the given statement.

Option C is INCORRECT since Federation is a collection of domains that have established trust. The level of trust may vary, but typically includes authentication and almost always includes

authorization. A typical federation might include a number of organizations that have established a trust for shared access to a set of resources.

Reference: https://docs.microsoft.com/en-us/azure/active-directory/hybrid/whatis-fed

Option D is INCORRECT since Ticketing is a process to raise support requests in Azure.

Question 2:
Which of the following is true when it comes to SaaS (Software as a service)?

- ○ You are responsible for scalability of the solution
- ○ You are responsible for deploying the solution
- ○ You are responsible for configuring the solution (Correct)
- ○ You are responsible for high availability of the solution

Explanation

C. You are responsible for configuring the solution *because SaaS provides a complete software solution that you purchase on a pay-as-you-go basis from a cloud service provider. You rent the use of an app for your organization, and your users connect to it over the Internet, usually with a web browser. All of the underlying infrastructure, middleware, app software, and app data are located in the service provider's data center. The service provider manages the hardware and software, and with the appropriate service agreement, will ensure the availability and the security of the app and your data as well. SaaS allows your organization to get quickly up and running with an app at minimal upfront cost.*

For more information, please visit:

https://azure.microsoft.com/en-us/overview/what-is-saas/

Question 3:
A company is planning on setting up an Enterprise Microsoft Azure Subscription.

Do they need to have a valid Microsoft account for associating the Azure Subscription?

- ○ Yes (Correct)
- ○ No

Explanation

A. Yes *because an Enterprise Azure account is a global unique entity that gets you access to Azure services and your Azure subscriptions. You can create multiple subscriptions in your*

Azure account to create separation e.g. for billing or management purposes. In your subscription(s) you can manage resources in resources groups. Azure subscription can have a trust relationship with an Azure Active Directory (Azure AD) instance. But a valid Microsoft account is required to associate with the Azure Subscription.

For more information, please reference:

https://docs.microsoft.com/en-us/azure/billing/billing-ea-portal-get-started

Question 4:
An IT administrator for a company has been given a powershell script.

This powershell script will be used to create several Virtual Machines in Azure.

You have to provide a machine to the IT administrator for running the powershell script.

You decide to provide a Linux machine which has the Azure CLI tools installed.

Would this solution fit the requirement?

- ○ Yes
- ○ No (Correct)

Explanation

B. No *because Azure PowerShell is basically an extension of Windows PowerShell. It lets Windows PowerShell users control Azure's robust functionality. From the command line, Azure PowerShell programmers use preset scripts called cmdlets to perform complex tasks like provisioning virtual machines (VMs) or creating cloud services.*

For more information, please visit:

https://docs.microsoft.com/en-us/powershell/azure/get-started-azureps?view=azps-3.1.0

Question 5:
An IT administrator for a company has been given a powershell script.

This powershell script will be used to create several Virtual Machines in Azure.

You have to provide a machine to the IT administrator for running the powershell script.

You decide to provide a ChromeOS based machine and use Azure Cloud Shell.

Would this solution fit the requirement?

- ○ Yes (Correct)
- ○ No

Explanation

A. Yes *because Azure Cloud Shell is an interactive, authenticated, browser-accessible shell for managing Azure resources. It provides the flexibility of choosing the shell experience that best suits the way you work, either Bash or PowerShell, accessible via Chrome.*

For more information, please visit:

https://docs.microsoft.com/en-us/azure/cloud-shell/overview

Question 6:
An IT administrator for a company has been given a powershell script.

This powershell script will be used to create several Virtual Machines in Azure.

You have to provide a machine to the IT administrator for running the powershell script.

You decide to provide a computer that has MacOS and Powershell Core 6.0 installed.

Would this solution fit the requirement?

- ○ Yes (Correct)
- ○ No

Explanation

A. Yes, *because you can run PowerShell on Mac OS X. PowerShell is a command-prompt in your terminal window, so to start it: Start the Terminal application, Now you can simply type powershell as a command and this will start the PowerShell engine and move you from the bash prompt ($) to the PowerShell prompt (PS).*

For more information, please reference:

https://docs.microsoft.com/en-us/powershell/azure/install-az-ps?view=azps-3.1.0

Question 7:
A company is planning on setting up a solution in Microsoft Azure.

The solution would have the following key requirement:

- An Integration solution for the deployment of code

Which of the following would be best suited for this requirement?

- ○ Azure Advisor

- ○ Azure Cognitive Services
- ○ Azure Application Insights
- ○ Azure Devops (Correct)

Explanation

D. Azure DevOps *because it provides developer services to support teams to plan work, collaborate on code development, and build and deploy applications. Developers can work in the cloud using Azure DevOps Services or on-premises using Azure DevOps Server. Azure DevOps Server was formerly named Visual Studio Team Foundation Server (TFS).*

Question 8:
A company is planning on setting up a solution in Microsoft Azure.

The solution would have the following key requirement:

- A tool that provides guidance and recommendations to improve an Azure environment

Which of the following would be best suited for this requirement?

- ○ Azure Advisor (Correct)
- ○ Azure Cognitive Services
- ○ Azure Application Insights
- ○ Azure Devops

Explanation

A. Azure Advisor *because this solution is a personalized cloud consultant that helps you follow best practices to optimize your Azure deployments. It analyzes your resource configuration and usage telemetry and then recommends solutions that can help you improve the cost effectiveness, performance, high availability, and security of your Azure resources.*

For more information, please visit:

https://docs.microsoft.com/en-us/azure/advisor/advisor-overview

Question 9:
A company has a requirement to deploy 10 different types of Azure resources for several departments.

All of the resource types and configurations are the same.

Which of the following could be used to automate the deployment of the resources?

- ○ Azure Resource Manager templates (Correct)
- ○ Virtual machine scale sets
- ○ Azure API Management service

- $\circ$ Management groups

Explanation

A. Azure Resource Manager templates *because Teams need to manage infrastructure and application code through a unified process.*

To meet these challenges, you can automate deployments and use the practice of infrastructure as code. In code, you define the infrastructure that needs to be deployed. The infrastructure code becomes part of your project. Just like application code, you store the infrastructure code in a source repository and version it. Any one on your team can run the code and deploy similar environments.

To implement infrastructure as code for your Azure solutions, use Azure Resource Manager templates. The template is a JavaScript Object Notation (JSON) file that defines the infrastructure and configuration for your project. The template uses declarative syntax, which lets you state what you intend to deploy without having to write the sequence of programming commands to create it. In the template, you specify the resources to deploy and the properties for those resources.

For more information, please visit:

https://docs.microsoft.com/en-us/azure/azure-resource-manager/template-deployment-overview

Question 10:
A company is planning on hosting solutions on within Microsoft Azure Cloud.

They need to implement MFA for identities hosted within Microsoft Azure.

Is it necessary to deploy a federation solution or sync on-premise identities to the cloud?

- $\circ$ Yes
- $\circ$ No (Correct)

Explanation

B. No *because several options are available for managing identity in a cloud environment. These options vary in cost and complexity. A key factor in structuring your cloud-based identity services is the level of integration required with your existing on-premises identity infrastructure.*

In Azure, Azure Active Directory (Azure AD) provides a base level of access control and identity management for cloud resources. However, if your organization's on-premises Active Directory infrastructure has a complex forest structure or customized organizational units (OUs), your cloud-based workloads might require directory synchronization with Azure AD for a consistent set of identities, groups, and roles between your on-premises and cloud environments. Additionally, support for applications that depend on legacy authentication mechanisms might require the deployment of Active Directory Domain Services (AD DS) in the cloud.

Cloud-based identity management is an iterative process. You could start with a cloud-native solution with a small set of users and corresponding roles for an initial deployment. As your migration matures, you might need to integrate your identity solution using directory synchronization or add domains services as part of your cloud deployments. Revisit your identity strategy in every iteration of your migration process.

Determine identity integration requirements

Question	Cloud baseline	Directory synchronization	Cloud-hosted domain services	Active Directory Federation Services
Do you currently lack an on-premises directory service?	Yes	No	No	No
Do your workloads need to use a common set of users and groups between the cloud and on-premises environment?	No	Yes	No	No
Do your workloads depend on legacy authentication mechanisms, such as Kerberos or NTLM?	No	No	Yes	Yes
Do you require single sign-on across multiple identity providers?	No	No	No	Yes

For more information, please visit:

https://docs.microsoft.com/en-us/azure/cloud-adoption-framework/decision-guides/identity/

Question 11:
A company has deployed their solutions on to Microsoft Azure.

They have users that connect to Azure AD via the Internet.

They have the requirement that if users try to login from an anonymous IP address, they are then prompted to change their password.

Which of the following should the company consider for this requirement?

- ○ Azure AD Connect Health
- ○ Azure AD Privileged Identity Management
- ○ Azure Advanced Threat Protection (ATP)
- ○ Azure AD Identity Protection (Correct)

Explanation

D. Azure AD Identity Protection *because Identity this is a tool that allows organizations to accomplish three key tasks:*

Automate the detection and remediation of identity-based risks.

Investigate risks using data in the portal.

Export risk detection data to third-party utilities for further analysis.

Identity Protection uses the learnings Microsoft has acquired from their position in organizations with Azure AD, the consumer space with Microsoft Accounts, and in gaming with Xbox to protect your users. Microsoft analyses 6.5 trillion signals per day to identify and protect customers from threats.

The signals generated by and fed to Identity Protection, can be further fed into tools like Conditional Access to make access decisions, or fed back to a security information and event management (SIEM) tool for further investigation based on your organization's enforced policies.

Risk detection and remediation

Identity Protection identifies risks in the following classifications:

Risk detection type	Description
Atypical travel	Sign in from an atypical location based on the user's recent sign-ins.
Anonymous IP address	Sign in from an anonymous IP address (for example: Tor browser, anonymizer VPNs).
Unfamiliar sign-in properties	Sign in with properties we've not seen recently for the given user.
Malware linked IP address	Sign in from a malware linked IP address
Leaked Credentials	This risk detection indicates that the user's valid credentials have been leaked
Azure AD threat intelligence	Microsoft's internal and external threat intelligence sources have identified a known attack pattern

For more information, please visit:

https://docs.microsoft.com/en-us/azure/active-directory/identity-protection/overview-identity-protection

Question 12:
A company plans to setup multiple resources within their Microsoft Azure subscription.

They want to implement tagging of resources in Microsoft Azure.

But they want to ensure that when resource groups are created, they have to contain a tag with a name of "organization" and value of "montana".

You recommend using *Azure locks* for implementing this requirement.

Would this recommendation fulfill the requirement?

- ○ Yes
- ○ **No** (Correct)

Explanation

B. No, *because Azure Locks, from an administrator perspective means you may need to lock a subscription, resource group, or resource to prevent other users in your organization from accidentally deleting or modifying critical resources. You can set the lock level to CanNotDelete or ReadOnly. In the portal, the locks are called Delete and Read-only respectively.*

CanNotDelete means authorized users can still read and modify a resource, but they can't delete the resource.

ReadOnly means authorized users can read a resource, but they can't delete or update the resource. Applying this lock is similar to restricting all authorized users to the permissions granted by the Reader role.

For more information on locking resources, please visit

https://docs.microsoft.com/en-us/azure/azure-resource-manager/resource-group-lock-resources

Question 13:
A company plans to setup multiple resources within their Microsoft Azure subscription.

They want to implement tagging of resources within Microsoft Azure.

But they want to ensure that when resource groups are created, they have to contain a tag with a name of "organization" and value of "montana".

You recommend using Azure Key Vault for implementing this requirement.

Would this recommendation fulfill the requirement?

- ○ Yes
- ○ **No** (Correct)

Explanation

B. No, *because Azure Key Vault is a tool for securely storing and accessing secrets. A secret is anything that you want to tightly control access to, such as API keys, passwords, or certificates. A vault is logical group of secrets.*

Here are other important terms:

Tenant: A tenant is the organization that owns and manages a specific instance of Microsoft cloud services. It's most often used to refer to the set of Azure and Office 365 services for an organization.

Vault owner: A vault owner can create a key vault and gain full access and control over it. The vault owner can also set up auditing to log who accesses secrets and keys. Administrators can control the key lifecycle. They can roll to a new version of the key, back it up, and do related tasks.

Vault consumer: A vault consumer can perform actions on the assets inside the key vault when the vault owner grants the consumer access. The available actions depend on the permissions granted.

Resource: A resource is a manageable item that's available through Azure. Common examples are virtual machine, storage account, web app, database, and virtual network. There are many more.

Resource group: A resource group is a container that holds related resources for an Azure solution. The resource group can include all the resources for the solution, or only those resources that you want to manage as a group. You decide how you want to allocate resources to resource groups, based on what makes the most sense for your organization.

Service principal: An Azure service principal is a security identity that user-created apps, services, and automation tools use to access specific Azure resources. Think of it as a "user identity" (username and password or certificate) with a specific role, and tightly controlled permissions. A service principal should only need to do specific things, unlike a general user identity. It improves security if you grant it only the minimum permission level that it needs to perform its management tasks.

Azure Active Directory (Azure AD): Azure AD is the Active Directory service for a tenant. Each directory has one or more domains. A directory can have many subscriptions associated with it, but only one tenant.

Azure tenant ID: A tenant ID is a unique way to identify an Azure AD instance within an Azure subscription.

Managed identities: Azure Key Vault provides a way to securely store credentials and other keys and secrets, but your code needs to authenticate to Key Vault to retrieve them. Using a managed identity makes solving this problem simpler by giving Azure services an automatically managed identity in Azure AD. You can use this identity to authenticate to Key Vault or any service that supports Azure AD authentication, without having any credentials in your code. For more information, see the following image and the overview of managed identities for Azure resources.

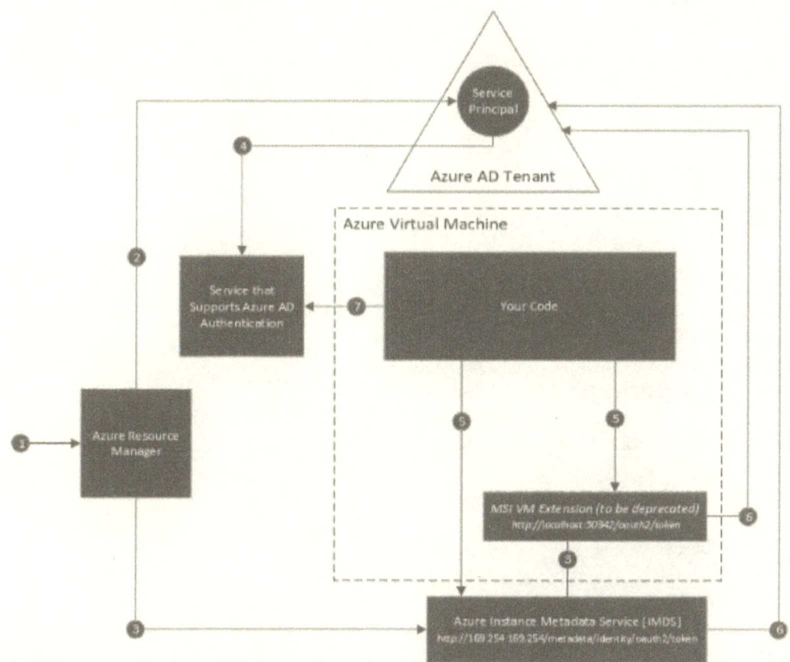

For more information, please visit:

https://docs.microsoft.com/en-us/azure/key-vault/basic-concepts

Question 14:
A company has created a Resource Group (RG) as shown below.

Larger image

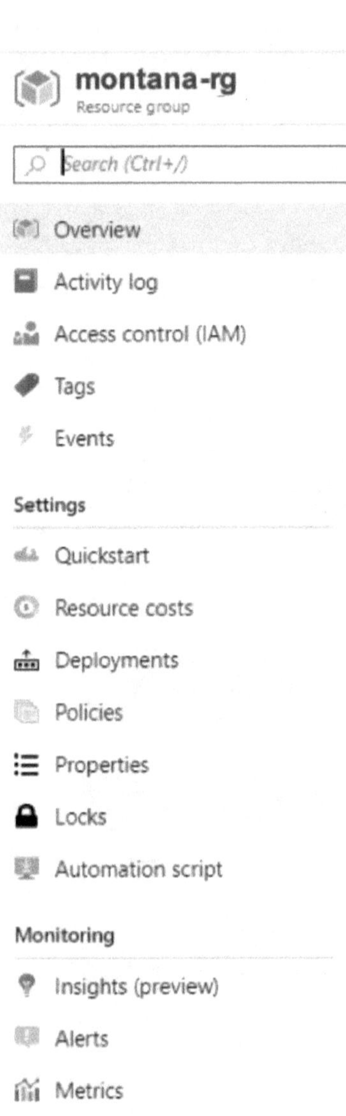

montana-rg
Resource group
Search (Ctrl+/)
Overview
Activity log
Access control (IAM)
Tags
Events
Settings
Quickstart
Resource costs
Deployments
Policies
Properties
Locks
Automation script
Monitoring
Insights (preview)
Alerts
Metrics
Diagnostic settings
Advisor recommendations

They want to ensure that resources within the Resource Group (RG) don't get accidentally deleted.

Which of the following would you use for this purpose?

- ○ Access Control
- ○ Policies
- ○ Locks (Correct)
- ○ Diagnostics settings

Explanation

B. Locks *because As an administrator, you may need to lock a subscription, resource group, or resource to prevent other users in your organization from accidentally deleting or modifying critical resources. You can set the lock level to CanNotDelete or ReadOnly. In the portal, the locks are called Delete and Read-only respectively.*

CanNotDelete means authorized users can still read and modify a resource, but they can't delete the resource.

ReadOnly means authorized users can read a resource, but they can't delete or update the resource. Applying this lock is similar to restricting all authorized users to the permissions granted by the Reader role.

For more information, please visit:

https://docs.microsoft.com/en-us/azure/azure-resource-manager/resource-group-lock-resources

Question 15:
A company wants to purchase a Microsoft Azure support plan.

Below is a key requirement from the support plan:

- Regular architecture reviews from Microsoft for the Azure environment

Which of the following plan would the company need to purchase to fulfill this requirement?

- ○ Basic
- ○ Developer
- ○ Professional Direct (Correct)
- ○ Standard

Explanation

C. Professional Direct *because regular architecture reviews from Microsoft for a company's Azure environment are included in this tier. See the comparisons within the visual below:*

The Basic *tier does not have architecture support.*

Developer and Standard tiers have only general guidance for Architecture support, hence they are incorrect in this scenario.

	Basic Request support	DEVELOPER Purchase support	STANDARD Purchase support	PROFESSIONAL DIRECT Purchase support
Price	Included for all Azure customers	$29 per month	$100 per month	$1,000 per month
Scope	Included for all Azure customers	Trial and non-production environments	Production workload environments	Business-critical dependence
Billing and subscription management support	✓	✓	✓	✓
24/7 self-help resources, including Microsoft Learn, Azure portal how-to videos, documentation, and community support	✓	✓	✓	✓
Ability to submit as many support tickets as you need	✓	✓	✓	✓
Azure Advisor—your free, personalized guide to Azure best practices	✓	✓	✓	✓
Azure health status and notifications	✓	✓	✓	✓
24/7 access to technical support by email and phone		Available during business hours by email only.	✓	✓
Case severity and response time		Minimal business impact (Sev C): Within eight business hours[1]	Minimal business impact (Sev C): Within eight business hours[1] Moderate business impact (Sev B): Within four hours Critical business impact (Sev A): Within one hour	Minimal business impact (Sev C): Within four business hours[1] Moderate business impact (Sev B): Within two hours Critical business impact (Sev A): Within one hour
Third-party software support with interoperability and configuration guidance and troubleshooting		✓	✓	✓
Architecture Support		General guidance	General guidance	Guidance from a pool of ProDirect delivery managers

For more information, please visit:

https://azure.microsoft.com/en-us/support/plans/

Question 16:
A company has a set of Virtual Machines (VMs) defined within Microsoft Azure.

One of the machines was down due to issues with the underlying Azure Infrastructure.

The server was down for an extended period of time and breached the standard SLA defined by Microsoft.

How will Microsoft reimburse the downtime cost?

- ○ **By directly sending money to the customer's bank account**
- ○ **By spinning up another Virtual Machine free of cost for the client**
- ○ **By providing service credits to the customer** (Correct)

- ○ By providing a service free of cost to use for a specific duration of time.

Explanation

C. By providing service credits to the customer because Microsoft Azure cloud service provider always refunded by giving "service credits" in case of breaches in their in SLAs. The "Service Credit" is the percentage of the applicable monthly service fees credited to customers following claim approval

For more information, please visit:

https://azure.microsoft.com/en-us/support/legal/sla/virtual-machines/v1_8/

Question 17:
A company is planning on moving to Microsoft Azure.

Senior management wants to get an idea on the cost that will be incurred if decided to host resources within Azure.

You recommend using the Azure Cost Management to get the required costing of the resources.

Would this recommendation fit the requirement?

- ○ Yes
- ○ **No** (Correct)

Explanation

B. No, because Azure Cost Management is a native Azure cost management solution. It helps you analyze costs, create and manage budgets, export data, and review and act on optimization recommendations to save money while already in production.

For more information, please visit:

https://docs.microsoft.com/en-us/azure/cost-management/overview

Question 18:
A company is planning on moving to Microsoft Azure.

Senior management wants to get an idea on the cost that would be incurred when hosting resources within Azure.

You recommend using the Cloudyn service to get the required costing of the resources.

Would this recommendation fit the requirement?

- ○ Yes
- ○ **No** (Correct)

Explanation

B. No, because Cloudyn, a Microsoft subsidiary, allows you to track cloud usage and expenditures for your Azure resources and other cloud providers including AWS and Google. Easy-to-understand dashboard reports help with cost allocation and showbacks/chargebacks as well. Cloudyn helps optimize your cloud spending by identifying underutilized resources that you can then manage and adjust.

For more information, please visit:

https://docs.microsoft.com/en-us/azure/cost-management/overview

Question 19:
A company is planning on setting up a solution within Microsoft Azure.

The solution would have the following key requirement:

- A simplified tool to build intelligent Artificial Intelligence applications

Which of the following would be best suited for this requirement?

- ○ Azure Advisor
- ○ Azure Cognitive Services (Correct)
- ○ Azure Application Insights
- ○ Azure Devops

Explanation

B. Azure Cognitive Services *because they are APIs, SDKs, and services available to help developers build intelligent applications without having direct AI or data science skills or knowledge. Azure Cognitive Services enable developers to easily add cognitive features into their applications. The goal of Azure Cognitive Services is to help developers create applications that can see, hear, speak, understand, and even begin to reason. The catalog of services within Azure Cognitive Services can be categorized into five main pillars - Vision, Speech, Language, Web Search, and Decision. Simplified, it can be used as a tool to build intelligent AI applications.*

For more information, please visit:

https://docs.microsoft.com/en-us/azure/cognitive-services/welcome

Question 20:
A company is planning on moving to Microsoft Azure.

The senior management wants to get an idea on the cost that would be incurred when hosting resources in Azure.

You recommend using the pricing calculator to get the required costing of the resources.

Would this recommendation fit the requirement?

- Yes (Correct)
- No

Explanation

Yes, the pricing calculator allows you to view the price for different sizes and configurations of your Azure Virtual Machines in terms of the machine's CPU, memory, storage, location and hours in use. Microsoft Azure has monthly releases of new updates and new features as well.

For more information, please visit:

https://azure.microsoft.com/en-us/pricing/calculator/

Question 21:
A company wants to host a mission critical application on a set of Virtual Machines within Microsoft Azure.

They want to ensure they can setup the infrastructure in Azure to guarantee the maximum possible up time for the application.

Which of the following can you make use of in Azure to fulfill this requirement?

Choose 2 answers from the options given below:

- ☐ Resource Groups
- ☐ Availability Zones (Correct)
- ☐ Availability Sets (Correct)
- ☐ Resource Tags

Explanation

B & C are correct, Availability Zones and Availability Sets.

An Availability Zone is a high-availability offering that protects your applications and data from data-center failures. Availability Zones are unique physical locations within an Azure region. Each zone is made up of one or more data-centers equipped with independent power, cooling, and networking

For more information, please visit:

https://docs.microsoft.com/en-us/azure/advisor/advisor-overview

An Availability Set is a logical grouping capability for isolating VM resources from each other when they're deployed. Azure makes sure that the VMs you place within an Availability Set run across multiple physical servers, compute racks, storage units, and network switches.

For more information, please visit:

https://docs.microsoft.com/en-us/azure/virtual-machines/windows/tutorial-availability-sets

Question 22:
A company is planning on hosting an application on a set of Virtual Machines in Microsoft Azure.

They want to ensure that the application survives a region wide failure within Azure.

Which of the following concept needs to be considered to fulfill this requirement?

- ○ Scalability
- ○ Disaster Recovery (Correct)
- ○ Agility
- ○ Elasticity

Explanation

B. Disaster Recovery is correct. Disaster recovery is the process of restoring application functionality in the wake of a catastrophic loss.

For more information, please visit:

https://docs.microsoft.com/en-us/azure/architecture/framework/resiliency/backup-and-recovery

Agility is the measure of IT's contribution and ability to adapt to day to day business situations.

For more information, please visit:

https://docs.microsoft.com/en-us/azure/cloud-adoption-framework/strategy/business-outcomes/agility-outcomes

Elasticity or elastic computing is the ability to quickly expand or decrease computer processing, memory, and storage resources to meet changing demands without worrying about capacity planning and engineering for peak usage. Typically controlled by system monitoring tools, elastic computing matches the amount of resources allocated to the amount of resources actually needed without disrupting operations. With cloud elasticity, a company avoids paying for unused capacity or idle resources and doesn't have to worry about investing in the purchase or maintenance of additional resources and equipment.

For more information, please visit:
https://azure.microsoft.com/en-us/overview/what-is-elastic-computing/

Scalability is the ability of a system to handle increased load, and is one of the pillars of software quality. Use this checklist to review your application architecture from a scalability standpoint.

For more information, please visit:

https://docs.microsoft.com/en-us/azure/architecture/checklist/scalability

Question 23:
A company is planning on implementing the architecture below:

Larger image

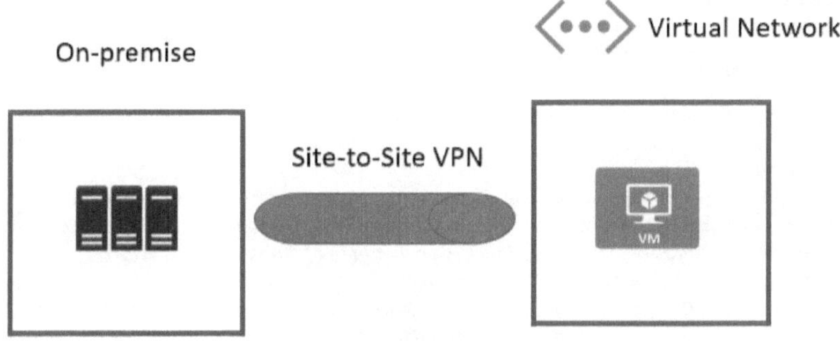

Which of the following best describes the above cloud model?

- ○ Private Cloud
- ○ Public Cloud
- ○ Government Cloud
- ○ Hybrid Cloud (Correct)

Explanation

D. Hybrid Cloud *is correct because a hybrid cloud is a computing environment that combines a public cloud and a private cloud by allowing data and applications to be shared between them. When computing and processing demand fluctuates, hybrid cloud computing gives businesses the ability to seamlessly scale their on-premises infrastructure up to the public cloud to handle any overflow—without giving third-party data-centers access to the entirety of their data. Organizations gain the flexibility and computing power of the public cloud for basic and non-sensitive computing tasks, while keeping business-critical applications and data on-premises, safely behind a company firewall.*

For more information, please visit:

https://azure.microsoft.com/en-us/overview/what-is-hybrid-cloud-computing/

Private Cloud is defined as computing services offered either over the Internet or a private internal network and only to select users instead of the general public. Also called an internal or corporate cloud, private cloud computing gives businesses many of the benefits of a public cloud - including self-service, scalability, and elasticity - with the additional control and customization available from dedicated resources over a computing infrastructure hosted on-premises. In addition, private clouds deliver a higher level of security and privacy through both company firewalls and internal hosting to ensure operations and sensitive data are not accessible to third-party providers. One drawback is that the company's IT department is held responsible for the cost and accountability of managing the private cloud. So private clouds require the same staffing, management, and maintenance expenses as traditional data-center ownership.

For more information, please visit:

https://azure.microsoft.com/en-us/overview/what-is-a-private-cloud/

Public Cloud *are the most common way of deploying cloud computing. The cloud resources (like servers and storage) are owned and operated by a third-party cloud service provider and delivered over the Internet. Microsoft Azure is an example of a public cloud. With a public cloud, all hardware, software, and other supporting infrastructure is owned and managed by the cloud provider. In a public cloud, you share the same hardware, storage, and network devices with other organizations or cloud "tenants." You access services and manage your account using a web browser. Public cloud deployments are frequently used to provide web-based email, online office applications, storage, and testing and development environments.*

For more information, please visit:

https://azure.microsoft.com/en-us/overview/what-are-private-public-hybrid-clouds/

Government Cloud *is a comprehensive cloud platform designed expressly for U.S. Federal, State, and Local Governments to meet the U.S. Government's thorough security and compliance regulations. It has the flexibility to run in government, public, or private clouds with an integrated open platform.*

For more information, please visit:

https://docs.microsoft.com/en-us/azure/azure-government/documentation-government-welcome

Question 24:
A company wants to create multiple data stores in Microsoft Azure.

They want to have storage layers that can be used to store data that is infrequently used.

Which of the following storage tiers for Azure BLOB storage would be suitable for this type of requirement?

Choose 2 answers from the options given below.

- [ ] Premium storage
- [ ] Hot storage
- [ ] Cool storage (Correct)
- [ ] Archive storage (Correct)

Explanation

C. Cool Storage & D. Archive Storage are correct because Azure storage offers different access tiers, which allow you to store blob object data in the most cost-effective manner. The available access tiers include:

Hot - Optimized for storing data that is accessed frequently.

Cool - Optimized for storing data that is infrequently accessed and stored for at least 30 days.

Archive - Optimized for storing data that is rarely accessed and stored for at least 180 days with flexible latency requirements (on the order of hours).

For more information, please visit:

https://docs.microsoft.com/en-us/azure/storage/blobs/storage-blob-storage-tiers

Question 25:
An IT Engineer needs to create a Virtual Machine in Microsoft Azure.

Currently the IT Engineer has an Android OS based workstation.

Which of the following can the IT Engineer use to create the desired Virtual Machine in Azure?

- ( ) Microsoft PowerApps
- ( ) Azure Cloud Shell (Correct)
- ( ) Azure Powershell
- ( ) Azure CLI

Explanation

B. Azure Cloud Shell is correct because the Azure Cloud Shell is an interactive, authenticated, browser-accessible shell for managing Azure resources. It provides the flexibility of choosing the shell experience that best suits the way you work, either Bash or PowerShell.

For more information, please visit:

https://docs.microsoft.com/en-us/azure/cloud-shell/overview

Azure PowerShell is basically an extension of Windows PowerShell. It lets Windows PowerShell users control Azure's robust functionality. From the command line, Azure PowerShell programmers use preset scripts called cmdlets to perform complex tasks like provisioning virtual machines (VMs) or creating cloud services.

For more information, please visit:

https://docs.microsoft.com/en-us/powershell/azure/?view=azps-3.1.0

Azure CLI *provides a command line and scripting environment for creating and managing Azure resources. The Azure CLI is available for macOS, Linux, and Windows operating systems.*

For more information, please visit:

https://docs.microsoft.com/en-us/cli/azure/install-azure-cli?view=azure-cli-latest

Microsoft Power Apps *is a suite of apps, services, connectors and data platform that provides a rapid application development environment to build custom apps for your business needs. Using PowerApps, you can quickly build custom business apps that connect to your business data stored either in the underlying data platform (Common Data Service) or in various online and on-premises data sources (SharePoint, Excel, Office 365, Dynamics 365, SQL Server, and so on).*

For more information, please visit:

https://docs.microsoft.com/en-us/powerapps/powerapps-overview

Question 26:
Whom amongst the following can use the services offered as part of "Azure Germany"?

- ○ Only Enterprises in Germany
- ○ Only users located in Germany
- ○ Only Enterprises and users located in Germany
- ○ All customers who intend to do business in Europe (Correct)

Explanation

E. All customers who intend to do business in Europe *because:*
Microsoft Azure Germany is built on the Microsoft "trusted cloud" principles of security, privacy, compliance, and transparency. It brings data residency, in transit and at rest in Germany, and data replication across German datacenters for business continuity.

Azure connects businesses to a global cloud with local services that help accelerate new investments, technology access, and innovation. Our new Frankfurt and Berlin datacenter regions will join 54 Azure datacenter regions with more than 130 edge node locations and 70,000 miles of fiber and undersea cable systems. Microsoft is committed to building security and compliance into our offerings from the ground up. Azure Germany meets relevant privacy certifications, including ISO/IEC 27018 for protection of personal data in the cloud, the EU/US Privacy Shield, and the European Union's General Data Protection Regulation (GDPR).

For more information, please visit:

https://docs.microsoft.com/en-us/azure/germany/

and

https://azure.microsoft.com/en-us/global-infrastructure/germany/

Question 27:
A company is planning on setting up an Azure Free Account.

Does the Basic Support plan come along with the Azure Free Account

- ○ Yes (Correct)
- ○ No

Explanation

A. Yes, because the Azure Basic support plan is available to all Microsoft Azure accounts.

	Basic Request support	DEVELOPER Purchase support	STANDARD Purchase support	PROFESSIONAL DIRECT Purchase support
Price	Included for all Azure customers	$29 per month	$100 per month	$1,000 per month
Scope	Included for all Azure customers	Trial and non-production environments	Production workload environments	Business-critical dependence
Billing and subscription management support	✓	✓	✓	✓
24/7 self-help resources, including Microsoft Learn, Azure portal how-to videos, documentation, and community support	✓	✓	✓	✓
Ability to submit as many support tickets as you need	✓	✓	✓	✓
Azure Advisor—your free, personalized guide to Azure best practices	✓	✓	✓	✓
Azure health status and notifications	✓	✓	✓	✓
24/7 access to technical support by email and phone		Available during business hours by email only.	✓	✓
Case severity and response time		Minimal business impact (Sev C): Within eight business hours[1]	Minimal business impact (Sev C): Within eight business hours[1] Moderate business impact (Sev B): Within four hours Critical business impact (Sev A): Within one hour	Minimal business impact (Sev C): Within four business hours[1] Moderate business impact (Sev B): Within two hours Critical business impact (Sev A): Within one hour
Third-party software support with interoperability and configuration guidance and troubleshooting		✓	✓	✓
Architecture Support		General guidance	General guidance	Guidance from a pool of ProDirect delivery managers
Operations Support				Service reviews and advisory consultation from a pool of ProDirect delivery managers
Training				Webinars led by Azure engineers
Proactive Guidance				From a pool of ProDirect delivery managers

For more information, please visit:

Question 28:
A company is planning on using their Microsoft Azure Free Account for hosting production-based resources.

Does the Azure Free Account allow you to host production-based resources?

- ○ Yes (Correct)
- ○ No

Explanation

A. Yes, *the Azure Free Account allows the hosting of up to 10 production resources for free.*

For more information, please visit:

https://azure.microsoft.com/en-us/free/free-account-faq/

Question 29:
Your company is planning on using Azure AD for authentication to the resources defined in Azure.

Does Azure AD have built-in capabilities for securing authentication and authorization to resources?

- ○ Yes (Correct)
- ○ No

Explanation

A. Yes, *Azure Active Directory (Azure AD) is Microsoft's cloud-based identity and access management service, which helps your employees sign in and access resources such as Microsoft Office 365, the Azure portal, and thousands of other SaaS applications with built-in capabilities for securing both authentication and authorization.*

For more information, please visit:

https://docs.microsoft.com/en-us/azure/active-directory/fundamentals/active-directory-whatis

Question 30:
You have an Azure subscription named Subscription1 that contains an Azure virtual machine named VM1. VM1 is in a resource group name for RG1.

VM1 runs services that will be used to deploy resources to RG1.

You need to ensure that a service running on VM1 can manage the resources in RG1 by using the identity of VM1.

What should you do first?

- ○ From the Azure portal, modify the Access control (IAM) settings of RG1.
- ○ From the Azure portal, modify the value of the Managed Service Identity option for VM1. (Correct)
- ○ From the Azure portal, modify the Access control (IAM) settings of VM1.
- ○ From the Azure portal, modify the Policies settings of RG1.

Explanation

Answer – B.

From the Azure portal, modify the value of the Managed Service Identity option for VM1 (since the question is asking for "using the identity of VM1")

Option A is INCORRECT because IAM used for access control of Azure services and modifying the IAM setting of the Resource Group RG1 will not help here

Option C is INCORRECT because IAM used for access control of Azure services and modifying the IAM setting of the Virtual Machine VM1 will not help here

Option D is INCORRECT because modifying the policy settings of the Resource Group RG1 will not help here

Please refer to the following links:

Managed Service Identity: https://docs.microsoft.com/en-us/azure/active-directory/managed-identities-azure-resources/overview

IAM: https://docs.microsoft.com/en-us/azure/architecture/security/identity

Question 31:
A company is planning on upgrading their current Microsoft Azure Free plan to the Basic plan.

Does the Free and Basic Azure AD plan come with the same standard support from Microsoft?

- 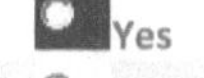 Yes
- ○ No (Correct)

Explanation

B. No *because only paid services come with standard support. Basic is a form of paid support tier as shown in the visual below.*

	FREE	OFFICE 365 APPS	PREMIUM P1	PREMIUM P2
Core Identity and Access Management				
Directory Objects[1]	500,000 Object Limit	No Object Limit	No Object Limit	No Object Limit
Single Sign-On (SSO) [2]	up to 10 apps	up to 10 apps	unlimited	unlimited
User provisioning	✔	✔	✔	✔
Federated Authentication (ADFS or 3rd party IDP)	✔	✔	✔	✔
User and group management (add/update/delete)	✔	✔	✔	✔
Device registration	✔	✔	✔	✔
Cloud Authentication (Pass-Through Auth, Password Hash sync, Seamless SSO)	✔	✔	✔	✔
Azure AD Connect sync (extend on premises directories to Azure AD)	✔	✔	✔	✔
Self-Service Password Change for cloud users	✔	✔	✔	✔
Azure AD Join: desktop SSO & administrator bitlocker recovery	✔	✔	✔	✔
Password Protection (global banned password)	✔	✔	✔	✔
Multi-Factor Authentication [3]	✔	✔	✔	✔
Basic security and usage reports	✔	✔	✔	✔
Business to Business Collaboration				
Azure AD features for guest users[4]	✔	✔	✔	✔

For more information, please visit:

https://azure.microsoft.com/en-us/pricing/details/active-directory/

Question 32:
A company wants to try out some services which are being offered by Microsoft Azure in Public Preview.

Do the services in Public Preview within Azure come with an SLA?

- ○ Yes
- ○ No (Correct)

Explanation

B. No, *because previews are provided "as-is," "with all faults," and "as available," and are excluded from the service level agreements and limited warranty.*

For more information, please visit:

https://azure.microsoft.com/en-us/support/legal/preview-supplemental-terms/

Question 33:
A company wants to try out some services which are being offered by Microsoft Azure in Public Preview.

Does Microsoft provide a separate Azure portal for trying out the services in Public Preview?

- ○ Yes (Correct)
- ● No

Explanation

A. Yes, *because Microsoft Azure offers preview features to you for evaluation purposes. A preview may include preview, beta, or other pre-release features, services, software, or regions. Previews are subject to reduced or different service terms, as set forth in your service agreement and the preview supplemental terms -https://azure.microsoft.com/en-us/support/legal/preview-supplemental-terms/ . Previews are made available to you on the condition that you agree to these terms of use, which supplement your agreement governing the use of Azure.*

So If you want to test public preview features you would go to for preview.portal.azure.com

If you want to implement the public preview solution, you'd use portal.azure.com

For more information, please visit:

https://azure.microsoft.com/en-us/support/legal/preview-supplemental-terms/

Question 34:
Your company needs to deploy and manage several Microsoft Azure Web apps using the Azure App service resource.

Which of the following URL's would you use to manage the Azure Web Apps?

- ○ https://portal.microsoft.com
- ○ https://portal.azure.com (Correct)
- ○ https://portal.azurewebsites.net
- ○ https://portal.azurewebsites.com

Explanation

B. https://portal.azure.com *is the correct answer.*

The Azure portal is a web-based, unified console that provides an alternative to command-line tools. With the Azure portal, you can manage your Azure subscription using a graphical user interface. You can build, manage, and monitor everything from simple web apps to complex cloud deployments. Create custom dashboards for an organized view of resources. Configure accessibility options for an optimal experience.

The Azure portal is designed for resiliency and continuous availability. It has a presence in every Azure datacenter. This configuration makes the Azure portal resilient to individual datacenter failures and avoids network slow-downs by being close to users. The Azure portal updates continuously and requires no downtime for maintenance activities.

The proper URL to access the portal would be: https://portal.azure.com

For more information, please visit:

https://docs.microsoft.com/en-us/azure/azure-portal/azure-portal-overview

Question 35:
A company needs to store 2TB of data that will be infrequently used.

The data needs to be accessed via PowerBI.

Choose 2 of the following options the company should consider as cost-effective data storage solutions to fulfill this need.

- ☐ Azure SQL Databases
- ☐ **Azure Synapse Analytics** (Correct)
- ☐ Azure PostgreSQL
- ☐ Azure CosmosDB
- ☐ **Azure Data Lake** (Correct)

Explanation

B & E are correct *because*

Azure Synapse Analytics is a limitless analytics service that brings together enterprise data warehousing and Big Data analytics. It gives you the freedom to query data on your terms, using either serverless on-demand or provisioned resources—at scale. Azure Synapse brings these two worlds together with a unified experience to ingest, prepare, manage, and serve data for immediate BI and machine learning needs

For more information, please reference:

https://docs.microsoft.com/en-us/azure/sql-data-warehouse/sql-data-warehouse-overview-what-is

Azure Data Lake is a highly scalable public cloud service that allows developers, scientists, business professionals and other Microsoft customers to gain insight from large, complex data sets. As with most data lake offerings, the service is composed of two parts: data storage and data analytics.

For more information, please reference:

https://docs.microsoft.com/en-us/azure/data-lake-store/data-lake-store-overview

Question 36:
A company wants to ensure that users in their company are authenticated when they access resources defined in their Microsoft Azure account.

Which of the following is the correct definition of authentication?

- ○ This specifies the type of service you can use in Azure
- ○ This specifies the type of data you can use in Azure
- ○ This is the act of providing legitimate credentials (Correct)
- ○ This specifies what you can do in Azure

Explanation

C. This is the act of providing legitimate credentials *because authentication is the process of proving you are who you say you are (i.e inputting your creds). Authentication is sometimes shortened to AuthN.*

For more information, please visit:

https://docs.microsoft.com/en-us/azure/active-directory/develop/authentication-scenarios

Question 37:
A company is planning on creating several Virtual Machines within Microsoft Azure.

They would be using the Azure Virtual Machine service.

Which of the following is the right category to which the Azure Virtual Machine service belongs to?

- ○ Infrastructure as a service (IaaS) (Correct)
- ○ Platform as a service (PaaS)
- ○ Software as a service (SaaS)
- ○ Function as a service (FaaS)

Explanation

A. Infrastructure as a service (IaaS) *because IaaS gives you a server in the cloud (virtual machine) that you have complete control over. With an Azure VM, you are responsible for managing everything from the Operating System on up to the application you are running.*

For more information, please visit:

https://azure.microsoft.com/en-us/blog/infrastructure-as-a-service-series-virtual-machines-and-windows/

Question 38:
You need to manage Microsoft Azure by using Azure Cloud Shell.

Larger image

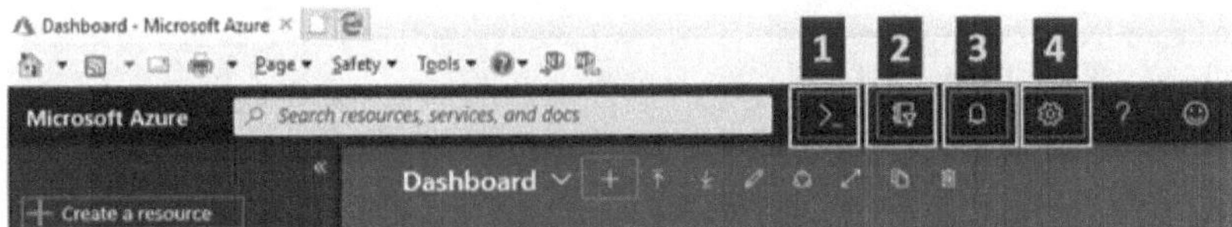

Which Azure portal icon should you select?

- ○ 1 (Correct)
- ○ 2
- ○ 3
- ○ 4

Explanation

A. 1 *because Azure Cloud Shell is an interactive, authenticated, browser-accessible shell for managing Azure resources. It provides the flexibility of choosing the shell experience that best suits the way you work, either Bash or PowerShell.*

Try from Azure portal using the Cloud Shell icon.

More for information, please visit:

https://docs.microsoft.com/en-us/azure/cloud-shell/overview

Question 39:
A company needs to create around 50 customized Virtual Machines.

Out of these 20 are Windows based Virtual machines and 30 are Ubuntu Machines.

Which of the following would help reduce the administrative effort required to deploy the machines?

- ○ Azure Load Balancer
- ○ Azure Web Apps
- ○ Azure Traffic Manager
- ○ Azure ScaleSets (Correct)

Explanation

D. Azure ScaleSets *because Azure virtual machine scale sets let you create and manage a group of identical, load balanced VMs. The number of VM instances can automatically increase or decrease in response to demand or a defined schedule.*

More for information, please visit:

https://docs.microsoft.com/en-us/azure/virtual-machine-scale-sets/overview

Question 40:
A company wants to make use of Microsoft Azure for deployment of various solutions.

They want to ensure that whenever users authenticate to Azure, they have to make use of Multi-Factor Authentication (MFA).

Which of the following can help them achieve this?

- ○ Azure AD Identity Protection (Correct)
- ○ Azure Security Center
- ○ Azure DDoS protection
- ○ Azure privileged identity management

Explanation

A. Azure Identity Protection *is a tool that allows organizations to accomplish three key tasks:*

Automate the detection and remediation of identity-based risks.

Investigate risks using data in the portal.

Export risk detection data to third-party utilities for further analysis.

Azure Active Directory Identity Protection accomplishes this and offers MFA.

For more information, please visit:

https://docs.microsoft.com/en-us/azure/active-directory/identity-protection/overview-identity-protection

Question 41:
A company is planning on hosting 2 Virtual Machines in Azure as shown below:

Virtual Machine Name	Virtual Machine Size
demovm	B1S
demovm1	B1S

When the virtual machine demovm is stopped, you will still incur costs for the storage attached to the Virtual Machine?

- ○ **Yes** (Correct)
- ○ No

Explanation

A. Yes, *because Azure continues to charge for the VM core hours while it is Stopped (but not Stopped (Deallocated), based on the size of the VM and the image you selected to create it. You continue to accrue charges for the VM's cloud service and the storage needed for the VM's OS disk and any attached data disks. Temporary (scratch) disk storage on the VM is free.*

More for information, please visit:

https://blogs.technet.microsoft.com/uspartner_ts2team/2014/10/10/azure-virtual-machines-stopping-versus-stopping-deallocating/

Question 42:
A company is planning on setting up a solution within Microsoft Azure.

The solution would have the following key requirement:

- A tool used to monitor Web applications hosted in production based environments

Which of the following would be best suited for this requirement?

- ○ Azure Advisor
- ○ Azure Cognitive Services
- ○ Azure Application Insights (Correct)
- ○ Azure Devops

Explanation

C. Azure Application Insights *because it is a a feature of Azure Monitor, is an extensible Application Performance Management (APM) service for web developers on multiple platforms. Use it to monitor your live web application. It will automatically detect performance anomalies. It includes powerful analytics tools to help you diagnose issues and to understand what users actually do with your app. It's designed to help you continuously improve performance and usability. It works for apps on a wide variety of platforms including .NET, Node.js and Java EE, hosted on-premises, hybrid, or any public cloud. It integrates with your DevOps process, and has connection points to a variety of development tools. It can monitor and analyze telemetry from mobile apps by integrating with Visual Studio App Center.*

For more information, please visit:

https://docs.microsoft.com/en-us/azure/azure-monitor/app/app-insights-overview

Question 43:
A company needs to implement a solution within Microsoft Azure.

Below are the key requirements for this solution:

- Ability to store JSON documents

- Ensure low latency access to data from around the world

Which of the following data solution would you consider for this requirement?

- Azure SQL Database
- Azure Cosmos DB (Correct)
- Azure SQL Datawarehouse
- SQL Server Stretch database

Explanation

B. Azure Cosmos DB, *because this DB is Microsoft's globally distributed, multi-model database service. With a click of a button, Cosmos DB enables you to elastically and independently scale throughput and storage across any number of Azure regions worldwide providing low latency. You can elastically scale throughput and storage, and take advantage of fast, single-digit-millisecond data access using your favorite API including SQL, MongoDB, Cassandra, Tables, or Gremlin. Cosmos DB provides comprehensive service level agreements (SLAs) for throughput, latency, availability, and consistency guarantees, something no other database service offers. In addition you have the ability to store JSON docs.*

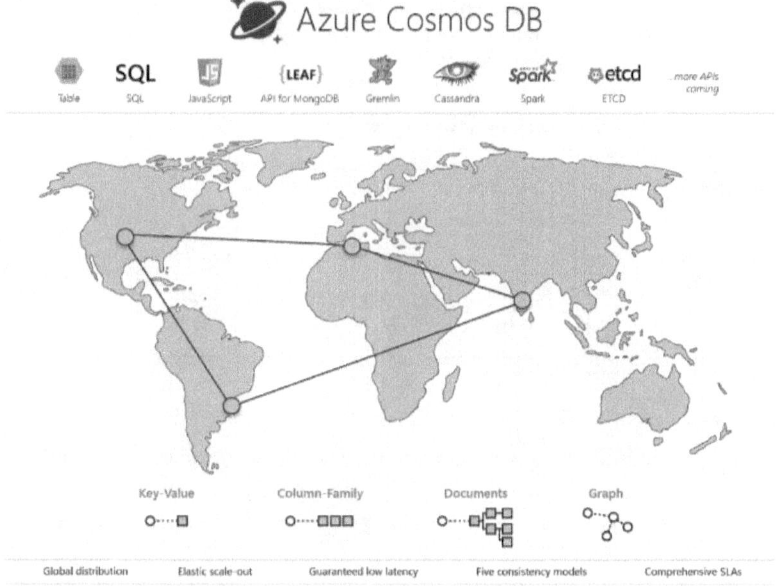

For more information, please visit:

https://docs.microsoft.com/en-us/azure/cosmos-db/introduction

Question 44:

A company is planning on deploying Microsoft Azure resources to a Resource Group (RG).

But the resources would belong to different locations.

Can you have resources that belong to the same resource group but be in multiple locations?

- ○ **Yes** (Correct)
- ○ **No**

Explanation

A. Yes, *because when creating a resource group, you need to provide a location for that resource group. You may be wondering, "Why does a resource group need a location? And, if the resources can have different locations than the resource group, why does the resource group location matter at all?" The resource group stores metadata about the resources. When you specify a location for the resource group, you're specifying where that metadata is stored. For compliance reasons, you may need to ensure that your data is stored in a particular region.*

If the resource group's region is temporarily unavailable, you can't update resources in the resource group because the metadata is unavailable. The resources in other regions will still function as expected, but you can't update them.

Resiliency of Azure Resource Manager

The Azure Resource Manager service is designed for resiliency and continuous availability. Resource Manager and control plane operations (requests sent to management.azure.com) in the REST API are:

- Distributed across regions. Some services are regional.

- Distributed across Availability Zones (as well regions) in locations that have multiple Availability Zones.

- Not dependent on a single logical data center.

- Never taken down for maintenance activities.

This resiliency applies to services that receive requests through Resource Manager. For example, Key Vault benefits from this resiliency.

For more information, please visit:

https://docs.microsoft.com/en-us/azure/azure-resource-manager/resource-group-overview

Question 45:
A company wants to have an Enterprise messaging solution integrated with their existing application hosted within Microsoft Azure.

Larger image

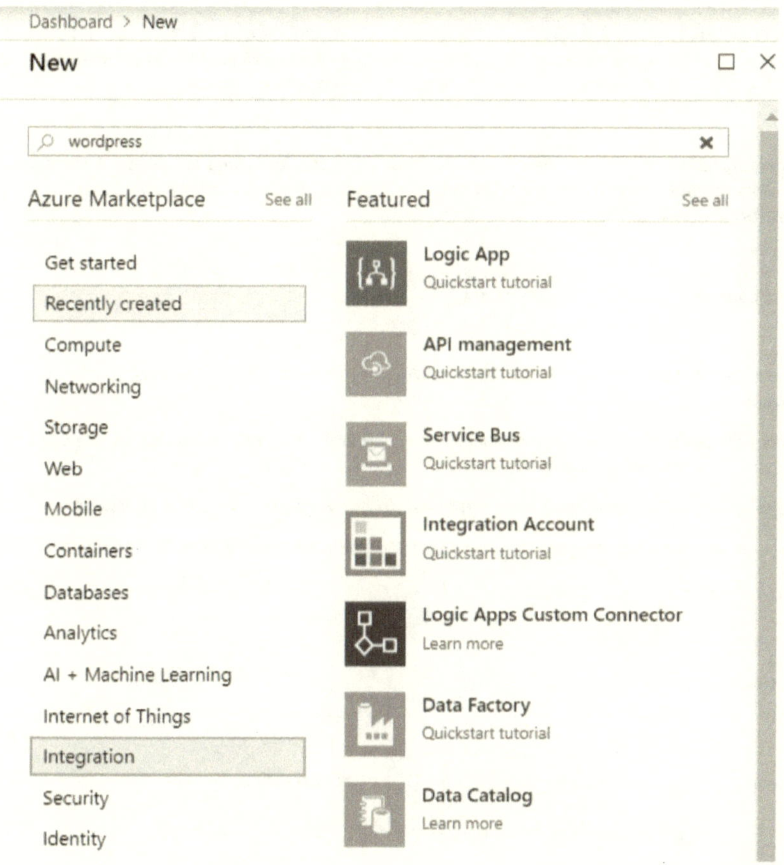

Which of the following from above should the company use for this requirement?

- ○ Logic App
- ○ API management
- ○ **Service Bus** (Correct)
- ○ Data Factory

Explanation

C. Service bus because Microsoft Azure Service Bus is a fully managed enterprise integration message broker. Service Bus can decouple applications and services. Service Bus offers a reliable and secure platform for asynchronous transfer of data and state.

Data is transferred between different applications and services using messages. A message is in binary format and can contain JSON, XML, or just text. For more information, see Integration Services.

Some common messaging scenarios are:

Messaging. Transfer business data, such as sales or purchase orders, journals, or inventory movements.

Decouple applications. Improve reliability and scalability of applications and services. Client and service don't have to be online at the same time.

Topics and subscriptions. Enable 1:n relationships between publishers and subscribers.

Message sessions. Implement workflows that require message ordering or message deferral.

Namespaces

A namespace is a container for all messaging components. Multiple queues and topics can be in a single namespace, and namespaces often serve as application containers.

Queues

Messages are sent to and received from queues. Queues store messages until the receiving application is available to receive and process them.

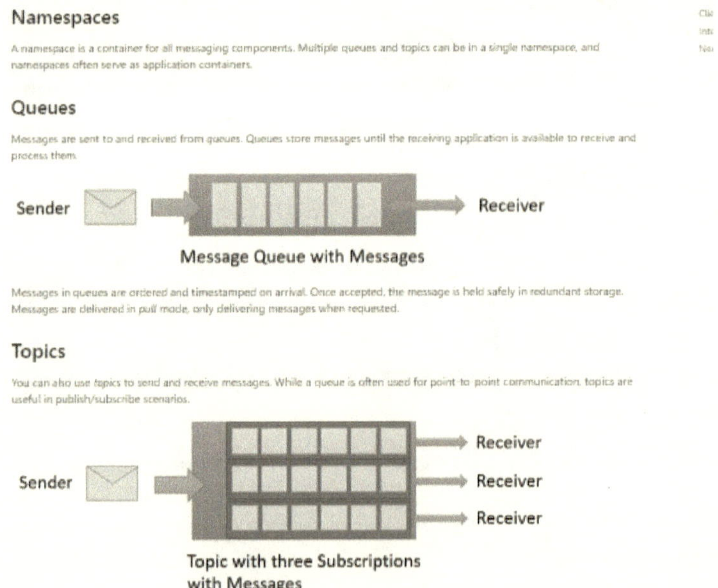

Messages in queues are ordered and timestamped on arrival. Once accepted, the message is held safely in redundant storage. Messages are delivered in pull mode, only delivering messages when requested.

Topics

You can also use topics to send and receive messages. While a queue is often used for point-to-point communication, topics are useful in publish/subscribe scenarios.

For more information, please visit:

https://docs.microsoft.com/en-us/azure/service-bus-messaging/service-bus-messaging-overview

Question 46:

A company is planning on hosting an application on a set of Virtual Machines.

The Virtual Machines are going to be running for a prolonged duration of time.

Which of the following should be considered to reduce the overall cost of Virtual Machine usage?

- ○ Premium Disks
- ○ Virtual Machine Scale sets
- ○ Azure Reservations (Correct)
- ○ Azure Resource Groups

Explanation

C. Azure Reservation *because they help you save money by committing to one-year or three-years plans for virtual machines, Azure Blob storage or Azure Data Lake Storage Gen2, SQL Database compute capacity, Azure Cosmos DB throughput, or other Azure resources. Committing allows you to get a discount on the resources you use. Reservations can significantly reduce your resource costs up to 72% on pay-as-you-go prices. Reservations provide a billing discount and don't affect the runtime state of your resources.*

If you have virtual machines, Blob storage data, Azure Cosmos DB, or SQL databases that use significant capacity or throughput, or that run for long periods of time, buying a reservation gives you the most cost-effective option. For example, when you continuously run four instances of a service without a reservation, you're charged at pay-as-you-go rates. When you buy a reservation for those resources, you immediately get the reservation discount. The resources are no longer charged at the pay-as-you-go rates.

Charges covered by reservation

Service plans:

- **Reserved Virtual Machine Instance** - A reservation only covers the virtual machine compute costs. It doesn't cover additional software, networking, or storage charges.
- **Azure Storage reserved capacity** - A reservation covers storage capacity for standard storage accounts for Blob storage or Azure Data Lake Gen2 storage. The reservation does not cover bandwidth or transaction rates.
- **Azure Cosmos DB reserved capacity** - A reservation covers throughput provisioned for your resources. It doesn't cover the storage and networking charges.
- **SQL Database reserved vCore** - Only the compute costs are included with a reservation. The license is billed separately.
- **SQL Data Warehouse** - A reservation covers cDWU usage. It doesn't cover storage or networking charges associated with the SQL Data Warehouse usage.
- **App Service stamp fee** - A reservation covers stamp usage. It doesn't apply to workers, so any other resources associated with the stamp are charged separately.
- Azure Database for MySQL
- Azure Database for PostgreSQL
- Azure Database for MariaDB
- Azure Data Explorer
- Premium SSD Managed Disks

For more information, please visit:

https://docs.microsoft.com/en-us/azure/billing/billing-save-compute-costs-reservations

Question 47:
A company has launched a set of Virtual Machines in their Pay-as-you-go Microsoft Azure subscription.

After launching a set of VM's they seem to be hitting a constraint of 20 vCPU's and are not able to provision additional Virtual Machines.

Which of the following can be done to allow the company to provision more Virtual Machines?

- ○ **Raise a support ticket with Microsoft** (Correct)
- ○ Increase the limit in the Azure portal
- ○ Increase the limit using the Azure CLI
- ○ Increase the limit in Azure Advisor

Explanation

A. Raise a support ticket with Microsoft *because you get easy access to Azure Support by going online to the Azure Portal and submitting a support request. This is the fastest way to hear back from a Support Engineer that will be ready to start helping you. Access to Subscription Management and billing support is included with your Microsoft Azure subscription, and Technical Support is provided through one of the Azure Support Plans.*

For more information, please visit:

https://azure.microsoft.com/en-us/support/faq/

Question 48:

A company wants to setup users in within their Microsoft Azure Account.

They have segregated their users into groups.

They now want to ensure they set the right permissions for users and administrators accordingly.

They need to manage the permissions effectively.

You recommend using Azure Policies.

Does this recommendation meet the requirement?

- ○ Yes
- ○ No (Correct)

Explanation

B. No *because Azure Policy is a service in Azure that you use to create, assign, and manage policies. These policies enforce different rules and effects over your resources, so those resources stay compliant with your corporate standards and service level agreements. Azure Policy meets this need by evaluating your resources for non-compliance with assigned policies. All data stored by Azure Policy is encrypted at rest.*

Policy definition

The journey of creating and implementing a policy in Azure Policy begins with creating a policy definition. Every policy definition has conditions under which it's enforced. And, it has a defined effect that takes place if the conditions are met.

In Azure Policy, we offer several built-in policies that are available by default. For example:

- **Allowed Storage Account SKUs**: Determines if a storage account being deployed is within a set of SKU sizes. Its effect is to deny all storage accounts that don't adhere to the set of defined SKU sizes.
- **Allowed Resource Type**: Defines the resource types that you can deploy. Its effect is to deny all resources that aren't part of this defined list.
- **Allowed Locations**: Restricts the available locations for new resources. Its effect is used to enforce your geo-compliance requirements.
- **Allowed Virtual Machine SKUs**: Specifies a set of virtual machine SKUs that you can deploy.
- **Add a tag to resources**: Applies a required tag and its default value if it's not specified by the deploy request.
- **Enforce tag and its value**: Enforces a required tag and its value to a resource.
- **Not allowed resource types**: Prevents a list of resource types from being deployed.

To implement these policy definitions (both built-in and custom definitions), you'll need to assign them. You can assign any of these policies through the Azure portal, PowerShell, or Azure CLI.

For more information, please visit:

https://docs.microsoft.com/en-us/azure/governance/policy/overview

Question 49:

A company wants to setup users within their Microsoft Azure Account.

They have segregated their users into groups.

They now want to ensure they set the right permissions for users and administrators accordingly. They need to manage the permissions effectively.

You recommend using Azure Role Based Access.

Does this recommendation meet the requirement?

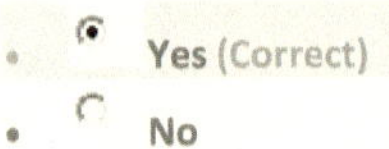

- Yes (Correct)
- No

Explanation

A. Yes, *because Azure role-based access control (RBAC) is the authorization system you use to manage access to Azure resources. To grant access, you assign roles to users, groups, service principals, or managed identities at a particular scope.*

Overview of Access control (IAM)

Access control (IAM) is the blade that you use to assign roles. It's also known as identity and access management and appears in several locations in the Azure portal. The following shows an example of the Access control (IAM) blade for a subscription.

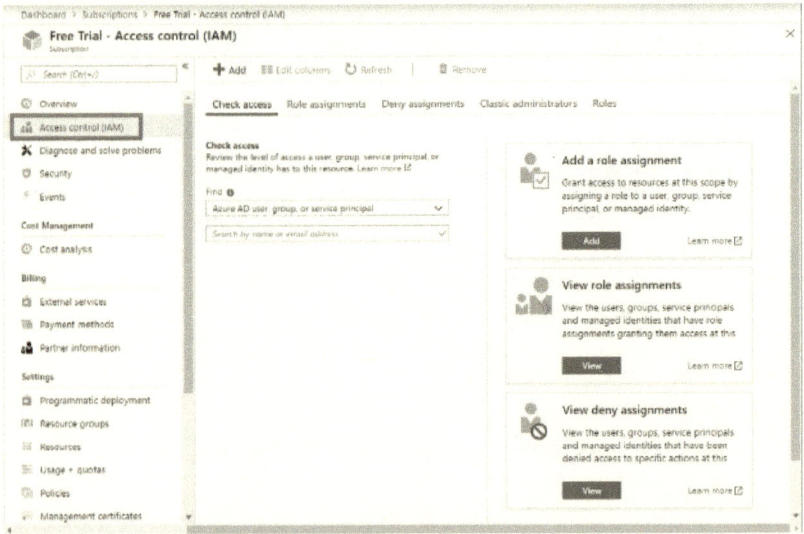

For more information, please visit:

https://docs.microsoft.com/en-us/azure/role-based-access-control/role-assignments-portal

Question 50:

A company wants to setup users within their Microsoft Azure Account.

They have segregated their users into groups.

They now want to ensure they set the right permissions for users and administrators accordingly.

They need to manage the permissions effectively.

You recommend using Azure Management Groups.

Does this recommendation meet the requirement?

- ○ Yes
- ○ No (Correct)

Explanation

B. No, *because Azure Management Groups refers to the tasks and processes required to maintain your business applications and the resources that support them. Azure has many services and tools that work together to provide complete management. These services aren't only for resources in Azure, but also in other clouds and on-premises. Understanding the different tools and how they work together is the first step in designing a complete management environment.*

The following diagram illustrates the different areas of management that are required to maintain any application or resource. These different areas can be thought of as a lifecycle. Each area is required in continuous succession over the lifespan of a resource. This resource lifecycle starts with the initial deployment, through continued operation, and finally when retired.

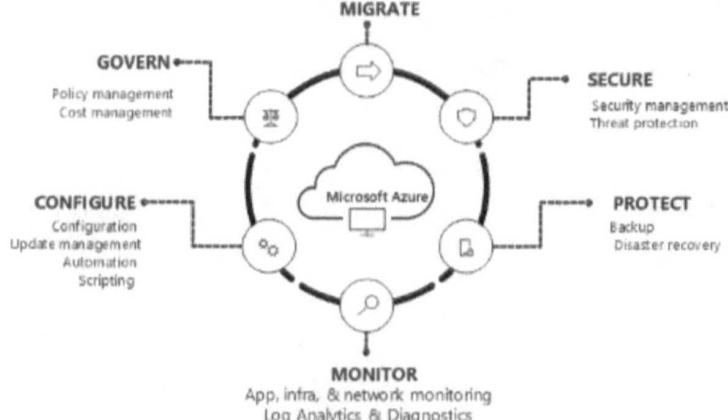

For more information, please visit:

https://docs.microsoft.com/en-us/azure/governance/azure-management

Question 51:

A company wants to host their applications on Microsoft Azure using serverless components.

They don't want to manage the underlying infrastructure for the application.

Which of the following could be used to host code that could be run on a serverless infrastructure?

- ○   Azure Logic Apps
- ○   Azure Service Bus
- ○   Azure Function App (Correct)
- ○   Azure Storage

Explanation

C. Azure Function App *because Azure Functions Apps are a solution for easily running small pieces of code, or "functions," in the cloud. You can write just the code you need for the problem at hand, without worrying about a whole application or the infrastructure to run it. Functions can make development even more productive, and you can use your development language of choice, such as C#, Java, JavaScript, PowerShell, and Python. Pay only for the time your code runs and trust Azure to scale as needed. Azure Functions lets you develop serverless applications on Microsoft Azure.*

For more information, please visit:

https://docs.microsoft.com/en-us/azure/azure-functions/functions-overview

Question 52:
A company wants to host their applications on Microsoft Azure using serverless components.

They don't want to manage the underlying infrastructure for the application.

Which of the following could be used to implement a workflow that could be run on a serverless infrastructure?

- ○   Azure Logic Apps (Correct)
- ○   Azure Service Bus
- ○   Azure Function App
- ○   Azure Storage

Explanation

A. Azure Logic Apps *because Azure Logic Apps is a cloud service that helps you schedule, automate, and orchestrate tasks, business processes, and workflows when you need to integrate apps, data, systems, and services across enterprises or organizations. Logic Apps simplifies how you design and build scalable solutions for app integration, data integration, system integration, enterprise application integration (EAI), and business-to-business (B2B) communication, whether in the cloud, on premises, or both.*

For more information, please visit:

Question 53:

A support engineer plans to perform several Azure management tasks by using the Azure CLI.

You install the CLI on a computer.

You need to tell the support engineer which tools to use to run the CLI.

Which two tools should you instruct the support engineer to use?

- ☐ **Command Prompt** (Correct)
- ☐ **Azure Storage Explorer**
- ☐ **Windows PowerShell** (Correct)
- ☐ **Windows Defender Firewall**
- ☐ **Network and Sharing Center**

Explanation

Correct Answers- A and C

Reference: https://docs.microsoft.com/en-us/cli/azure/install-azure-cli-windows?view=azure-cli-latest

Install Azure CLI on Windows

05/01/2019 • 3 minutes to read •

For Windows the Azure CLI is installed via an MSI, which gives you access to the CLI through the Windows Command Prompt (CMD) or PowerShell. When installing for Windows Subsystem for Linux (WSL), packages are available for your Linux distribution. See the main install page for the list of supported package managers or how to install manually under WSL.

The current version of the Azure CLI is **2.0.76**. For information about the latest release, see the release notes. To find your installed version and see if you need to update, run `az --version`.

Option B is INCORRECT since Microsoft Azure Storage Explorer is a standalone app that makes it easy to work with Azure Storage data on Windows, macOS, and Linux.

Reference:https://docs.microsoft.com/en-us/azure/vs-azure-tools-storage-manage-with-storage-explorer?tabs=windows

Option D is INCORRECT since Windows Defender Firewall cannot be used to run CLI commands

Reference: https://docs.microsoft.com/en-us/windows/security/threat-protection/windows-firewall/configure-the-windows-firewall-log

Option E is INCORRECT since Network and Sharing center is used for networking and cannot be used to run CLI commands

Question 54:
Your company is planning on hosting resources in Azure. Is it possible for outside users to have access to resources in Azure?

- ◯ **Yes** (Correct)
- ◯ **No**

Explanation

Yes, since Azure has other capabilities in place that can allow other users to access Azure-based resources. For example, Azure has the feature of Azure AD Business to Business collaboration where the users don't have to be defined in Azure.

The Microsoft documentation mentions the following on Azure B2B

Collaborate with any partner using their identities

With Azure AD B2B, the partner uses their own identity management solution, so there is no external administrative overhead for your organization.

- The partner uses their own identities and credentials; Azure AD is not required.
- You don't need to manage external accounts or passwords.
- You don't need to sync accounts or manage account lifecycles.

For more information on Azure B2B, please visit the below URL

https://docs.microsoft.com/en-us/azure/active-directory/b2b/what-is-b2b

Question 55:
Your company has several business units.

Each business unit requires 20 different Microsoft Azure Resources for daily operation.

All the business units require the same types of Azure resources.

You need to recommend a solution to automate the creation of the Azure resources.

What should you include in the recommendation?

- ◯ **Azure virtual machine scale sets**
- ◯ **Azure API Management service**
- ◯ **Azure Management groups**
- ◯ **Azure Resources Manager templates** (Correct)

Explanation

D. Azure Resource Manager templates *because since moving to the cloud, many companies have adopted agile development methods. These teams iterate quickly. They need to repeatedly deploy their solutions to the cloud, and know their infrastructure is in a reliable state. As infrastructure has become part of the iterative process, the division between operations and development has disappeared. Teams need to manage infrastructure and application code through a unified process.*

To meet these challenges, you can automate deployments and use the practice of infrastructure as code. In code, you define the infrastructure that needs to be deployed. The infrastructure code becomes part of your project. Just like application code, you store the infrastructure code in a source repository and version it. Any one on your team can run the code and deploy similar environments.

To implement infrastructure as code for your Azure solutions, use Azure Resource Manager templates. The template is a JavaScript Object Notation (JSON) file that defines the infrastructure and configuration for your project. The template uses declarative syntax, which lets you state what you intend to deploy without having to write the sequence of programming commands to create it. In the template, you specify the resources to deploy and the properties for those resources.

Why choose Resource Manager templates?

If you're trying to decide between using Resource Manager templates and one of the other infrastructure as code services, consider the following advantages of using templates:

* **Declarative syntax**: Resource Manager templates allow you to create and deploy an entire Azure infrastructure declaratively. For example, you can deploy not only virtual machines, but also the network infrastructure, storage systems and any other resources you may need.

* **Repeatable results**: Repeatedly deploy your infrastructure throughout the development lifecycle and have confidence your resources are deployed in a consistent manner. Templates are idempotent, which means you can deploy the same template many times and get the same resource types in the same state. You can develop one template that represents the desired state, rather than developing lots of separate templates to represent updates.

* **Orchestration**: You don't have to worry about the complexities of ordering operations. Resource Manager orchestrates the deployment of interdependent resources so they're created in the correct order. When possible, Resource Manager deploys resources in parallel so your deployments finish faster than serial deployments. You deploy the template through one command, rather than through multiple imperative commands.

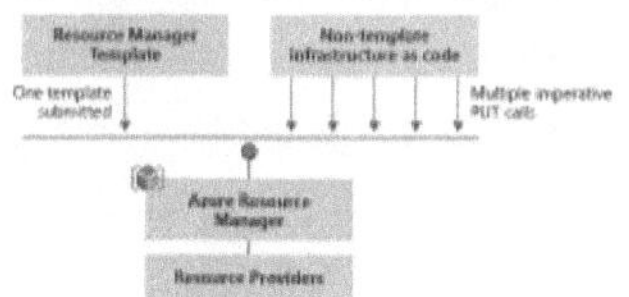

* **Built-in validation**: Your template is deployed only after passing validation. Resource Manager checks the template before starting the deployment to make sure the deployment will succeed. Your deployment is less likely to stop in a half-finished state.

* **Modular files**: You can break your templates into smaller, reusable components and link them together at deployment time. You can also nest one template inside another templates.

* **Create any Azure resource**: You can immediately use new Azure services and features in templates. As soon as a resource provider introduces new resources, you can deploy those resources through templates. You don't have to wait for tools or modules to be updated before using the new services.

* **Tracked deployments**: In the Azure portal, you can review the deployment history and get information about the template deployment. You can see the template that was deployed, the parameter values passed in, and any output values. Other infrastructure as code services aren't tracked through the portal.

For more information, please visit:

https://docs.microsoft.com/en-us/azure/azure-resource-manager/template-deployment-overview

Question 21:
A company is planning on setting up a solution within Microsoft Azure.

The solution would have the following key requirement:

- Provide an efficient way to distribute web content to users across the world

Which of the following would be best suited for this requirement?

- ○ **Azure Content Delivery Network** (Correct)
- ○ Azúre SQL Datawarehouse
- ○ Azure Load Balancer
- ○ Azure HD Insight

Explanation

A. Azure Content Delivery Network *because Azure Content Delivery Network (CDN) is a global CDN solution for delivering high-bandwidth content. It can be hosted in Azure or any other location. With Azure CDN, you can cache static objects loaded from Azure Blob storage, a web application, or any publicly accessible web server, by using the closest point of presence (POP) server. Azure CDN can also accelerate dynamic content, which cannot be cached, by leveraging various network and routing optimizations. Better performance and improved user experience for end users, especially when using applications in which multiple round-trips are required to load content.*

Large scaling to better handle instantaneous high loads, such as the start of a product launch event.

Distribution of user requests and serving of content directly from edge servers so that less traffic is sent to the origin server.

How it works

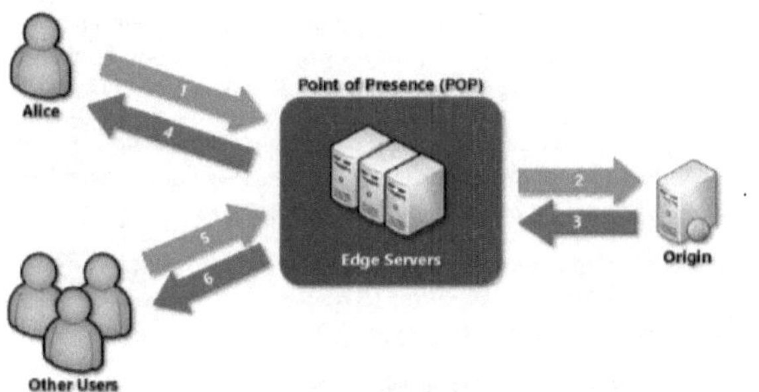

1. A user (Alice) requests a file (also called an asset) by using a URL with a special domain name, such as *<endpoint name>*.azureedge.net. This name can be an endpoint hostname or a custom domain. The DNS routes the request to the best performing POP location, which is usually the POP that is geographically closest to the user.

2. If no edge servers in the POP have the file in their cache, the POP requests the file from the origin server. The origin server can be an Azure Web App, Azure Cloud Service, Azure Storage account, or any publicly accessible web server.

3. The origin server returns the file to an edge server in the POP.

4. An edge server in the POP caches the file and returns the file to the original requestor (Alice). The file remains cached on the edge server in the POP until the time-to-live (TTL) specified by its HTTP headers expires. If the origin server didn't specify a TTL, the default TTL is seven days.

5. Additional users can then request the same file by using the same URL that Alice used, and can also be directed to the same POP.

6. If the TTL for the file hasn't expired, the POP edge server returns the file directly from the cache. This process results in a faster, more responsive user experience.

For more information, please visit:

https://docs.microsoft.com/en-us/azure/cdn/cdn-overview

Question 22:
A company is planning on setting up a solution within Microsoft Azure.

The solution would have the following key requirement:

- Provide the ability to distribute user traffic to a set of backend Virtual Machines

Which of the following would be best suited for this requirement?

- ○ Azure Content Delivery Network
- ○ Azure SQL Datawarehouse
- ○ Azure Load Balancer (Correct)
- ○ Azure HD Insight

Explanation

C. Azure Load Balancer because Azure Load Balancer operates at layer four of the Open Systems Interconnection (OSI) model. It is the single point of contact for clients. Load Balancer distributes new inbound flows that arrive at the Load Balancer's front end to back-end pool instances, according to specified load balacing rules and health probes. The back-end pool instances can be Azure Virtual Machines or instances in a Virtual Machine Scale Set (VMSS).

With Azure Load Balancer, you can scale your applications and create high availabile services. Load Balancer supports both, inbound and outbound scenarios, provides low latency and high throughput, and scales up to millions of flows for all TCP and UDP applications.

A public Load Balancer can provide outbound connections for virtual machines (VMs) inside your virtual network by translating their private IP addresses to public IP addresses. Public Load Balancers are used to load balancer internet traffic to your VMs.

An internal (or private) Load Balancer can be used for scenarios where only private IP addresses are needed at the front end. Internal Load Balancers are used to load balance traffic inside a virtual network. You can also reach a Load Balancer front end from an on-premises network in a hybrid scenario.

For more information, please visit:

https://docs.microsoft.com/en-us/azure/load-balancer/load-balancer-overview

Question 23:
A company is planning on setting up a solution within Microsoft Azure.

The solution would have the following key requirement:

- Provide a cloud service that makes it easy, fast, and cost-effective to analyse massive amounts of data.

Which of the following would be best suited for this requirement?

- ○ Azure Content Delivery Network
- ○ Azure SQL Datawarehouse
- ○ Azure Load Balancer
- ○ Azure HD Insight (Correct)

Explanation

D. Azure HD Insight because Azure HD Insight is a managed, full-spectrum, open-source analytics service in the cloud for enterprises. You can use open-source frameworks such as Hadoop, Apache Spark, Apache Hive, LLAP, Apache Kafka, Apache Storm, R, and more.

Why should I use Azure HDInsight?

This section lists the capabilities of Azure HDInsight.

Capability	Description
Cloud native	Azure HDInsight enables you to create optimized clusters for Hadoop, Spark, interactive query (LLAP), Kafka, Storm, HBase, and ML Services on Azure. HDInsight also provides an end-to-end SLA on all your production workloads.
Low-cost and scalable	HDInsight enables you to scale workloads up or down. You can reduce costs by creating clusters on demand and paying only for what you use. You can also build data pipelines to operationalize your jobs. Decoupled compute and storage provide better performance and flexibility.
Secure and compliant	HDInsight enables you to protect your enterprise data assets with Azure Virtual Network, encryption, and integration with Azure Active Directory. HDInsight also meets the most popular industry and government compliance standards.
Monitoring	Azure HDInsight integrates with Azure Monitor logs to provide a single interface with which you can monitor all your clusters.
Global availability	HDInsight is available in more regions than any other big data analytics offering. Azure HDInsight is also available in Azure Government, China, and Germany, which allows you to meet your enterprise needs in key sovereign areas.
Productivity	Azure HDInsight enables you to use rich productive tools for Hadoop and Spark with your preferred development environments. These development environments include Visual Studio, VSCode, Eclipse, and IntelliJ for Scala, Python, R, Java, and .NET support. Data scientists can also collaborate using popular notebooks such as Jupyter and Zeppelin.
Extensibility	You can extend the HDInsight clusters with installed components (Hue, Presto, and so on) by using script actions, by adding edge nodes, or by integrating with other big data certified applications. HDInsight enables seamless integration with the most popular big data solutions with a one-click deployment.

For more information, please visit:

https://docs.microsoft.com/en-us/azure/hdinsight/hdinsight-overview

Question 24:
A company is planning on hosting a set of resources within their Microsoft Azure subscription.

They are currently aware that most Azure Services can provide an SLA of 99.9%.

Which of the following technique could be used to increase the up-time for resources hosted in Azure?

- ○ Adding resources to multiple regions (Correct)
- ○ Adding resources to the same data center
- ○ Adding resources to the same resource group
- ○ Adding resources to the same subscription

Explanation

A. Adding resources to multiple regions *because Regions are a set of data centres deployed within a latency-defined perimeter and connected through a dedicated regional low-latency network.*

With more global regions than any other cloud provider, Azure gives customers the flexibility to deploy apps where they need to. Azure is generally available in 52 regions around the world, with plans announced for 2 additional regions.

For more information, please visit:

https://azure.microsoft.com/en-au/global-infrastructure/regions/

Question 25:

A company is planning on using Microsoft Azure Cloud for hosting resources.

Which of the following is a key advantage of hosting resources in the Azure private cloud?

- All users across the world can access the resources in your Azure account
- Different departments in your organization can have a segmentation of resources defined in Azure (Correct)
- Only privileged users can have access to resources in your Azure account
- You pay a capital upfront cost when using resources in the public cloud

Explanation

B. Different departments in your organization can have a segmentation of resources defined in Azure *because*

A private cloud consists of computing resources used exclusively by one business or organization. The private cloud can be physically located at your organization's on-site datacenter, or it can be hosted by a third-party service provider. But in a private cloud, the services and infrastructure are always maintained on a private network and the hardware and software are dedicated solely to your organization. In this way, a private cloud can make it easier for an organization to customize its resources to meet specific IT requirements. Private clouds are often used by government agencies, financial institutions, any other mid- to large-size organizations with business-critical operations seeking enhanced control over their environment.

Advantages of a private clouds:

More flexibility—your organization can customize its cloud environment to meet specific business needs.

Improved security—resources are not shared with others, so higher levels of control and security are possible.

High scalability—private clouds still afford the scalability and efficiency of a public cloud.

For more information, please visit:

https://azure.microsoft.com/en-us/overview/what-are-private-public-hybrid-clouds/

Question 26:

A company is planning on setting up a solution within Microsoft Azure.

The solution would have the following key requirement:

- Provides serverless computing functionalities

Which of the following would be best suited for this requirement?

- ○ Azure Machine Learning
- ○ Azure IoT Hub
- ○ Azure AI Bot
- ○ Azure Functions (Correct)

Explanation

D. Azure Functions *because Azure Functions is a solution for easily running small pieces of code, or "functions," in the cloud. You can write just the code you need for the problem at hand, without worrying about a whole application or the infrastructure to run it. Functions can make development even more productive, and you can use your development language of choice, such as C#, Java, JavaScript, PowerShell, and Python. Pay only for the time your code runs and trust Azure to scale as needed. Azure Functions lets you develop serverless applications on Microsoft Azure.*

For more information, please visit:

https://docs.microsoft.com/en-us/azure/azure-functions/functions-overview

Question 27:
A company has a number of resources hosted within Microsoft Azure.

They want to push all the events from various resources into a centralized repository so that the events can be correlated later on.

Which of the following services would you use for this requirement?

- ○ Azure Event Hubs
- ○ Azure Analysis Services
- ○ Azure Advisor
- ○ Azure Log Analytics (Correct)

Explanation

C. Azure Log Analytics *because The Azure Log Analytics agent, previously referred to as the Microsoft Monitoring Agent (MMA) or OMS Linux agent, was developed for comprehensive management across on-premises machines, computers monitored by System Center Operations Manager, and virtual machines in any cloud to push logs to a centralized repository for analysis. The Windows and Linux agents attach to an Azure Monitor and store collected log data from different sources in your Log Analytics workspace, as well as any unique logs or metrics as defined in a monitoring solution.*

For more information, please visit:

https://docs.microsoft.com/en-us/azure/azure-monitor/platform/log-analytics-agent

Question 28:
A company has a Virtual Machine (VM) defined as demovm.

This Virtual Machine (VM) was created with the standard settings.

An application is installed on demovm.

It now needs to be ensured that the application can be accessed over the Internet via HTTP.

You propose the solution to modify the DDoS protection plan

Would this solution fit the requirement?

- ○ Yes
- ○ No (Correct)

Explanation

B. No, *because Azure DDoS Protection is something that prevents and mitigates DDoS attacks automatically tuned to protect your specific Azure resources. Protection is simple to enable on any new or existing Virtual Network and requires no application or resource changes. Azure DDos has nothing to do with accessing an Azure VM over the Internet via HTTP.*

For more information, please visit:

https://azure.microsoft.com/en-us/services/ddos-protection/

Question 29:
A company has a Virtual Machine (VM) defined as demovm.

This Virtual Machine (VM) was created with the standard settings.

An application is installed on demovm. It now needs to be ensured that the application can be accessed over the Internet via HTTP using a prioritised security rule.

You make modifications to the Azure firewall.

Would this solution fit the requirement?

- ○ Yes
- ○ No (Correct)

Explanation

NO, because only "Security Groups" have priority rules to allow inbound and outbound traffic and this CANNOT be done via "Azure Firewall".

Question 30:
A company has a Virtual Machine (VM) defined as demovm.

This Virtual Machine (VM) was created with the standard settings.

An application is installed on demovm. It now needs to be ensured that the application can be accessed over the Internet via HTTP.

You modify the Azure Traffic Manager profile.

Would this solution fit the requirement?

- ○ Yes
- ○ No (Correct)

Explanation

B. No, *because Azure Traffic Manager is a DNS-based traffic load balancer that enables you to distribute traffic optimally to services across global Azure regions, while providing high availability and responsiveness.*

Traffic Manager uses DNS to direct client requests to the most appropriate service endpoint based on a traffic-routing method and the health of the endpoints. An endpoint is any Internet-facing service hosted inside or outside of Azure. Traffic Manager provides a range of traffic-routing methods and endpoint monitoring options to suit different application needs and automatic failover models. Traffic Manager is resilient to failure, including the failure of an entire Azure region. Modifying this won't make the Azure VM accessible from the internet.

For more information, please visit:

https://docs.microsoft.com/en-us/azure/traffic-manager/traffic-manager-overview

Question 31:
A company has a Virtual Machine (VM) defined as demovm.

This Virtual Machine (VM) was created with the standard settings.

An application is installed on demovm. It now needs to be ensured that the application can be accessed over the Internet via HTTP.

You modify the Network Security Groups.

Would this solution fit the requirement?

- ○ Yes (Correct)
- ○ No

Explanation

A. Yes, *using Network Security Groups, you can filter network traffic to and from Azure resources in an Azure virtual network with a network security group. A network security group contains security rules that allow or deny inbound network traffic to, or outbound network traffic from, several types of Azure resources.*

Security rules

A network security group contains zero, or as many rules as desired, within Azure subscription limits. Each rule specifies the following properties:

Property	Explanation
Name	A unique name within the network security group.
Priority	A number between 100 and 4096. Rules are processed in priority order, with lower numbers processed before higher numbers, because lower numbers have higher priority. Once traffic matches a rule, processing stops. As a result, any rules that exist with lower priorities (higher numbers) that have the same attributes as rules with higher priorities are not processed.
Source or destination	Any, or an individual IP address, classless inter-domain routing (CIDR) block (10.0.0.0/24, for example), service tag, or application security group. If you specify an address for an Azure resource, specify the private IP address assigned to the resource. Network security groups are processed after Azure translates a public IP address to a private IP address for inbound traffic, and before Azure translates a private IP address to a public IP address for outbound traffic. Learn more about Azure IP addresses. Specifying a range, a service tag, or application security group, enables you to create fewer security rules. The ability to specify multiple individual IP addresses and ranges (you cannot specify multiple service tags or application groups) in a rule is referred to as augmented security rules. Augmented security rules can only be created in network security groups created through the Resource Manager deployment model. You cannot specify multiple IP addresses and IP address ranges in network security groups created through the classic deployment model. Learn more about Azure deployment models.
Protocol	TCP, UDP, ICMP or Any.
Direction	Whether the rule applies to inbound, or outbound traffic.
Port range	You can specify an individual or range of ports. For example, you could specify 80 or 10000-10005. Specifying ranges enables you to create fewer security rules. Augmented security rules can only be created in network security groups created through the Resource Manager deployment model. You cannot specify multiple ports or port ranges in the same security rule in network security groups created through the classic deployment model.
Action	Allow or deny

For more information, please visit:

https://docs.microsoft.com/en-us/azure/virtual-network/security-overview

Question 32:
A company is looking at the possibility of using Azure Government for development of their cloud-based solutions.

Which of the following customers are allowed to use Azure Government?

Choose 2 answers from the options given below

- ☐ **A Canadian government contractor**
- ☐ **A European government contractor**
- ☐ **A United States government entity** (Correct)
- ☐ **A United States government contractor** (Correct)
- ☐ **A European government entity**

Explanation

C & D *because US government agencies or their partners interested in cloud services that meet government security and compliance requirements, can be confident that Microsoft Azure Government provides world-class security, protection, and compliance services. Azure Government delivers a dedicated cloud enabling government agencies and their partners to transform mission-critical workloads to the cloud. Azure Government services handle data* *that is subject to certain government regulations and requirements, such as FedRAMP, NIST 800.171 (DIB), ITAR, IRS 1075, DoD L4, and CJIS. In order to provide you with the highest level of security and compliance, Azure Government uses physically isolated datacenters and networks (located in U.S. only).*

For more information, please visit:

https://docs.microsoft.com/en-us/azure/azure-government/documentation-government-welcome

Question 33:
A company plans to purchase a Microsoft Azure Support plan.

Below is a key requirement for the support plan:

- Ensure that for high severity cases, there is a minimum initial response time of 10 minutes

A recommendation is made to purchase the Basic Support plan Would this recommendation fulfill the requirement

- ○ Yes
- ○ No (Correct)

Explanation

B. No, *because the Basic support tier doesn't include Case Severity/Response Times compared to the Developer, Standard, and Professional Direct plans.*

	Basic Request support	DEVELOPER Purchase support	STANDARD Purchase support	PROFESSIONAL DIRECT Purchase support
Price	Included for all Azure customers	$29 per month	$100 per month	$1,000 per month
Scope	Included for all Azure customers	Trial and non-production environments	Production workload environments	Business-critical dependence
Billing and subscription management support	✓	✓	✓	✓
24/7 self-help resources, including Microsoft Learn, Azure portal how-to videos, documentation, and community support	✓	✓	✓	✓
Ability to submit as many support tickets as you need	✓	✓	✓	✓
Azure Advisor—your free, personalized guide to Azure best practices	✓	✓	✓	✓
Azure health status and notifications	✓	✓	✓	✓
24/7 access to technical support by email and phone		Available during business hours by email only.	✓	✓
Case severity and response time		Minimal business impact (Sev C): Within eight business hours[1]	Minimal business impact (Sev C): Within eight business hours[1] Moderate business impact (Sev B): Within four hours Critical business impact (Sev A): Within one hour	Minimal business impact (Sev C): Within four business hours[1] Moderate business impact (Sev B): Within two hours Critical business impact (Sev A): Within one hour
Third-party software support with interoperability and configuration guidance and troubleshooting		✓	✓	✓
Architecture Support		General guidance	General guidance	Guidance from a pool of ProDirect delivery managers
Operations Support				Service reviews and advisory consultation from a pool of ProDirect delivery managers
Training				Webinars led by Azure engineers
Proactive Guidance				From a pool of ProDirect delivery managers

For more information, please visit:

https://azure.microsoft.com/en-us/support/plans/

Question 34:
A company plans to purchase a Microsoft Azure Support plan. Below is a key requirement for the support plan:

- Ensure that for high severity cases, there is a minimum initial response time of less than 1 hour.

- Ensure that the support plan is the most cost-effective.

A recommendation is made to purchase the Professional Direct Support plan

Would this recommendation fulfill the requirement?

- ○ Yes
- ○ No (Correct)

Explanation

B. No. Although, the Professional Direct Support plan DOES include a 1-hour window for critical business impact but is not a cost-effective option here. The Standard support plan also has a 1-hour window for critical business impact and is less costly as compared to the Professional Direct support plan.

Therefore, choosing the Professional Direct support plan won't fulfill both of our requirements.

	Basic Request support	DEVELOPER Purchase support	STANDARD Purchase support	PROFESSIONAL DIRECT Purchase support
Price	Included for all Azure customers	$29 per month	$100 per month	$1,000 per month
Scope	Included for all Azure customers	Trial and non-production environments	Production workload environments	Business-critical dependence
Billing and subscription management support	✓	✓	✓	✓
24/7 self-help resources, including Microsoft Learn, Azure portal how-to videos, documentation, and community support	✓	✓	✓	✓
Ability to submit as many support tickets as you need	✓	✓	✓	✓
Azure Advisor—your free, personalized guide to Azure best practices	✓	✓	✓	✓
Azure health status and notifications	✓	✓	✓	✓
24/7 access to technical support by email and phone		Available during business hours by email only.	✓	✓
Case severity and response time		Minimal business impact (Sev C): Within eight business hours[1]	Minimal business impact (Sev C): Within eight business hours[1] Moderate business impact (Sev B): Within four hours Critical business impact (Sev A): Within one hour	Minimal business impact (Sev C): Within four business hours[1] Moderate business impact (Sev B): Within two hours Critical business impact (Sev A): Within one hour
Third-party software support with interoperability and configuration guidance and troubleshooting		✓	✓	✓
Architecture Support		General guidance	General guidance	Guidance from a pool of ProDirect delivery managers
Operations Support				Service reviews and advisory consultation from a pool of ProDirect delivery managers
Training				Webinars led by Azure engineers
Proactive Guidance				From a pool of ProDirect delivery managers

For more information, please visit:

https://azure.microsoft.com/en-us/support/plans/

Question 35:
A company plans to purchase a Microsoft Azure Support plan.

Below is a key requirement for the support plan:

- Ensure that for moderate severity cases, there is a minimum initial response time of 2 hours.

A recommendation is made to purchase the Professional Direct support plan.

Would this recommendation fulfill the requirement?

- ○ **Yes** (Correct)
- ○ No

Explanation

A. Yes, *the Professional Direct* **plan would ensure that for moderate severity cases, there is a minimum initial response time of 2 hours.**

	Basic	DEVELOPER	STANDARD	PROFESSIONAL DIRECT
	Request support	Purchase support	Purchase support	Purchase support
Price	Included for all Azure customers	$29 per month	$100 per month	$1,000 per month
Scope	Included for all Azure customers	Trial and non-production environments	Production workload environments	Business-critical dependence
Billing and subscription management support	✓	✓	✓	✓
24/7 self-help resources, including Microsoft Learn, Azure portal how-to videos, documentation, and community support	✓	✓	✓	✓
Ability to submit as many support tickets as you need	✓	✓	✓	✓
Azure Advisor—your free, personalized guide to Azure best practices	✓	✓	✓	✓
Azure health status and notifications	✓	✓	✓	✓
24/7 access to technical support by email and phone		Available during business hours by email only.	✓	✓
Case severity and response time		Minimal business impact (Sev C): Within eight business hours[1]	Minimal business impact (Sev C): Within eight business hours[1] Moderate business impact (Sev B): Within four hours Critical business impact (Sev A): Within one hour	Minimal business impact (Sev C): Within four business hours[1] Moderate business impact (Sev B): Within two hours Critical business impact (Sev A): Within one hour
Third-party software support with interoperability and configuration guidance and troubleshooting		✓	✓	✓
Architecture Support		General guidance	General guidance	Guidance from a pool of ProDirect delivery managers
Operations Support				Service reviews and advisory consultation from a pool of ProDirect delivery managers
Training				Webinars led by Azure engineers
Proactive Guidance				From a pool of ProDirect delivery managers

For more information, please visit:

https://azure.microsoft.com/en-us/support/plans/

Question 36:
A company is planning on deploying a web server and database server as shown in the architecture diagram below.

You have to ensure that traffic restrictions are in place so that the database server can only communicate with the web server.

Larger image

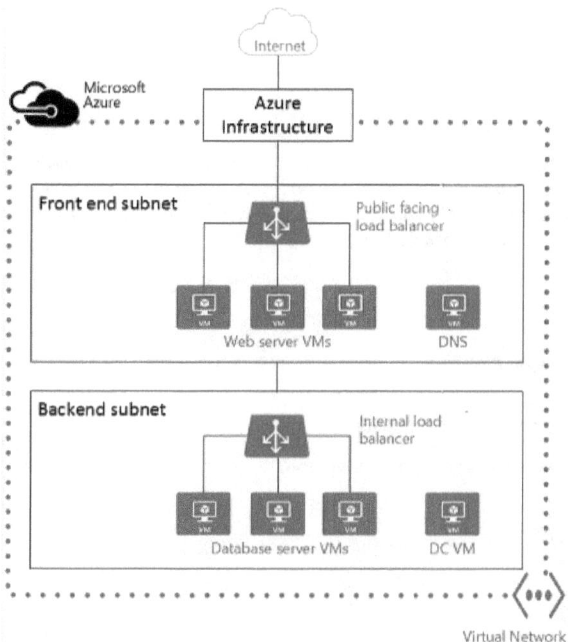

Which of the following would you recommend for implementing these restrictions?

- ○ Network security groups (NSGs) (Correct)
- ○ Azure Service Bus
- ○ A local network gateway
- ○ A Virtual Private Gateway

Explanation

A. Network security groups (NSGs) *because with NSGs you can filter network traffic to and from Azure resources in an Azure virtual network with a network security group. A network security group contains security rules that allow or deny inbound network traffic to, or outbound network traffic from, several types of Azure resources.*

For more information, please visit:

https://docs.microsoft.com/en-us/azure/virtual-network/security-overview

Question 37:
A company wants to make use of a Microsoft Azure service in private preview.

Are Azure services in private preview available to all customers?

- ○ Yes
- ○ **No** (Correct)

Explanation

B. No, *because the private preview is only available to certain Azure customers for evaluation purposes. The public preview is available to all Azure customers. ... Azure features that have been successfully evaluated and tested will typically be released to customers as part of the generally available product integrated into Azure.*

For more information, please visit:

https://azure.microsoft.com/en-us/support/legal/preview-supplemental-terms/

Question 38:
A company wants to make use of a Microsoft Azure service in public preview.

Are Azure services in public preview available to all customers?

- ○ **Yes** (Correct)
- ○ No

Explanation

A. Yes, *Azure may include preview, beta, or other pre-release features, services, software, or regions offered by Microsoft to obtain customer feedback ("Previews"). Previews are made available to you on the condition that you agree to these terms of use, which supplement your agreement governing use of Azure. Public preview is available to all Azure customers.*

PREVIEWS ARE PROVIDED "AS-IS," "WITH ALL FAULTS," AND "AS AVAILABLE," AND ARE EXCLUDED FROM THE SERVICE LEVEL AGREEMENTS AND LIMITED WARRANTY. Previews may not be covered by customer support. Previews may be subject to reduced or different security, compliance and privacy commitments, as further explained in the Microsoft Online Services Privacy Statement, Microsoft Azure Trust Center, the Online Services Terms, and any additional notices provided with the Preview. Customers should not use Previews to process Personal Data or other data that is subject to heightened compliance requirements. Certain named Previews may also be subject to additional terms set forth below, if any. We may change or discontinue Previews at any time without notice. We also may choose not to release a Preview into "General Availability."

For more information, please visit:

https://azure.microsoft.com/en-us/support/legal/preview-supplemental-terms/

Question 39:
A company is planning on setting up a Microsoft Azure account.

Can they purchase multiple Azure subscriptions and tie them to the single Azure account?

- ⊙ Yes (Correct)
- ⊙ No

Explanation

A. Yes, *because a billing account is created when you sign up to use Azure. You use your billing account to manage your invoices, payments, and track costs. You can have access to multiple billing accounts. For example, you might have signed up for Azure for your personal projects. You could also have access through your organization's Enterprise Agreement or Microsoft Customer Agreement. For each of these scenarios, you would have a separate billing account.*

Azure portal currently supports the following type of billing accounts:

Microsoft Online Services Program: A billing account for a Microsoft Online Services Program is created when you sign up for Azure through the Azure website. For example, when you sign up for an Azure Free Account, account with pay-as-you-go rates or as a Visual studio subscriber.

Enterprise Agreement: A billing account for an Enterprise Agreement is created when your organization signs an Enterprise Agreement (EA) to use Azure.

Microsoft Customer Agreement: A billing account for a Microsoft Customer Agreement is created when your organization works with a Microsoft representative to sign a Microsoft Customer Agreement. Some customers in select regions, who sign up through the Azure website for an account with pay-as-you-go rates or upgrade their Azure Free Account may have a billing account for a Microsoft Customer Agreement as well. For more information, see Get started with your billing account for Microsoft Customer Agreement.

Microsoft Online Services Program

Scope	Definition
Billing account	Represents a single owner (Account administrator) for one or more Azure subscriptions. An Account Administrator is authorized to perform various billing tasks like create subscriptions, view invoices or change the billing for subscriptions.
Subscription	Represents a grouping of Azure resources. Invoice is generated at this scope. It has its own payment methods that are used to pay its invoice.

For more information, please visit:

https://docs.microsoft.com/en-us/azure/billing/billing-view-all-accounts

Question 40:
A company has multiple Microsoft Azure subscriptions.

They want to merge the subscriptions into one.

Do they need to contact Microsoft to merge the subscriptions?

- ○ Yes
- ○ **No** (Correct)

Explanation

B. No, *you don't need to contact Microsoft for this request. You can transfer subscriptions between your accounts. Your accounts are conceptually considered accounts of two different users so you can use the above steps to transfer subscriptions between your accounts. Using "Cost Management + Billing" within the Azure Portal.*

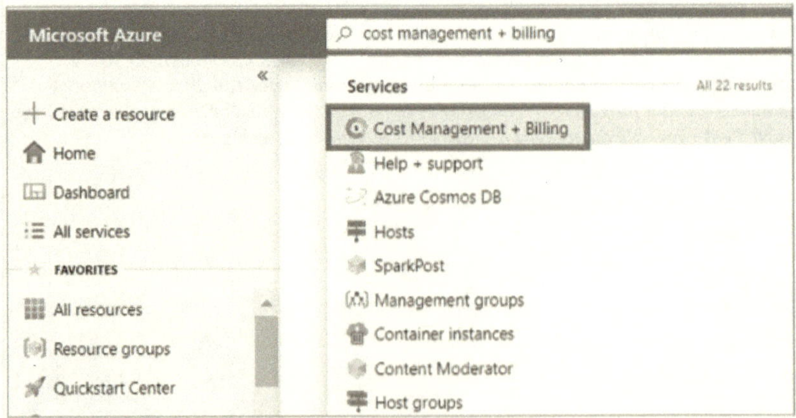

For more information, please visit:

Question 41:

A company needs to deploy several Virtual Machines (VMs).

Each of these Virtual Machines (VMs) will have the same set of permissions.

To minimize the administrative overhead, in which method would you deploy the Azure Virtual Machines?

- ○ Azure policies
- ○ Azure Virtual Machine Scale sets
- ○ Azure Resource Manager (Correct)
- ○ Azure Tags

Explanation

C. *Azure Resource Manager because Azure Resource Manager is the deployment and management service for Azure. It provides a management layer that enables you to create, update, and delete resources in your Azure subscription. You use management features, like access control, locks, and tags, to secure and organize your resources after deployment.*

Consistent management layer

When a user sends a request from any of the Azure tools, APIs, or SDKs, Resource Manager receives the request. It authenticates and authorizes the request. Resource Manager sends the request to the Azure service, which takes the requested action. Because all requests are handled through the same API, you see consistent results and capabilities in all the different tools.

The following image shows the role Azure Resource Manager plays in handling Azure requests.

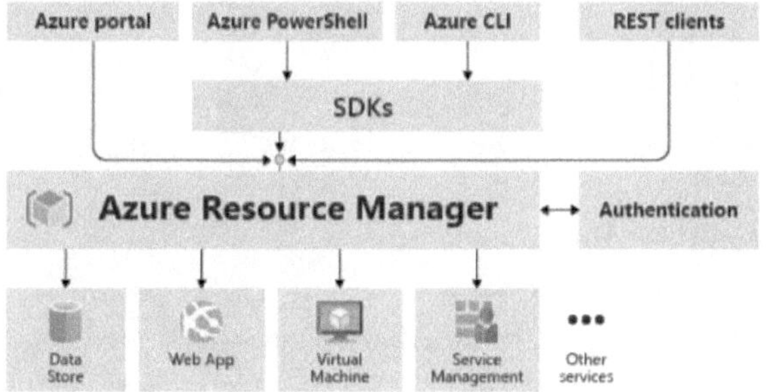

All capabilities that are available in the portal are also available through PowerShell, Azure CLI, REST APIs, and client SDKs. Functionality initially released through APIs will be represented in the portal within 180 days of initial release.

For more information, please visit:

https://docs.microsoft.com/en-us/azure/azure-resource-manager/resource-group-overview

Question 42:
An application consists of a set of virtual machines hosted in a Virtual Network.

In a month, the application seems to have a load of around 20% for 3 weeks.

During the last week, the load on the application reached 80%.

Which of the following concept would you implement to ensure least cost and efficiency of the underlying application infrastructure?

- ○ High availability
- ○ Elasticity (Correct)
- ○ Disaster recovery
- ○ Fault tolerance

Explanation

B. Elasticity *because Elastic computing is the ability to quickly expand or decrease computer processing, memory, and storage resources to meet changing demands without worrying about capacity planning and engineering for peak usage. Typically controlled by system monitoring tools, elastic computing matches the amount of resources allocated to the amount of resources actually needed without disrupting operations. With cloud elasticity, a company avoids paying for unused capacity or idle resources and doesn't have to worry about investing in the purchase or maintenance of additional resources and equipment.*

While security and limited control are concerns to take into account when considering elastic cloud computing, it has many benefits. Elastic computing is more efficient than your typical IT infrastructure, is typically automated so it doesn't have to rely on human administrators around the clock, and offers continuous availability of services by avoiding unnecessary slowdowns or service interruptions.

For more information, please visit:

https://azure.microsoft.com/en-us/overview/what-is-elastic-computing/

Question 43:
A company wants to start using Microsoft Azure.

They want to make use of availability zones within Azure.

Which of the following is associated with the concept of availability zones within Microsoft Azure?

- ○ Region failure
- ○ Resource failure

- ○ **Data Center failure** (Correct)
- ○ Azure failure

Explanation

C. Data Center failure *because Availability Zones is a high-availability offering that protects your applications and data from datacenter failures. Availability Zones are unique physical locations within an Azure region. Each zone is made up of one or more datacenters equipped with independent power, cooling, and networking. To ensure resiliency, there's a minimum of three separate zones in all enabled regions. The physical separation of Availability Zones within a region protects applications and data from datacenter failures. Zone-redundant services replicate your applications and data across Availability Zones to protect from single-points-of-failure. With Availability Zones, Azure offers industry best 99.99% VM uptime SLA.*

An Availability Zone in an Azure region is a combination of a fault domain and an update domain. For example, if you create three or more VMs across three zones in an Azure region, your VMs are effectively distributed across three fault domains and three update domains. The Azure platform recognizes this distribution across update domains to make sure that VMs in different zones are not updated at the same time.

Build high-availability into your application architecture by co-locating your compute, storage, networking, and data resources within a zone and replicating in other zones. Azure services that support Availability Zones fall into two categories:

Zonal services – you pin the resource to a specific zone (for example, virtual machines, managed disks, Standard IP addresses), or

Zone-redundant services – platform replicates automatically across zones (for example, zone-redundant storage, SQL Database).

To achieve comprehensive business continuity on Azure, build your application architecture using the combination of Availability Zones with Azure region pairs. You can synchronously replicate your applications and data using Availability Zones within an Azure region for high-availability and asynchronously replicate across Azure regions for disaster recovery protection.

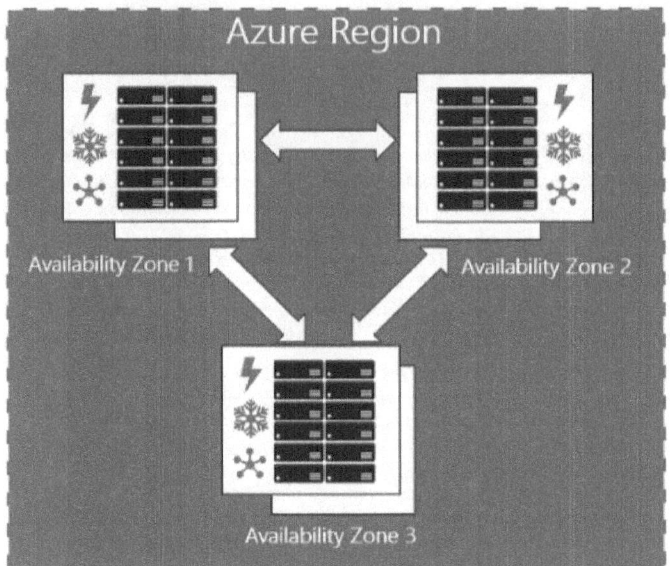

For more information, please visit:

https://docs.microsoft.com/en-us/azure/availability-zones/az-overview

Question 44:
A company wants to start using Microsoft Azure.

They want to make use of availability zones within Azure.

If they deploy resources across all regions in Azure, can they make use of availability zones in all regions in Azure?

- ○ Yes
- ○ No (Correct)

Explanation

B. No, *because Availability Zones are physically separate locations within an Azure region. Each Availability Zone is made up of one or more datacenters equipped with independent power, cooling, and networking. Availability Zones allow customers to run mission-critical applications with high availability and low-latency replication although their are not enough availability zones world wide though to implement due to the lack of a availability zone not within a specific region.*

There are dedicated regions for US Government as per the image below – US Gov Arizona, US Gov Iowa, US Gov Texas, US Gov Virginia, US DoD East and US DoD Central.

You cannot deploy resources in these regions as these are dedicated to US Government. The question asks for "...........make use of availability zones in all regions in Azure"

The answer is NO because the normal user is not used to deploy resources in these regions, let alone using the availability zones in these regions

For more information, please visit:

https://azure.microsoft.com/en-us/global-infrastructure/regions/

Question 45:
A company is planning on creating resources for different departments within Microsoft Azure.

They want to ensure that they get the bills by the departments.

Which of the following should you consider implementing for this requirement?

- ○ Azure locks
- ○ Azure Tags (Correct)
- ○ Azure Monitor
- ○ Azure Advisor

Explanation

B. Azure Tags because with Azure Tags, you apply tags to your Azure resources to logically organize them into a taxonomy. Each tag consists of a name and a value pair. For example, you can apply the name "Environment" and the value "Production" to all the resources in production.

After you apply tags, you can retrieve all the resources in your subscription with that tag name and value. Tags enable you to retrieve related resources from different resource groups. This approach is helpful when you need to organize resources for billing or management such as certain departments like HR or Accounting.

Limitations

The following limitations apply to tags:

- Not all resource types support tags. To determine if you can apply a tag to a resource type, see Tag support for Azure resources.

- Each resource or resource group can have a maximum of 50 tag name/value pairs. If you need to apply more tags than the maximum allowed number, use a JSON string for the tag value. The JSON string can contain many values that are applied to a single tag name. A resource group can contain many resources that each have 50 tag name/value pairs.

- The tag name is limited to 512 characters, and the tag value is limited to 256 characters. For storage accounts, the tag name is limited to 128 characters, and the tag value is limited to 256 characters.

- Generalized VMs don't support tags.

- Tags applied to the resource group are not inherited by the resources in that resource group.

- Tags can't be applied to classic resources such as Cloud Services.

- Tag names can't contain these characters: <, >, %, &, \, ?, /

For more information, please visit:

https://docs.microsoft.com/en-us/azure/azure-resource-manager/resource-group-using-tags

Question 46:
A company needs to create a set of resources within Microsoft Azure.

For IT Administrators, there is a requirement in which they may only create resources in a certain region.

Which of the following can help achieve this?

- ○ Azure Tags
- ○ Azure Policies (Correct)
- ○ Azure Resource Groups
- ○ Azure Locks

Explanation

B. Azure Policies *because Azure Policies is really governance validation that your organization can achieve its goals through effective and efficient use of IT. It meets this need by creating clarity between business goals and IT projects.*

Does your company experience a significant number of IT issues that never seem to get resolved? Good IT governance involves planning your initiatives and setting priorities on a strategic level to help manage and prevent issues. This strategic need is where Azure Policy comes in.

Azure Policy is a service in Azure that you use to create, assign, and manage policies. These policies enforce different rules and effects over your resources, so those resources stay compliant with your corporate standards and service level agreements. Azure Policy meets this need by evaluating your resources for non-compliance with assigned policies. All data stored by Azure Policy is encrypted at rest.

For example, you can have a policy to allow only a certain SKU size of virtual machines in your environment. Once this policy is implemented, new and existing resources are evaluated for compliance. With the right type of policy, existing resources can be brought into compliance. This would also apply to the IT administrator in the question who can only create resources in a certain region.

A policy assignment is a policy definition that has been assigned to take place within a specific scope. This scope could range from a management group to a resource group. The term *scope* refers to all the resource groups, subscriptions, or management groups that the policy definition is assigned to. Policy assignments are inherited by all child resources. This design means that a policy applied to a resource group is also applied to resources in that resource group. However, you can exclude a subscope from the policy assignment.

For example, at the subscription scope, you can assign a policy that prevents the creation of networking resources. You could exclude a resource group in that subscription that is intended for networking infrastructure. You then grant access to this networking resource group to users that you trust with creating networking resources.

In another example, you might want to assign a resource type allow list policy at the management group level. And then assign a more permissive policy (allowing more resource types) on a child management group or even directly on subscriptions. However, this example wouldn't work because policy is an explicit deny system. Instead, you need to exclude the child management group or subscription from the management group-level policy assignment. Then, assign the more permissive policy on the child management group or subscription level. If any policy results in a resource getting denied, then the only way to allow the resource is to modify the denying policy.

For more information, please visit:

https://docs.microsoft.com/en-us/azure/governance/policy/overview

Question 47:
A company is planning on using the Microsoft Azure Content Delivery Service.

Which of the following is the right cloud concept to which the Azure Content Delivery service belongs to?

- ○ Infrastructure as a service (IaaS)
- ○ Platform as a service (PaaS) (Correct)

- ○ Software as a service (SaaS)
- ○ Function as a service (FaaS)

Explanation

B. Platform as a service (PaaS) that is what Azure Content Delivery Network (CDN) is. It's a global CDN solution for delivering high-bandwidth content. It can be hosted in Azure or any other location. With Azure CDN, you can cache static objects loaded from Azure Blob storage, a web application, or any publicly accessible web server, by using the closest point of presence (POP) server. Azure CDN can also accelerate dynamic content, which cannot be cached, by leveraging various network and routing optimizations.

How it works

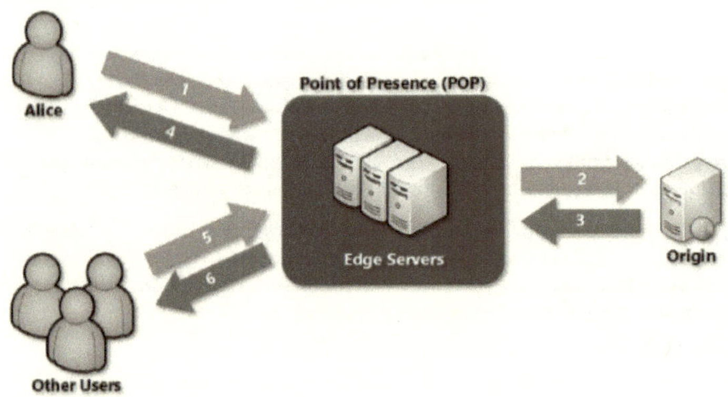

For more information, please visit:

https://docs.microsoft.com/en-us/azure/cdn/cdn-overview

Question 48:
A company wants to host an application within Microsoft Azure.

The application connects to a database in Azure.

The company would like to store the database password in a secure location.

You recommend the usage of the Azure Key Vault for storage of the password.

Would this fulfill the requirement?

- ○ Yes (Correct)
- ○ No

Explanation

A. Yes, because Azure Key Vault is a tool for securely storing and accessing secrets. A secret is anything that you want to tightly control access to, such as API keys, passwords, or certificates. A vault is logical group of secrets.

Here are other important terms:

Tenant: A tenant is the organization that owns and manages a specific instance of Microsoft cloud services. It's most often used to refer to the set of Azure and Office 365 services for an organization.

Vault owner: A vault owner can create a key vault and gain full access and control over it. The vault owner can also set up auditing to log who accesses secrets and keys. Administrators can control the key lifecycle. They can roll to a new version of the key, back it up, and do related tasks.

Vault consumer: A vault consumer can perform actions on the assets inside the key vault when the vault owner grants the consumer access. The available actions depend on the permissions granted.

Resource: A resource is a manageable item that's available through Azure. Common examples are virtual machine, storage account, web app, database, and virtual network. There are many more.

Resource group: A resource group is a container that holds related resources for an Azure solution. The resource group can include all the resources for the solution, or only those resources that you want to manage as a group. You decide how you want to allocate resources to resource groups, based on what makes the most sense for your organization.

Service principal: An Azure service principal is a security identity that user-created apps, services, and automation tools use to access specific Azure resources. Think of it as a "user identity" (username and password or certificate) with a specific role, and tightly controlled permissions. A service principal should only need to do specific things, unlike a general user identity. It improves security if you grant it only the minimum permission level that it needs to perform its management tasks.

Azure Active Directory (Azure AD): Azure AD is the Active Directory service for a tenant. Each directory has one or more domains. A directory can have many subscriptions associated with it, but only one tenant.

Azure tenant ID: A tenant ID is a unique way to identify an Azure AD instance within an Azure subscription.

Managed identities: Azure Key Vault provides a way to securely store credentials and other keys and secrets, but your code needs to authenticate to Key Vault to retrieve them. Using a managed identity makes solving this problem simpler by giving Azure services an automatically managed identity in Azure AD. You can use this identity to authenticate to Key Vault or any service that supports Azure AD authentication, without having any credentials in your code. For more information, see the following image and the overview of managed identities for Azure resources.

For more information, please visit:

https://docs.microsoft.com/en-us/azure/key-vault/basic-concepts

Question 49:

A company wants to host an application within Microsoft Azure.

The application connects to a database in Azure.

The company to store the database password in a secure location.

You recommend the usage of the Azure Security Center for storage of the password.

Would this fulfill the requirement?

- ○ Yes
- ○ **No** (Correct)

Explanation

B. No, *because the Azure Security Center is a unified infrastructure security management system that strengthens the security posture of your data centers, and provides advanced threat protection across your hybrid workloads in the cloud - whether they're in Azure or not - as well as on premises.*

Keeping your resources safe is a joint effort between your cloud provider, Azure, and you, the customer. You have to make sure your workloads are secure as you move to the cloud, and at the same time, when you move to IaaS (infrastructure as a service) there is more customer responsibility than there was in PaaS (platform as a service), and SaaS (software as a service). Azure Security Center provides you the tools needed to harden your network, secure your services and make sure you're on top of your security posture.

Azure Security Center addresses the three most urgent security challenges:

Rapidly changing workloads – It's both a strength and a challenge of the cloud. On the one hand, end users are empowered to do more. On the other, how do you make sure that the ever-changing services people are using and creating are up to your security standards and follow security best practices?

Increasingly sophisticated attacks - Wherever you run your workloads, the attacks keep getting more sophisticated. You have to secure your public cloud workloads, which are, in effect, an Internet facing workload that can leave you even more vulnerable if you don't follow security best practices.

Security skills are in short supply - The number of security alerts and alerting systems far outnumbers the number of administrators with the necessary background and experience to make sure your environments are protected. Staying up-to-date with the latest attacks is a constant challenge, making it impossible to stay in place while the world of security is an ever-changing front.

For more information, please visit:

https://docs.microsoft.com/en-us/azure/security-center/security-center-intro

Question 50:
A company wants to host an application within Microsoft Azure.

The application connects to a database in Azure.

The company to store the database password in a secure location.

You recommend the usage of the Azure Advisor for storage of the password.

Would this fulfill the requirement?

- ○ Yes
- ○ No (Correct)

Explanation

B. No, *because Azure Advisor is a personalized cloud consultant that helps you follow best practices to optimize your Azure deployments. It analyzes your resource configuration and usage telemetry and then recommends solutions that can help you improve the cost effectiveness, performance, high availability, and security of your Azure resources.*

With Advisor, you can:

-Get proactive, actionable, and personalized best practices recommendations.

-Improve the performance, security, and high availability of your resources, as you identify opportunities to reduce your overall Azure spend.

-Get recommendations with proposed actions inline.

The Advisor dashboard displays personalized recommendations for all your subscriptions. You can apply filters to display recommendations for specific subscriptions and resource types. The recommendations are divided into four categories:

- **High Availability**: To ensure and improve the continuity of your business-critical applications. For more information, see Advisor High Availability recommendations.

- **Security**: To detect threats and vulnerabilities that might lead to security breaches. For more information, see Advisor Security recommendations.

- **Performance**: To improve the speed of your applications. For more information, see Advisor Performance recommendations.

- **Cost**: To optimize and reduce your overall Azure spending. For more information, see Advisor Cost recommendations.

- **Operational Excellence**: To help you achieve process and workflow efficiency, resource manageability and deployment best practices. . For more information, see Advisor Operational Excellence recommendations.

For more information, please visit:

https://docs.microsoft.com/en-us/azure/advisor/advisor-overview

Question 51:
A company needs to connect their on-premise data center to an Azure Virtual Network using a Site-to-Site connection.

Larger image

Virtual network
Quickstart tutorial

Load Balancer
Learn more

Application Gateway
Learn more

Virtual network gateway
Learn more

Which of the following would you create as part of this implementation?

- ○ Virtual Network
- ○ Load Balancer
- ○ Application Gateway
- ○ Virtual Network Gateway (Correct)

Explanation

C. Virtual Network Gateway *because with a VPN gateway is a specific type of virtual network gateway that is used to send encrypted traffic between an Azure virtual network and an on-premises location over the public Internet. You can also use a VPN gateway to send encrypted traffic between Azure virtual networks over the Microsoft network. Each virtual network can have only one VPN gateway. However, you can create multiple connections to the same VPN gateway. When you create multiple connections to the same VPN gateway, all VPN tunnels share the available gateway bandwidth.*

Site-to-Site and Multi-Site (IPsec/IKE VPN tunnel)

Site-to-Site

A Site-to-Site (S2S) VPN gateway connection is a connection over IPsec/IKE (IKEv1 or IKEv2) VPN tunnel. S2S connections can be used for cross-premises and hybrid configurations. A S2S connection requires a VPN device located on-premises that has a public IP address assigned to it. For information about selecting a VPN device, see the VPN Gateway FAQ - VPN devices.

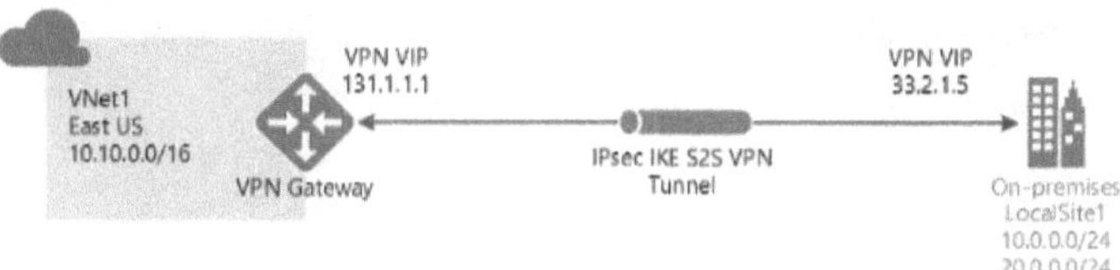

For more information, please visit:

https://docs.microsoft.com/en-us/azure/vpn-gateway/vpn-gateway-about-vpngateways

Question 52:
A company is planning on setting up a private cloud network.

Which of the following is an advantage of setting up a private cloud network?

- ○ A Private Cloud environment can only support an Infrastructure as a service model
- ○ A Private Cloud environment can only support a Platform as a service model
- ○ The Private Cloud environment can be rolled out to the general public
- ○ The Private Cloud environment can be rolled out to select users (Correct)

Explanation

D. The Private Cloud environment can be rolled out to select users *is correct because a private cloud consists of computing resources used exclusively by one business or organization. The private cloud can be physically located at your organization's on-site datacenter, or it can be hosted by a third-party service provider. But in a private cloud, the services and infrastructure are always maintained on a private network and the hardware and software are dedicated solely to your organization. In this way, a private cloud can make it easier for an organization to customize its resources to meet specific IT requirements. Private clouds are often used by government agencies, financial institutions, any other mid- to large-size organizations with business-critical operations seeking enhanced control over their environment.*

Advantages of a private clouds:

More flexibility—your organization can customize its cloud environment to meet specific business needs.

Improved security—resources are not shared with others, so higher levels of control and security are possible.

High scalability—private clouds still afford the scalability and efficiency of a public cloud.

For more information, please visit:

https://azure.microsoft.com/en-us/overview/what-are-private-public-hybrid-clouds/

Question 53:
A company wants to setup resources within Microsoft Azure.

They want a way to manage identities within Azure.

Which of the following is used as an Identity Management solution in Azure?

- ○ **Azure AD** (Correct)
- ○ Azure Advisor
- ○ Azure Security Center
- ○ Azure Monitor

Explanation

A. Azure AD is correct because Azure Active Directory is Microsoft's cloud-based identity and access management service, which helps your employees sign in and access resources in:

External resources, such as Microsoft Office 365, the Azure portal, and thousands of other SaaS applications.

Internal resources, such as apps on your corporate network and intranet, along with any cloud apps developed by your own organization.

Who uses Azure AD?

Azure AD is intended for:

- **IT admins.** As an IT admin, you can use Azure AD to control access to your apps and your app resources, based on your business requirements. For example, you can use Azure AD to require multi-factor authentication when accessing important organizational resources. Additionally, you can use Azure AD to automate user provisioning between your existing Windows Server AD and your cloud apps, including Office 365. Finally, Azure AD gives you powerful tools to automatically help protect user identities and credentials and to meet your access governance requirements. To get started, sign up for a free 30-day Azure Active Directory Premium trial.

- **App developers.** As an app developer, you can use Azure AD as a standards-based approach for adding single sign-on (SSO) to your app, allowing it to work with a user's pre-existing credentials. Azure AD also provides APIs that can help you build personalized app experiences using existing organizational data. To get started, sign up for a free 30-day Azure Active Directory Premium trial. For more information, you can also see Azure Active Directory for developers.

- **Microsoft 365, Office 365, Azure, or Dynamics CRM Online subscribers.** As a subscriber, you're already using Azure AD. Each Microsoft 365, Office 365, Azure, and Dynamics CRM Online tenant is automatically an Azure AD tenant. You can immediately start to manage access to your integrated cloud apps.

For more information, please visit:

https://docs.microsoft.com/en-us/azure/active-directory/fundamentals/active-directory-whatis

Question 54:
You are planning on setting up a Microsoft Azure Free account.

Which of the following is not true when it comes to what is offered with an Azure Free account?

- ○ 200 USD free credit to use for 30 days
- ○ Free access to certain Azure products for 12 months
- ○ Free access to all Azure products after the 12 month expiration period (Correct)
- ○ Access to certain products that are always free

Explanation

C. Free access to all Azure products after the 12 month expiration period *because the Azure free account includes free access to Azure products for only 12 months, you don't keep access to those products unless you pay, but when you sign up, you get $200 credit to spend for the first 30 days and access to more than 25 products that are always free.*

What happens at the end of the 12 months of free products?

For 12 months after you upgrade your account, certain amounts of popular products for compute, networking, storage, and databases are free. After 12 months, any of these products you may be using will continue to run, and you'll be billed at the standard pay-as-you-go rates.

For more information, please visit:

https://azure.microsoft.com/en-us/free/free-account-faq/

Question 55:
Fill in the blank with the correct Azure service to correctly complete the statement below:

____________ **is a simplified tool to build intelligent Artificial Intelligence (AI) applications.**

- ○ Azure Advisor
- ○ Azure Cognitive Services (Correct)
- ○ Azure DevOps
- ○ Azure Application Insights

Explanation

B. Azure Cognitive Services *because Azure Cognitive Services are APIs, SDKs, and services available to help developers build intelligent applications without having direct AI or data science skills or knowledge. Azure Cognitive Services enable developers to easily add cognitive features into their applications. The goal of Azure Cognitive Services is to help developers create applications that can see, hear, speak, understand, and even begin to reason. The catalog of services within Azure Cognitive Services can be categorized into five main pillars - Vision, Speech, Language, Web Search, and Decision.*

For more information, please visit:

https://docs.microsoft.com/en-us/azure/cognitive-services/welcome

Question 1:
An IT Engineer needs to create a Virtual Machine within Microsoft Azure.

Currently the IT Engineer has a Windows desktop and has installed the Azure Command Line interface.

From which of the following could the IT engineer use the Azure Command Line Interface?

Choose 2 answers from the options given below

- ☐ **Powershell** (Correct)
- ☐ **File and Print Explorer**
- ☐ **Command Prompt** (Correct)
- ☐ **Google Chrome**

Explanation

A & C because the Azure command-line interface (CLI) is Microsoft's cross-platform command-line experience for managing Azure resources. The Azure CLI is designed to be easy to learn and get started with, but powerful enough to be a great tool for building custom automation to use Azure resources.

Azure PowerShell is a set of cmdlets that allow for manging Azure resources directly from the PowerShell command line. Azure PowerShell is designed to make it easy to learn and get started with, but provides powerful features for automation. Written in .NET Standard, Azure PowerShell works with PowerShell 5.1 on Windows, and PowerShell 6.x and higher on all platforms.

For more information, please visit:

https://docs.microsoft.com/en-us/powershell/azure/?view=azps-3.1.0

and

https://docs.microsoft.com/en-us/cli/azure/install-azure-cli?view=azure-cli-latest

Question 2:
A company is planning on setting up a Microsoft Azure Free Account.

Does the Standard Support plan come along with the Microsoft Azure Free Account?

- ○ Yes
- ○ No (Correct)

Explanation

B. No, because Azure Standard support is intended for customers running production workloads and offers unlimited 24/7 technical and billing support for your entire organization. It isn't a free service, it's one of 4 support tiers.

For more information, please visit:

Question 3:
A customer is planning on creating several Free Microsoft Azure Accounts.

Is a customer allowed a maximum of 10 Free Microsoft Azure account?

- ○ Yes
- ○ **No** (Correct)

Explanation

B. No, *because there is a limit of one account with 12 months free access to products and $200 credit per new customer. You can, however, use as many products as you like beyond the free amounts by upgrading your account to pay-as-you-go pricing.*

For more information, please visit:

https://azure.microsoft.com/en-us/free/free-account-faq/

Question 4:
Your company is planning on hosting resources within Microsoft Azure.

Is it possible for outside users to have access to resources within Azure, or do the users have to be specifically defined in Azure AD only?

- ○ Yes, only Azure AD defined users can access Azure resources
- ○ No, users from the outside can also get access to Azure resources (Correct)
- ○ Both A and B
- ○ Neither A nor B

Explanation

B. No, users from the outside can also get access to Azure resources *because of Azure role-based access control (RBAC) which allows better security management for large organizations and for small and medium-sized businesses working with external collaborators, vendors, or freelancers that need access to specific resources in your environment, but not necessarily to the entire infrastructure or any billing-related scopes. You can use the capabilities in Azure Active Directory B2B to collaborate with external guest users and you can use RBAC to grant just the permissions that guest users need in your environment.*

For more information, please visit:

https://docs.microsoft.com/en-us/azure/role-based-access-control/role-assignments-external-users

Question 5:
A company is planning on purchasing Azure AD Premium for their Microsoft Azure account.

Does the Azure AD Premium tier come with an SLA of 99.9%?

- ○ **Yes** (Correct)
- ○ **No**

Explanation

A. Yes, *because Microsoft guarantees at least 99.9% availability of the Azure Active Directory Basic and Premium services. The services are considered available in the following scenarios:*

Users are able to login to the service, login to the Access Panel, access applications on the Access Panel and reset passwords.

IT administrators are able to create, read, write and delete entries in the directory or provision or de-provision users to applications in the directory.

No SLA is provided for the Free tier of Azure Active Directory.

For more information, please visit:

https://azure.microsoft.com/en-ca/support/legal/sla/active-directory/v1_0/

Question 6:
A company wants to try out some services which are being offered by Microsoft Azure in Public Preview.

Should the company deploy resources which are part of Public Preview in their production environment?

- ○ Yes
- ○ **No** (Correct)

Explanation

B. No. *Azure may include preview, beta, or other pre-release features, services, software, or regions offered by Microsoft to obtain customer feedback ("Previews"). Previews are made available to you on the condition that you agree to these terms of use, which supplement your agreement governing use of Azure.*

PREVIEWS ARE PROVIDED "AS-IS," "WITH ALL FAULTS," AND "AS AVAILABLE," AND ARE EXCLUDED FROM THE SERVICE LEVEL AGREEMENTS AND LIMITED WARRANTY which is the main reason not to release in your production enviorment as you have no binding SLA. Previews may not be covered by customer support. Previews may be subject to reduced or different security, compliance and privacy commitments, as further explained in the Microsoft Online Services Privacy Statement, Microsoft Azure Trust Center, the Online Services Terms, and any additional notices provided with the Preview. Customers should not use Previews to process Personal Data or other data that is subject to heightened compliance requirements. Certain named Previews may also be subject to additional terms set forth below, if any. We

For more information, please visit:

https://azure.microsoft.com/en-us/support/legal/preview-supplemental-terms/

Question 7:
A company is planning on using Azure SQL Data Warehouse for hosting their sales historical data.

Which of the following is a feature of the Azure SQL Data Warehouse architecture?

- ○ High Availability
- ○ Scalability (Correct)
- ○ Disaster Recovery
- ○ Visualization

Explanation

B. Scalability *because the architecture of SQL Data Warehouse separates storage and compute, allowing each to scale independently. As a result, you can scale compute to meet performance demands independent of data storage. You can also pause and resume compute resources. A natural consequence of this architecture is that billing for compute and storage is separate. If you don't need to use your data warehouse for a while, you can save compute costs by pausing compute.*

For more information, please visit:

https://docs.microsoft.com/en-us/azure/sql-data-warehouse/sql-data-warehouse-manage-compute-overview

Question 8:
A company is planning on creating several SQL Databases within Microsoft Azure.

They would be using the Azure SQL Database service.

Which of the following is the right category to which the Azure SQL Database service belongs?

- ○ Infrastructure as a service (IaaS)
- ○ Platform as a service (PaaS) (Correct)
- ○ Software as a service (SaaS)
- ○ Function as a service (FaaS)

Explanation

B. Platform as a service (PaaS) *because Azure SQL Database is a fully managed Platform as a Service (PaaS) Database Engine that handles most of the database management functions* *such as upgrading, patching, backups, and monitoring without user involvement. Azure SQL Database is always running on the latest stable version of SQL Server Database Engine and patched OS with 99.99% availability. PaaS capabilities that are built-in into Azure SQL database enable you to focus on the domain specific database administration and optimization activities that are critical for your business.*

Business continuity Azure SQL Database enables your business to continue operating in the face of disruption, particularly to its computing infrastructure.	**High availability** Azure SQL Database guarantees that your databases are up and running 99.99% of time, without worrying about maintenance and downtimes.	**Automated backups** Azure SQL Database automatically creates database backups and uses Azure read-access geo-redundant storage (RA-GRS) to provide geo-redundancy.
Long term backup retention Azure SQL Database enables you store specified SQL database full backups for up to 10 years.	**Geo-replication** Azure SQL Database enables you to create readable replicas of your database in the same or different data center (region).	**Scale resources** Azure SQL Database enables you to easily add more resources (CPU, memory, storage) without long provisioning.

For more information, please visit:

https://docs.microsoft.com/en-us/azure/sql-database/sql-database-paas-index

Question 9:

A company is planning on using Azure Storage Accounts. They have the following requirement:

- Storage of 2 TB of data

- Storage of a million files

Would using an Azure Storage Account fulfill these requirements?

- ○ **Yes** (Correct)
- ○ **No**

Explanation

A. Yes, *because an Azure storage account contains all of your Azure Storage data objects: blobs, files, queues, tables, and disks. The storage account provides a unique namespace for your Azure Storage data that is accessible from anywhere in the world over HTTP or HTTPS. Data in your Azure storage account is durable and highly available, secure, and massively scalable.*

The following table describes the types of storage accounts and their capabilities:

Storage account type	Supported services	Supported performance tiers	Supported access tiers	Replication options	Deployment model [1]	Encryption [2]
General-purpose V2	Blob, File, Queue, Table, Disk, and Data Lake Gen2 [6]	Standard, Premium [5]	Hot, Cool, Archive [3]	LRS, GRS, RA-GRS, ZRS, GZRS (preview), RA-GZRS (preview) [4]	Resource Manager	Encrypted
General-purpose V1	Blob, File, Queue, Table, and Disk	Standard, Premium [5]	N/A	LRS, GRS, RA-GRS	Resource Manager, Classic	Encrypted
BlockBlobStorage	Blob (block blobs and append blobs only)	Premium	N/A	LRS, ZRS [4]	Resource Manager	Encrypted
FileStorage	File only	Premium	N/A	LRS, ZRS [4]	Resource Manager	Encrypted
BlobStorage	Blob (block blobs and append blobs only)	Standard	Hot, Cool, Archive [3]	LRS, GRS, RA-GRS	Resource Manager	Encrypted

For more information, please visit:

https://docs.microsoft.com/en-us/azure/storage/common/storage-account-overview

Question 10:

A company is planning on using Azure Storage Accounts. They have the following requirement:

- Replication of data to another region

Do Azure Storage Accounts automatically replicate data to another region?

- ○ Yes (Correct)
- ○ No

Explanation

A, Yes.

When you create a storage account in Azure, the default replication that is chosen is RA-GRS and therefore storage accounts automatically replicate data to another region.

Question 11:

A company wants to make use of Microsoft Azure to deploy various business solutions.

They want to ensure that suspicious attacks and threats to resources within their Microsoft Azure account are prevented.

Which of the following helps prevent such attacks by using built-in sensors in Azure?

- ○ Azure AD Identity Protection
- ○ Azure DDoS attacks
- ○ Azure privileged identity management

- ○ **Azure Advanced Threat Protection** (Correct)

Explanation

D. Azure Advanced Threat Protection *because Azure Advanced Threat Protection (ATP) is a cloud-based security solution that leverages your on-premises Active Directory signals to identify, detect, and investigate advanced threats, compromised identities, and malicious insider actions directed at your organization. Azure ATP enables SecOp analysts and security professionals struggling to detect advanced attacks in hybrid environments to:*

Monitor users, entity behavior, and activities with learning-based analytics

Protect user identities and credentials stored in Active Directory

Identify and investigate suspicious user activities and advanced attacks throughout the kill chain

Provide clear incident information on a simple timeline for fast triage

For more information, please visit:

https://docs.microsoft.com/en-us/azure-advanced-threat-protection/what-is-atp

Question 12:
A company is planning on hosting resources within Microsoft Azure.

They want to ensure that Azure complies with the rules and regulations of the region for hosting resources.

Which of the following can assist the company in getting the required compliance reports?

- ○ Azure AD
- ○ **Microsoft Trust Center** (Correct)
- ○ Azure Advisor
- ○ Azure Security Center

Explanation

B. Microsoft Trust Center *because within this resource, you can take advantage of more than 90 compliance certifications, including over 50 specific to global regions and countries, such as the US, the European Union, Germany, Japan, the United Kingdom, India, and China. And, get more than 35 compliance offerings specific to the needs of key industries, including health, government, finance, education, manufacturing, and media. Your emerging compliance needs are covered, too: Microsoft engages globally with governments, regulators, standards bodies, and non-governmental organizations.*

Explore Azure compliance offerings in the Microsoft Trust Center.

Global	US Government	Region / Country Specific		Industry Specific	
CIS Benchmark	CJIS	BIR 2012 (Netherlands)	IT-Grundschutz (Germany)	23 NYCRR 500 (US)	GLBA (US)
CSA STAR Attestation	CNSSI	CS (Germany)	LOPD (Spain)	AFM/DNB (Netherlands)	GxP (US)
CSA STAR Certification	DFARS	CS Mark Gold (Japan)	MeitY (India)	AMF/ACPR (France)	HIPAA (US)
CSA STAR Self-Assessment	DoD L 2,4,5	Cyber Essentials Plus (US)	MTCS Level 3 (Singapore)	APRA (Australia)	HITRUST (US)
ISO 20000	DoE 10	DJCP (China)	My Number Act (Japan)	CDSA	KNF (Poland)
ISO 22301	EAR	EN 301 549 (EU)	New Zealand CC Framework	CFTC 131 (US)	MARS-E (US)
ISO 27001	FDA CFR Title 21	ENISA IAF (EU)	PASF (UK)	DPP (UK)	MAS/ABS (Singapore)
ISO 27017	FedRAMP	ENS (Spain)	PIPEDA (Canada)	EBA (EU)	MPAA (US)
ISO 27018	FIPS 140-2	EU Model Clauses	PDPA (Argentina)	FACT (UK)	NBB/FSMA (Belgium)
ISO 9001	IRS 1075	EU-US Privacy Shield	TISAX (Germany)	FCA/PRA (UK)	NEN 7510 (Netherlands)
SOC 1,2,3	ITAR	GB 18030 (China)	TRUCS (China)	FERPA (US)	NHS IG (UK)
WCAG 2.0	NIST CSF	G-Cloud OFFICIAL (UK)	TruSight	FFIEC (US)	OSFI (Canada)
	NIST 800-171	GDPR		FINMA (Switzerland)	PCI DSS
	Section 508 VPATs	HDS (France)		FINRA (US)	RBI/IRDAI (India)
		IRAP (Australia)		FISC (Japan)	SEC 17a-4 (US)
		ISMS (Korea)		FSA (Denmark)	Shared Assessments
					SOX (US)

For more information, please visit:
https://azure.microsoft.com/en-us/overview/trusted-cloud/compliance/

Question 13:

A company has just deployed a set of Virtual Machines (VMs) to host a production software for their end users.

The company needs to have a solution that will allow them to know the health of their VMs at all times so they can implement alerts and redundancy.

Which solution would best fulfil this need for the company?

- ○ Azure Advisor
- ○ Azure AD
- ○ Azure Power BI
- ○ **Azure Monitor** (Correct)

Explanation

D. Azure Monitor *because Microsoft Azure includes services for specific roles or tasks in the monitoring space, but it doesn't provide in-depth health perspectives of operating systems (OSs) hosted on Azure virtual machines (VMs). Although you can use Azure Monitor for different conditions, it's not designed to model and represent the health of core components, or the overall health of VMs.*

By using Azure Monitor for VMs health, you can actively monitor the availability and performance of a Windows or Linux guest OS. The health feature uses a model that represents key components and their relationships, provides criteria that specifies how to measure component health, and sends an alert when it detects an unhealthy condition.

Viewing the overall health state of an Azure VM and the underlying OS can be observed from two perspectives: directly from a VM, or across all VMs in a resource group from Azure Monitor.

For more information, please reference:
https://docs.microsoft.com/en-us/azure/azure-monitor/insights/vminsights-health

Question 14:
A company is planning on hosting 2 Virtual Machines within Microsoft Azure as shown below:

Virtual Machine Name	Virtual Machine Size
demovm	B1S
demovm1	B1S

Would both the Virtual Machines always generate the same monthly costs?

- ○ Yes
- ○ **No** (Correct)

Explanation

B. No, because VMs usually use some form of storage, such as Azure Managed Disks, which are the new and recommended disk storage offering for use with Azure virtual machines for persistent storage of data. You can use multiple Managed Disks with each virtual machine. Microsoft offers four types of Managed Disks — Ultra Disk, Premium SSD Managed Disks, Standard SSD Managed Disks, Standard HDD Managed Disks. If one VM stops and the other runs, the cost will not be the same. If one VM has storage and the other does not, the cost will not be the same. If you scale in or out one VM, the cost will not be the same.

For more information, please visit:

https://azure.microsoft.com/en-us/pricing/details/managed-disks/

Question 15:
A company has a set of resources deployed to Microsoft Azure.

They want to make use of the Azure Advisor tool.

Would the Azure Advisor tool give recommendations on how to configure Virtual Network settings?

- ○ Yes
- ○ **No** (Correct)

Explanation

B. No, *because Advisor is a personalized cloud consultant that helps you follow best practices to optimize your Azure deployments. It analyzes your resource configuration and usage telemetry and then recommends solutions that can help you improve the cost effectiveness, performance, high availability, and security of your Azure resources.*

With Advisor, you can:

Get proactive, actionable, and personalized best practices recommendations.

Improve the performance, security, and high availability of your resources, as you identify opportunities to reduce your overall Azure spend.

Get recommendations with proposed actions inline.

For more information, please visit:

https://docs.microsoft.com/en-us/azure/advisor/advisor-overview

Question 16:
A company is planning on deploying resources to Microsoft Azure.

Which of the following in Azure provides a common platform for deploying objects to the Azure Cloud Infrastructure and also allows implementing consistency across the environment?

- ○ Azure Resource Groups
- ○ Azure policies
- ○ Azure Management Groups
- ○ Azure Resource Manager (Correct)

Explanation

D. Azure Resource Manager *because Azure Resource Manager is the deployment and management service for Azure. It provides a management layer that enables you to create, update, and delete resources in your Azure subscription. You use management features, like access control, locks, and tags, to secure and organize your resources after deployment.*

The benefits of using Resource Manager include:

Manage your infrastructure through declarative templates rather than scripts.

Deploy, manage, and monitor all the resources for your solution as a group, rather than handling these resources individually.

Redeploy your solution throughout the development lifecycle and have confidence your resources are deployed in a consistent state.

Define the dependencies between resources so they're deployed in the correct order.

Apply access control to all services in your resource group because Role-Based Access Control (RBAC) is natively integrated into the management platform.

Apply tags to resources to logically organize all the resources in your subscription.

Clarify your organization's billing by viewing costs for a group of resources sharing the same tag.

For more information, please visit:

https://docs.microsoft.com/en-us/azure/azure-resource-manager/resource-group-overview

Question 17:
A company is planning on setting up a solution within Microsoft Azure.

The solution would have the following key requirement:

- Provide a digital online assistant that provides speech support

Which of the following would be best suited for this requirement?

- ○ Azure Machine Learning
- ○ Azure IoT Hub
- ○ Azure AI Bot Service (Correct)
- ○ Azure Functions

Explanation

C. Azure AI Bot Service *because Azure Bot Service and Bot Framework provide tools to build, test, deploy, and manage intelligent bots, all in one place. Through the use of modular and extensible framework provided by the SDK, tools, templates, and AI services developers can create bots that use speech, understand natural language, handle questions and answers, and more.*

For more information, please visit:

https://docs.microsoft.com/en-us/azure/bot-service/bot-service-overview-introduction?view=azure-bot-service-4.0

Question 18:
A company has multiple subscriptions.

They want to create resources in the different subscriptions.

Is it possible to create resources in multiple subscriptions?

- ○ Yes (Correct)
- ○ No

Explanation

A. Yes, *because typically, you deploy all the resources in your template to a single resource group. However, there are scenarios where you want to deploy a set of resources together but place them in different resource groups or subscriptions. For example, you may want to deploy the backup virtual machine for Azure Site Recovery to a separate resource group and location.*

Resource Manager enables you to use nested templates to target different subscriptions and resource groups than the subscription and resource group used for the parent template.

You can deploy to only five resource groups in a single deployment. Typically, this limitation means you can deploy to one resource group specified for the parent template, and up to four resource groups in nested or linked deployments. However, if your parent template contains only nested or linked templates and does not itself deploy any resources, then you can include up to five resource groups in nested or linked deployments.

For more information, please visit:

https://docs.microsoft.com/en-us/azure/azure-resource-manager/resource-manager-cross-resource-group-deployment

Question 19:
A company is planning on setting up a solution within Microsoft Azure.

The solution would have the following key requirement:

- Provide a data store that can be used to store and perform analytics on petabytes of data

Which of the following would be best suited for this requirement?

- ○ Azure Content Delivery Network
- ○ Azure SQL Data Warehouse (Correct)
- ○ Azure Load Balancer
- ○ Azure HD Insight

Explanation

B. Azure SQL Data Warehouse *because it is a cloud-based enterprise data warehouse that leverages massively parallel processing (MPP) to quickly run complex queries across petabytes of data. Use SQL Data Warehouse as a key component of a big data solution. Import big data into SQL Data Warehouse with simple PolyBase T-SQL queries, and then use the power of MPP to run high-performance analytics. As you integrate and analyze, the data warehouse will become the single version of truth your business can count on for insights.*

You can access Azure SQL Data Warehouse (SQL DW) from Azure Databricks using the SQL Data Warehouse connector (referred to as the SQL DW connector), a data source implementation for Apache Spark that uses Azure Blob storage, and PolyBase in SQL DW to transfer large volumes of data efficiently between an Azure Databricks cluster and a SQL DW instance.

For more information, please visit:

https://docs.microsoft.com/en-us/azure/databricks/data/data-sources/azure/sql-data-warehouse

Question 20:
A company is planning on setting up a solution within Microsoft Azure.

The solution would have the following key requirement:

- Uses past training's to provide predictions that have high probability

Which of the following would be best suited for this requirement?

- ○ **Azure Machine Learning** (Correct)
- ○ **Azure IoT Hub**
- ○ **Azure AI Bot**
- ○ **Azure Functions**

Explanation

A. Azure Machine Learning *because Microsoft Azure Machine Learning Studio is a collaborative, drag-and-drop tool you can use to build, test, and deploy predictive analytics solutions on your data. Machine Learning Studio publishes models as web services that can easily be consumed by custom apps or BI tools such as Excel.*

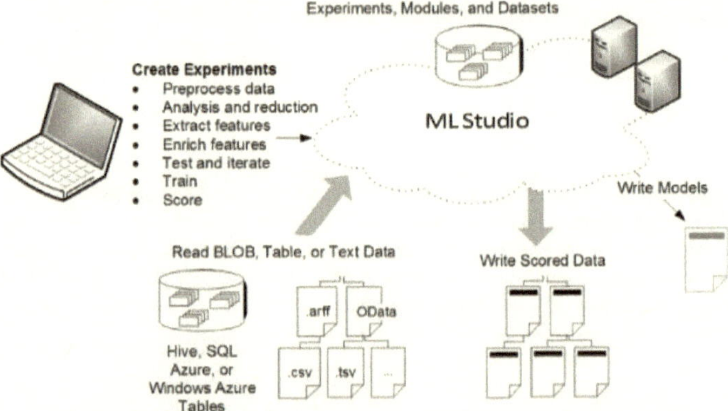

For more information, please visit:

https://docs.microsoft.com/en-us/azure/machine-learning/studio/what-is-ml-studio

Question 21:
A company is planning on setting up a solution within Microsoft Azure.

The solution would have the following key requirement:

- Provide an efficient way to distribute web content to users across the world

Which of the following would be best suited for this requirement?

- ○ **Azure Content Delivery Network** (Correct)
- ○ **Azure SQL Datawarehouse**
- ○ **Azure Load Balancer**
- ○ **Azure HD Insight**

Explanation

A. Azure Content Delivery Network *because Azure Content Delivery Network (CDN) is a global CDN solution for delivering high-bandwidth content. It can be hosted in Azure or any other location. With Azure CDN, you can cache static objects loaded from Azure Blob storage, a web application, or any publicly accessible web server, by using the closest point of presence (POP) server. Azure CDN can also accelerate dynamic content, which cannot be cached, by leveraging various network and routing optimizations. Better performance and improved user experience for end users, especially when using applications in which multiple round-trips are required to load content.*

Large scaling to better handle instantaneous high loads, such as the start of a product launch event.

Distribution of user requests and serving of content directly from edge servers so that less traffic is sent to the origin server.

How it works

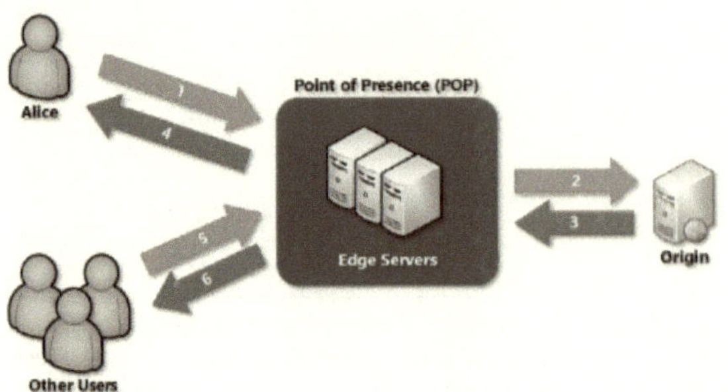

1. A user (Alice) requests a file (also called an asset) by using a URL with a special domain name, such as *<endpoint name>*.azureedge.net. This name can be an endpoint hostname or a custom domain. The DNS routes the request to the best performing POP location, which is usually the POP that is geographically closest to the user.

2. If no edge servers in the POP have the file in their cache, the POP requests the file from the origin server. The origin server can be an Azure Web App, Azure Cloud Service, Azure Storage account, or any publicly accessible web server.

3. The origin server returns the file to an edge server in the POP.

4. An edge server in the POP caches the file and returns the file to the original requestor (Alice). The file remains cached on the edge server in the POP until the time-to-live (TTL) specified by its HTTP headers expires. If the origin server didn't specify a TTL, the default TTL is seven days.

5. Additional users can then request the same file by using the same URL that Alice used, and can also be directed to the same POP.

6. If the TTL for the file hasn't expired, the POP edge server returns the file directly from the cache. This process results in a faster, more responsive user experience.

For more information, please visit:

https://docs.microsoft.com/en-us/azure/cdn/cdn-overview

Question 22:
A company is planning on setting up a solution within Microsoft Azure.

The solution would have the following key requirement:

- Provide the ability to distribute user traffic to a set of backend Virtual Machines

Which of the following would be best suited for this requirement?

- ○ **Azure Content Delivery Network**
- ○ **Azure SQL Datawarehouse**
- ○ **Azure Load Balancer** (Correct)
- ○ **Azure HD Insight**

Explanation

C. Azure Load Balancer *because Azure Load Balancer operates at layer four of the Open Systems Interconnection (OSI) model. It is the single point of contact for clients. Load Balancer* *distributes new inbound flows that arrive at the Load Balancer's front end to back-end pool instances, according to specified load balacing rules and health probes. The back-end pool instances can be Azure Virtual Machines or instances in a Virtual Machine Scale Set (VMSS).*

With Azure Load Balancer, you can scale your applications and create high availabile services. Load Balancer supports both, inbound and outbound scenarios, provides low latency and high throughput, and scales up to millions of flows for all TCP and UDP applications.

A public Load Balancer can provide outbound connections for virtual machines (VMs) inside your virtual network by translating their private IP addresses to public IP addresses. Public Load Balancers are used to load balancer internet traffic to your VMs.

An internal (or private) Load Balancer can be used for scenarios where only private IP addresses are needed at the front end. Internal Load Balancers are used to load balance traffic inside a virtual network. You can also reach a Load Balancer front end from an on-premises network in a hybrid scenario.

For more information, please visit:

https://docs.microsoft.com/en-us/azure/load-balancer/load-balancer-overview

Question 23:
A company is planning on setting up a solution within Microsoft Azure.

The solution would have the following key requirement:

- Provide a cloud service that makes it easy, fast, and cost-effective to analyse massive amounts of data.

Which of the following would be best suited for this requirement?

- ○ Azure Content Delivery Network
- ○ Azure SQL Datawarehouse
- ○ Azure Load Balancer
- ○ Azure HD Insight (Correct)

Explanation

D. Azure HD Insight *because Azure HD Insight is a managed, full-spectrum, open-source analytics service in the cloud for enterprises. You can use open-source frameworks such as Hadoop, Apache Spark, Apache Hive, LLAP, Apache Kafka, Apache Storm, R, and more.*

Why should I use Azure HDInsight?

This section lists the capabilities of Azure HDInsight.

Capability	Description
Cloud native	Azure HDInsight enables you to create optimized clusters for Hadoop, Spark, Interactive query (LLAP), Kafka, Storm, HBase, and ML Services on Azure. HDInsight also provides an end-to-end SLA on all your production workloads.
Low-cost and scalable	HDInsight enables you to scale workloads up or down. You can reduce costs by creating clusters on demand and paying only for what you use. You can also build data pipelines to operationalize your jobs. Decoupled compute and storage provide better performance and flexibility.
Secure and compliant	HDInsight enables you to protect your enterprise data assets with Azure Virtual Network, encryption, and integration with Azure Active Directory. HDInsight also meets the most popular industry and government compliance standards.
Monitoring	Azure HDInsight integrates with Azure Monitor logs to provide a single interface with which you can monitor all your clusters.
Global availability	HDInsight is available in more regions than any other big data analytics offering. Azure HDInsight is also available in Azure Government, China, and Germany, which allows you to meet your enterprise needs in key sovereign areas.
Productivity	Azure HDInsight enables you to use rich productive tools for Hadoop and Spark with your preferred development environments. These development environments include Visual Studio, VSCode, Eclipse, and IntelliJ for Scala, Python, R, Java, and .NET support. Data scientists can also collaborate using popular notebooks such as Jupyter and Zeppelin.
Extensibility	You can extend the HDInsight clusters with installed components (Hue, Presto, and so on) by using script actions, by adding edge nodes, or by integrating with other big data certified applications. HDInsight enables seamless integration with the most popular big data solutions with a one-click deployment.

For more information, please visit:

https://docs.microsoft.com/en-us/azure/hdinsight/hdinsight-overview

Question 24:
A company is planning on hosting a set of resources within their Microsoft Azure subscription.

They are currently aware that most Azure Services can provide an SLA of 99.9%.

Which of the following technique could be used to increase the up-time for resources hosted in Azure?

- ○ **Adding resources to multiple regions** (Correct)
- ○ **Adding resources to the same data center**
- ○ **Adding resources to the same resource group**
- ○ **Adding resources to the same subscription**

Explanation

A. Adding resources to multiple regions because Regions are a set of data centres deployed within a latency-defined perimeter and connected through a dedicated regional low-latency network.

With more global regions than any other cloud provider, Azure gives customers the flexibility to deploy apps where they need to. Azure is generally available in 52 regions around the world, with plans announced for 2 additional regions.

For more information, please visit:

https://azure.microsoft.com/en-au/global-infrastructure/regions/

Question 25:
A company is planning on using Microsoft Azure Cloud for hosting resources.

Which of the following is a key advantage of hosting resources in the Azure private cloud?

- All users across the world can access the resources in your Azure account
- Different departments in your organization can have a segmentation of resources defined in Azure (Correct)
- Only privileged users can have access to resources in your Azure account
- You pay a capital upfront cost when using resources in the public cloud

Explanation

B. Different departments in your organization can have a segmentation of resources defined in Azure *because*

A private cloud consists of computing resources used exclusively by one business or organization. The private cloud can be physically located at your organization's on-site datacenter, or it can be hosted by a third-party service provider. But in a private cloud, the services and infrastructure are always maintained on a private network and the hardware and software are dedicated solely to your organization. In this way, a private cloud can make it easier for an organization to customize its resources to meet specific IT requirements. Private clouds are often used by government agencies, financial institutions, any other mid- to large-size organizations with business-critical operations seeking enhanced control over their environment.

Advantages of a private clouds:

More flexibility—your organization can customize its cloud environment to meet specific business needs.

Improved security—resources are not shared with others, so higher levels of control and security are possible.

High scalability—private clouds still afford the scalability and efficiency of a public cloud.

For more information, please visit:

https://azure.microsoft.com/en-us/overview/what-are-private-public-hybrid-clouds/

Question 26:
A company is planning on setting up a solution within Microsoft Azure.

The solution would have the following key requirement:

- Provides serverless computing functionalities

Which of the following would be best suited for this requirement?

- Azure Machine Learning
- Azure IoT Hub

- ○ Azure AI Bot
- ○ Azure Functions (Correct)

Explanation

D. Azure Functions *because Azure Functions is a solution for easily running small pieces of code, or "functions," in the cloud. You can write just the code you need for the problem at hand, without worrying about a whole application or the infrastructure to run it. Functions can make development even more productive, and you can use your development language of choice, such as C#, Java, JavaScript, PowerShell, and Python. Pay only for the time your code runs and trust Azure to scale as needed. Azure Functions lets you develop serverless applications on Microsoft Azure.*

For more information, please visit:

https://docs.microsoft.com/en-us/azure/azure-functions/functions-overview

Question 27:
A company has a number of resources hosted within Microsoft Azure.

They want to push all the events from various resources into a centralized repository so that the events can be correlated later on.

Which of the following services would you use for this requirement?

- ○ Azure Event Hubs
- ○ Azure Analysis Services
- ○ Azure Advisor
- ○ Azure Log Analytics (Correct)

Explanation

C. Azure Log Analytics *because The Azure Log Analytics agent, previously referred to as the Microsoft Monitoring Agent (MMA) or OMS Linux agent, was developed for comprehensive management across on-premises machines, computers monitored by System Center Operations Manager, and virtual machines in any cloud to push logs to a centralized repository for analysis. The Windows and Linux agents attach to an Azure Monitor and store collected log data from different sources in your Log Analytics workspace, as well as any unique logs or metrics as defined in a monitoring solution.*

For more information, please visit:

https://docs.microsoft.com/en-us/azure/azure-monitor/platform/log-analytics-agent

Question 28:
A company has a Virtual Machine (VM) defined as demovm.

This Virtual Machine (VM) was created with the standard settings.

An application is installed on demovm.

It now needs to be ensured that the application can be accessed over the Internet via HTTP.

You propose the solution to modify the DDoS protection plan

Would this solution fit the requirement?

- ○ Yes
- ○ **No** (Correct)

Explanation

B. No, *because Azure DDoS Protection is something that prevents and mitigates DDoS attacks automatically tuned to protect your specific Azure resources. Protection is simple to enable on any new or existing Virtual Network and requires no application or resource changes. Azure DDos has nothing to do with accessing an Azure VM over the Internet via HTTP.*

For more information, please visit:

https://azure.microsoft.com/en-us/services/ddos-protection/

Question 29:
A company has a Virtual Machine (VM) defined as demovm.

This Virtual Machine (VM) was created with the standard settings.

An application is installed on demovm. It now needs to be ensured that the application can be accessed over the Internet via HTTP using a prioritised security rule.

You make modifications to the Azure firewall.

Would this solution fit the requirement?

- ○ Yes
- ○ **No** (Correct)

Explanation

NO, because only "Security Groups" have priority rules to allow inbound and outbound traffic and this CANNOT be done via "Azure Firewall".

Question 30:
A company has a Virtual Machine (VM) defined as demovm.

This Virtual Machine (VM) was created with the standard settings.

An application is installed on demovm. It now needs to be ensured that the application can be accessed over the Internet via HTTP.

You modify the Azure Traffic Manager profile.

Would this solution fit the requirement?

- ○ Yes

- ○ **No** (Correct)

Explanation

B. No, because Azure Traffic Manager is a DNS-based traffic load balancer that enables you to distribute traffic optimally to services across global Azure regions, while providing high availability and responsiveness.

Traffic Manager uses DNS to direct client requests to the most appropriate service endpoint based on a traffic-routing method and the health of the endpoints. An endpoint is any Internet-facing service hosted inside or outside of Azure. Traffic Manager provides a range of traffic-routing methods and endpoint monitoring options to suit different application needs and automatic failover models. Traffic Manager is resilient to failure, including the failure of an entire Azure region. Modifying this won't make the Azure VM accessible from the internet.

For more information, please visit:

https://docs.microsoft.com/en-us/azure/traffic-manager/traffic-manager-overview

Question 31:
A company has a Virtual Machine (VM) defined as demovm.

This Virtual Machine (VM) was created with the standard settings.

An application is installed on demovm. It now needs to be ensured that the application can be accessed over the Internet via HTTP.

You modify the Network Security Groups.

Would this solution fit the requirement?

- ○ **Yes** (Correct)
- ○ **No**

Explanation

A. Yes, using Network Security Groups, you can filter network traffic to and from Azure resources in an Azure virtual network with a network security group. A network security group contains security rules that allow or deny inbound network traffic to, or outbound network traffic from, several types of Azure resources.

Security rules

A network security group contains zero, or as many rules as desired, within Azure subscription limits. Each rule specifies the following properties:

Property	Explanation
Name	A unique name within the network security group.
Priority	A number between 100 and 4096. Rules are processed in priority order, with lower numbers processed before higher numbers, because lower numbers have higher priority. Once traffic matches a rule, processing stops. As a result, any rules that exist with lower priorities (higher numbers) that have the same attributes as rules with higher priorities are not processed.
Source or destination	Any, or an individual IP address, classless inter-domain routing (CIDR) block (10.0.0.0/24, for example), service tag, or application security group. If you specify an address for an Azure resource, specify the private IP address assigned to the resource. Network security groups are processed after Azure translates a public IP address to a private IP address for inbound traffic, and before Azure translates a private IP address to a public IP address for outbound traffic. Learn more about Azure IP addresses. Specifying a range, a service tag, or application security group, enables you to create fewer security rules. The ability to specify multiple individual IP addresses and ranges (you cannot specify multiple service tags or application groups) in a rule is referred to as augmented security rules. Augmented security rules can only be created in network security groups created through the Resource Manager deployment model. You cannot specify multiple IP addresses and IP address ranges in network security groups created through the classic deployment model. Learn more about Azure deployment models.
Protocol	TCP, UDP, ICMP or Any.
Direction	Whether the rule applies to inbound, or outbound traffic.
Port range	You can specify an individual or range of ports. For example, you could specify 80 or 10000-10005. Specifying ranges enables you to create fewer security rules. Augmented security rules can only be created in network security groups created through the Resource Manager deployment model. You cannot specify multiple ports or port ranges in the same security rule in network security groups created through the classic deployment model.
Action	Allow or deny

For more information, please visit:

https://docs.microsoft.com/en-us/azure/virtual-network/security-overview

Question 32:
A company is looking at the possibility of using Azure Government for development of their cloud-based solutions.

Which of the following customers are allowed to use Azure Government?

Choose 2 answers from the options given below

- ☐ A Canadian government contractor
- ☐ A European government contractor
- ☐ A United States government entity (Correct)
- ☐ A United States government contractor (Correct)
- ☐ A European government entity

Explanation

C & D *because US government agencies or their partners interested in cloud services that meet government security and compliance requirements, can be confident that Microsoft Azure Government provides world-class security, protection, and compliance services. Azure Government delivers a dedicated cloud enabling government agencies and their partners to transform mission-critical workloads to the cloud. Azure Government services handle data that is subject to certain government regulations and requirements, such as FedRAMP, NIST*

Question 33:
A company plans to purchase a Microsoft Azure Support plan.

Below is a key requirement for the support plan:

- Ensure that for high severity cases, there is a minimum initial response time of 10 minutes

A recommendation is made to purchase the Basic Support plan Would this recommendation fulfill the requirement

- ○ Yes
- ○ **No** (Correct)

Explanation

B. No, *because the Basic support tier doesn't include Case Severity/Response Times compared to the Developer, Standard, and Professional Direct plans.*

	Basic Request support	DEVELOPER Purchase support	STANDARD Purchase support	PROFESSIONAL DIRECT Purchase support
Price	Included for all Azure customers	$29 per month	$100 per month	$1,000 per month
Scope	Included for all Azure customers	Trial and non-production environments	Production workload environments	Business-critical dependence
Billing and subscription management support	✔	✔	✔	✔
24/7 self-help resources, including Microsoft Learn, Azure portal how-to videos, documentation, and community support	✔	✔	✔	✔
Ability to submit as many support tickets as you need	✔	✔	✔	✔
Azure Advisor—your free, personalized guide to Azure best practices	✔	✔	✔	✔
Azure health status and notifications	✔	✔	✔	✔
24/7 access to technical support by email and phone		Available during business hours by email only.	✔	✔
Case severity and response time		Minimal business impact (Sev C): Within eight business hours[1]	Minimal business impact (Sev C): Within eight business hours[1] Moderate business impact (Sev B): Within four hours Critical business impact (Sev A): Within one hour	Minimal business impact (Sev C): Within four business hours[1] Moderate business impact (Sev B): Within two hours Critical business impact (Sev A): Within one hour
Third-party software support with interoperability and configuration guidance and troubleshooting		✔	✔	✔
Architecture Support		General guidance	General guidance	Guidance from a pool of ProDirect delivery managers
Operations Support				Service reviews and advisory consultation from a pool of ProDirect delivery managers
Training				Webinars led by Azure engineers
Proactive Guidance				From a pool of ProDirect delivery managers

For more information, please visit:

https://azure.microsoft.com/en-us/support/plans/

Question 34:

A company plans to purchase a Microsoft Azure Support plan. Below is a key requirement for the support plan:

- Ensure that for high severity cases, there is a minimum initial response time of less than 1 hour.

- Ensure that the support plan is the most cost-effective.

A recommendation is made to purchase the Professional Direct Support plan

Would this recommendation fulfill the requirement?

- ○ Yes
- ○ No (Correct)

Explanation

B. No. Although, *the Professional Direct Support plan DOES include a 1-hour window for critical business impact but is not a cost-effective option here. The Standard support plan also has a 1-hour window for critical business impact and is less costly as compared to the Professional Direct support plan.*

Therefore, choosing the Professional Direct support plan won't fulfill both of our requirements.

	Basic Request support	DEVELOPER Purchase support	STANDARD Purchase support	PROFESSIONAL DIRECT Purchase support
Price	Included for all Azure customers	$29 per month	$100 per month	$1,000 per month
Scope	Included for all Azure customers	Trial and non-production environments	Production workload environments	Business-critical dependence
Billing and subscription management support	✓	✓	✓	✓
24/7 self-help resources, including Microsoft Learn, Azure portal how-to videos, documentation, and community support	✓	✓	✓	✓
Ability to submit as many support tickets as you need	✓	✓	✓	✓
Azure Advisor—your free, personalized guide to Azure best practices	✓	✓	✓	✓
Azure health status and notifications	✓	✓	✓	✓
24/7 access to technical support by email and phone		Available during business hours by email only	✓	✓
Case severity and response time		Minimal business impact (Sev C): Within eight business hours[1]	Minimal business impact (Sev C): Within eight business hours[1] Moderate business impact (Sev B): Within four hours Critical business impact (Sev A): Within one hour	Minimal business impact (Sev C): Within four business hours[1] Moderate business impact (Sev B): Within two hours Critical business impact (Sev A): Within one hour
Third-party software support with interoperability and configuration guidance and troubleshooting		✓	✓	✓
Architecture Support		General guidance	General guidance	Guidance from a pool of ProDirect delivery managers
Operations Support				Service reviews and advisory consultation from a pool of ProDirect delivery managers
Training				Webinars led by Azure engineers
Proactive Guidance				From a pool of ProDirect delivery managers

For more information, please visit:

https://azure.microsoft.com/en-us/support/plans/

Question 35:
A company plans to purchase a Microsoft Azure Support plan.

Below is a key requirement for the support plan:

- Ensure that for moderate severity cases, there is a minimum initial response time of 2 hours.

A recommendation is made to purchase the Professional Direct support plan.

Would this recommendation fulfill the requirement?

- ○ **Yes** (Correct)
- ○ No

Explanation

A. Yes, *the Professional Direct plan would ensure that for moderate severity cases, there is a minimum initial response time of 2 hours.*

	Basic Request support	DEVELOPER Purchase support	STANDARD Purchase support	PROFESSIONAL DIRECT Purchase support
Price	Included for all Azure customers	$29 per month	$100 per month	$1,000 per month
Scope	Included for all Azure customers	Trial and non-production environments	Production workload environments	Business-critical dependence
Billing and subscription management support	✓	✓	✓	✓
24/7 self help resources, including Microsoft Learn, Azure portal how-to videos, documentation, and community support	✓	✓	✓	✓
Ability to submit as many support tickets as you need	✓	✓	✓	✓
Azure Advisor—your free, personalized guide to Azure best practices	✓	✓	✓	✓
Azure health status and notifications	✓	✓	✓	✓
24/7 access to technical support by email and phone		Available during business hours by email only.	✓	✓
Case severity and response time		Minimal business impact (Sev C): Within eight business hours¹	Minimal business impact (Sev C): Within eight business hours¹ Moderate business impact (Sev B): Within four hours Critical business impact (Sev A): Within one hour	Minimal business impact (Sev C): Within four business hours¹ Moderate business impact (Sev B): Within two hours Critical business impact (Sev A): Within one hour
Third-party software support with interoperability and configuration guidance and troubleshooting		✓	✓	✓
Architecture Support		General guidance	General guidance	Guidance from a pool of ProDirect delivery managers
Operations Support				Service reviews and advisory consultation from a pool of ProDirect delivery managers
Training				Webinars led by Azure engineers
Proactive Guidance				From a pool of ProDirect delivery managers

For more information, please visit:

https://azure.microsoft.com/en-us/support/plans/

Question 36:
A company is planning on deploying a web server and database server as shown in the architecture diagram below.

You have to ensure that traffic restrictions are in place so that the database server can only communicate with the web server.

Larger image

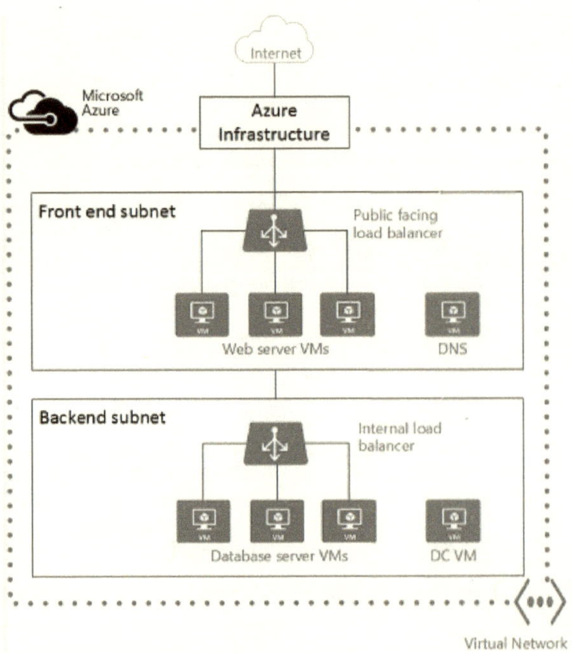

Which of the following would you recommend for implementing these restrictions?

- ○ Network security groups (NSGs) (Correct)
- ○ Azure Service Bus
- ○ A local network gateway
- ○ A Virtual Private Gateway

Explanation

A. Network security groups (NSGs) because with NSGs you can filter network traffic to and from Azure resources in an Azure virtual network with a network security group. A network security group contains security rules that allow or deny inbound network traffic to, or outbound network traffic from, several types of Azure resources.

For more information, please visit:

https://docs.microsoft.com/en-us/azure/virtual-network/security-overview

Question 37:
A company wants to make use of a Microsoft Azure service in private preview.

Are Azure services in private preview available to all customers?

- ○ Yes
- ○ **No** (Correct)

Explanation

B. No, *because the private preview is only available to certain Azure customers for evaluation purposes. The public preview is available to all Azure customers. ... Azure features that have been successfully evaluated and tested will typically be released to customers as part of the generally available product integrated into Azure.*

For more information, please visit:

https://azure.microsoft.com/en-us/support/legal/preview-supplemental-terms/

Question 38:
A company wants to make use of a Microsoft Azure service in public preview.

Are Azure services in public preview available to all customers?

- ○ **Yes** (Correct)
- ○ No

Explanation

A. Yes, *Azure may include preview, beta, or other pre-release features, services, software, or regions offered by Microsoft to obtain customer feedback ("Previews"). Previews are made available to you on the condition that you agree to these terms of use, which supplement your agreement governing use of Azure. Public preview is available to all Azure customers.*

PREVIEWS ARE PROVIDED "AS-IS," "WITH ALL FAULTS," AND "AS AVAILABLE," AND ARE EXCLUDED FROM THE SERVICE LEVEL AGREEMENTS AND LIMITED WARRANTY. Previews may not be covered by customer support. Previews may be subject to reduced or different security, compliance and privacy commitments, as further explained in the Microsoft Online Services Privacy Statement, Microsoft Azure Trust Center, the Online Services Terms, and any additional notices provided with the Preview. Customers should not use Previews to process Personal Data or other data that is subject to heightened compliance requirements. Certain named Previews may also be subject to additional terms set forth below, if any. We may change or discontinue Previews at any time without notice. We also may choose not to release a Preview into "General Availability."

For more information, please visit:

https://azure.microsoft.com/en-us/support/legal/preview-supplemental-terms/

Question 39:

A company is planning on setting up a Microsoft Azure account.

Can they purchase multiple Azure subscriptions and tie them to the single Azure account?

- ○ **Yes** (Correct)
- ○ No

Explanation

A. **Yes,** *because a billing account is created when you sign up to use Azure. You use your billing account to manage your invoices, payments, and track costs. You can have access to multiple billing accounts. For example, you might have signed up for Azure for your personal projects. You could also have access through your organization's Enterprise Agreement or Microsoft Customer Agreement. For each of these scenarios, you would have a separate billing account.*

Azure portal currently supports the following type of billing accounts:

Microsoft Online Services Program: A billing account for a Microsoft Online Services Program is created when you sign up for Azure through the Azure website. For example, when you sign up for an Azure Free Account, account with pay-as-you-go rates or as a Visual studio subscriber.

Enterprise Agreement: A billing account for an Enterprise Agreement is created when your organization signs an Enterprise Agreement (EA) to use Azure.

Microsoft Customer Agreement: A billing account for a Microsoft Customer Agreement is created when your organization works with a Microsoft representative to sign a Microsoft Customer Agreement. Some customers in select regions, who sign up through the Azure website for an account with pay-as-you-go rates or upgrade their Azure Free Account may have a billing account for a Microsoft Customer Agreement as well. For more information, see Get started with your billing account for Microsoft Customer Agreement.

Microsoft Online Services Program

Scope	Definition
Billing account	Represents a single owner (Account administrator) for one or more Azure subscriptions. An Account Administrator is authorized to perform various billing tasks like create subscriptions, view invoices or change the billing for subscriptions.
Subscription	Represents a grouping of Azure resources. Invoice is generated at this scope. It has its own payment methods that are used to pay its invoice.

For more information, please visit:

https://docs.microsoft.com/en-us/azure/billing/billing-view-all-accounts

Question 40:
A company has multiple Microsoft Azure subscriptions.

They want to merge the subscriptions into one.

Do they need to contact Microsoft to merge the subscriptions?

- ○ Yes
- ○ **No** (Correct)

Explanation

B. No, *you don't need to contact Microsoft for this request. You can transfer subscriptions between your accounts. Your accounts are conceptually considered accounts of two different users so you can use the above steps to transfer subscriptions between your accounts. Using "Cost Management + Billing" within the Azure Portal.*

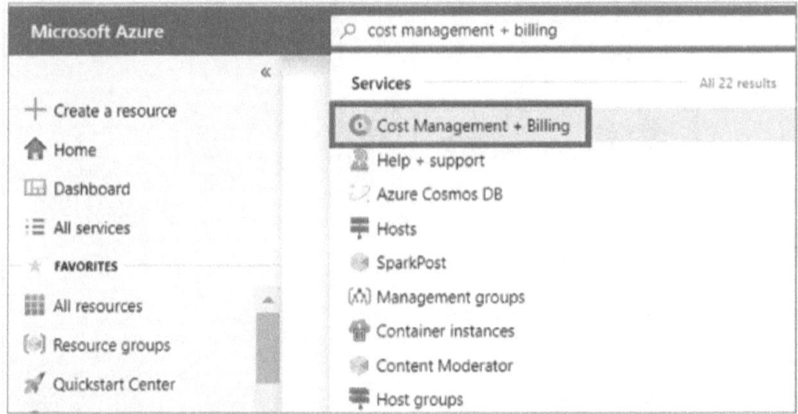

For more information, please visit:

https://docs.microsoft.com/en-us/azure/billing/billing-subscription-transfer

---

Question 41:
A company needs to deploy several Virtual Machines (VMs).

Each of these Virtual Machines (VMs) will have the same set of permissions.

To minimize the administrative overhead, in which method would you deploy the Azure Virtual Machines?

- ○ Azure policies

- ○ Azure Virtual Machine Scale sets
- ○ **Azure Resource Manager** (Correct)
- ○ Azure Tags

Explanation

C. *Azure Resource Manager because Azure Resource Manager is the deployment and management service for Azure. It provides a management layer that enables you to create, update, and delete resources in your Azure subscription. You use management features, like access control, locks, and tags, to secure and organize your resources after deployment.*

Consistent management layer

When a user sends a request from any of the Azure tools, APIs, or SDKs, Resource Manager receives the request. It authenticates and authorizes the request. Resource Manager sends the request to the Azure service, which takes the requested action. Because all requests are handled through the same API, you see consistent results and capabilities in all the different tools.

The following image shows the role Azure Resource Manager plays in handling Azure requests.

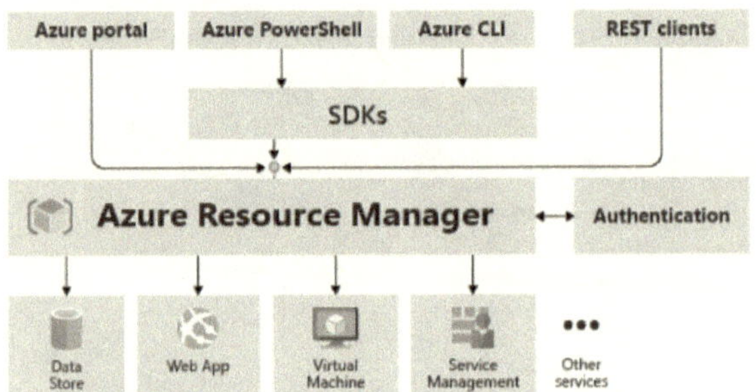

All capabilities that are available in the portal are also available through PowerShell, Azure CLI, REST APIs, and client SDKs. Functionality initially released through APIs will be represented in the portal within 180 days of initial release.

For more information, please visit:

https://docs.microsoft.com/en-us/azure/azure-resource-manager/resource-group-overview

Question 42:
An application consists of a set of virtual machines hosted in a Virtual Network.

In a month, the application seems to have a load of around 20% for 3 weeks.

During the last week, the load on the application reached 80%.

Which of the following concept would you implement to ensure least cost and efficiency of the underlying application infrastructure?

- ○ High availability
- ○ **Elasticity** (Correct)

- ○ Disaster recovery
- ○ Fault tolerance

Explanation

B. Elasticity *because Elastic computing is the ability to quickly expand or decrease computer processing, memory, and storage resources to meet changing demands without worrying about capacity planning and engineering for peak usage. Typically controlled by system monitoring tools, elastic computing matches the amount of resources allocated to the amount of resources actually needed without disrupting operations. With cloud elasticity, a company avoids paying for unused capacity or idle resources and doesn't have to worry about investing in the purchase or maintenance of additional resources and equipment.*

While security and limited control are concerns to take into account when considering elastic cloud computing, it has many benefits. Elastic computing is more efficient than your typical IT infrastructure, is typically automated so it doesn't have to rely on human administrators around the clock, and offers continuous availability of services by avoiding unnecessary slowdowns or service interruptions.

For more information, please visit:

https://azure.microsoft.com/en-us/overview/what-is-elastic-computing/

Question 43:
A company wants to start using Microsoft Azure.

They want to make use of availability zones within Azure.

Which of the following is associated with the concept of availability zones within Microsoft Azure?

- ○ Region failure
- ○ Resource failure
- ○ Data Center failure (Correct)
- ○ Azure failure

Explanation

C. Data Center failure *because Availability Zones is a high-availability offering that protects your applications and data from datacenter failures. Availability Zones are unique physical locations within an Azure region. Each zone is made up of one or more datacenters equipped with independent power, cooling, and networking. To ensure resiliency, there's a minimum of three separate zones in all enabled regions. The physical separation of Availability Zones within a region protects applications and data from datacenter failures. Zone-redundant services replicate your applications and data across Availability Zones to protect from single-points-of-failure. With Availability Zones, Azure offers industry best 99.99% VM uptime SLA.*

An Availability Zone in an Azure region is a combination of a fault domain and an update domain. For example, if you create three or more VMs across three zones in an Azure region, your VMs are effectively distributed across three fault domains and three update domains. The Azure platform recognizes this distribution across update domains to make sure that VMs in different zones are not updated at the same time.

Build high-availability into your application architecture by co-locating your compute, storage, networking, and data resources within a zone and replicating in other zones. Azure services that support Availability Zones fall into two categories:

Zonal services – you pin the resource to a specific zone (for example, virtual machines, managed disks, Standard IP addresses), or

Zone-redundant services – platform replicates automatically across zones (for example, zone-redundant storage, SQL Database).

To achieve comprehensive business continuity on Azure, build your application architecture using the combination of Availability Zones with Azure region pairs. You can synchronously replicate your applications and data using Availability Zones within an Azure region for high-availability and asynchronously replicate across Azure regions for disaster recovery protection.

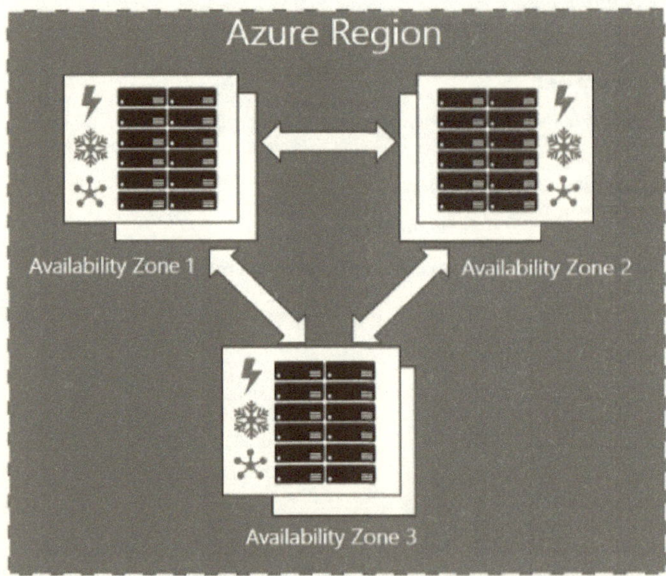

For more information, please visit:

https://docs.microsoft.com/en-us/azure/availability-zones/az-overview

Question 44:
A company wants to start using Microsoft Azure.

They want to make use of availability zones within Azure.

If they deploy resources across all regions in Azure, can they make use of availability zones in all regions in Azure?

- ○ Yes
- ○ **No** (Correct)

Explanation

B. No, *because Availability Zones are physically separate locations within an Azure region. Each Availability Zone is made up of one or more datacenters equipped with independent power, cooling, and networking. Availability Zones allow customers to run mission-critical applications with high availability and low-latency replication although their are not enough availability zones world wide though to implement due to the lack of a availability zone not within a specific region.*

There are dedicated regions for US Government as per the image below – US Gov Arizona, US Gov Iowa, US Gov Texas, US Gov Virginia, US DoD East and US DoD Central.

You cannot deploy resources in these regions as these are dedicated to US Government. The question asks for "............make use of availability zones in all regions in Azure"

The answer is NO because the normal user is not used to deploy resources in these regions, let alone using the availability zones in these regions

For more information, please visit:

https://azure.microsoft.com/en-us/global-infrastructure/regions/

Question 45:
A company is planning on creating resources for different departments within Microsoft Azure.

They want to ensure that they get the bills by the departments.

Which of the following should you consider implementing for this requirement?

- ○ Azure locks
- ○ **Azure Tags** (Correct)
- ○ Azure Monitor
- ○ Azure Advisor

Explanation

B. Azure Tags *because with Azure Tags, you apply tags to your Azure resources to logically organize them into a taxonomy. Each tag consists of a name and a value pair. For example, you can apply the name "Environment" and the value "Production" to all the resources in production.*

After you apply tags, you can retrieve all the resources in your subscription with that tag name and value. Tags enable you to retrieve related resources from different resource groups. This approach is helpful when you need to organize resources for billing or management such as certain departments like HR or Accounting.

Limitations

The following limitations apply to tags:

- Not all resource types support tags. To determine if you can apply a tag to a resource type, see Tag support for Azure resources.

- Each resource or resource group can have a maximum of 50 tag name/value pairs. If you need to apply more tags than the maximum allowed number, use a JSON string for the tag value. The JSON string can contain many values that are applied to a single tag name. A resource group can contain many resources that each have 50 tag name/value pairs.

- The tag name is limited to 512 characters, and the tag value is limited to 256 characters. For storage accounts, the tag name is limited to 128 characters, and the tag value is limited to 256 characters.

- Generalized VMs don't support tags.

- Tags applied to the resource group are not inherited by the resources in that resource group.

- Tags can't be applied to classic resources such as Cloud Services.

- Tag names can't contain these characters: <, >, %, &, \, ?, /

For more information, please visit:

https://docs.microsoft.com/en-us/azure/azure-resource-manager/resource-group-using-tags

Question 46:

A company needs to create a set of resources within Microsoft Azure.

For IT Administrators, there is a requirement in which they may only create resources in a certain region.

Which of the following can help achieve this?

- ○ Azure Tags
- ○ Azure Policies (Correct)
- ○ Azure Resource Groups
- ○ Azure Locks

Explanation

B. Azure Policies *because Azure Policies is really governance validation that your organization can achieve its goals through effective and efficient use of IT. It meets this need by creating clarity between business goals and IT projects.*

Does your company experience a significant number of IT issues that never seem to get resolved? Good IT governance involves planning your initiatives and setting priorities on a strategic level to help manage and prevent issues. This strategic need is where Azure Policy comes in.

Azure Policy is a service in Azure that you use to create, assign, and manage policies. These policies enforce different rules and effects over your resources, so those resources stay compliant with your corporate standards and service level agreements. Azure Policy meets this need by evaluating your resources for non-compliance with assigned policies. All data stored by Azure Policy is encrypted at rest.

For example, you can have a policy to allow only a certain SKU size of virtual machines in your environment. Once this policy is implemented, new and existing resources are evaluated for compliance. With the right type of policy, existing resources can be brought into compliance. This would also apply to the IT administrator in the question who can only create resources in a certain region.

A policy assignment is a policy definition that has been assigned to take place within a specific scope. This scope could range from a management group to a resource group. The term *scope* refers to all the resource groups, subscriptions, or management groups that the policy definition is assigned to. Policy assignments are inherited by all child resources. This design means that a policy applied to a resource group is also applied to resources in that resource group. However, you can exclude a subscope from the policy assignment.

For example, at the subscription scope, you can assign a policy that prevents the creation of networking resources. You could exclude a resource group in that subscription that is intended for networking infrastructure. You then grant access to this networking resource group to users that you trust with creating networking resources.

In another example, you might want to assign a resource type allow list policy at the management group level. And then assign a more permissive policy (allowing more resource types) on a child management group or even directly on subscriptions. However, this example wouldn't work because policy is an explicit deny system. Instead, you need to exclude the child

Question 47:
A company is planning on using the Microsoft Azure Content Delivery Service.

Which of the following is the right cloud concept to which the Azure Content Delivery service belongs to?

- ○ Infrastructure as a service (IaaS)
- ○ Platform as a service (PaaS) (Correct)
- ○ Software as a service (SaaS)
- ○ Function as a service (FaaS)

Explanation

B. Platform as a service (PaaS) *that is what Azure Content Delivery Network (CDN) is. It's a
global CDN solution for delivering high-bandwidth content. It can be hosted in Azure or any
other location. With Azure CDN, you can cache static objects loaded from Azure Blob storage,
a web application, or any publicly accessible web server, by using the closest point of presence
(POP) server. Azure CDN can also accelerate dynamic content, which cannot be cached, by
leveraging various network and routing optimizations.*

How it works

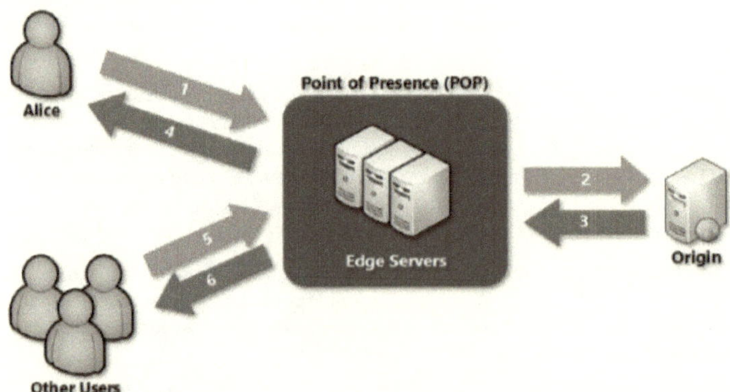

For more information, please visit:

https://docs.microsoft.com/en-us/azure/cdn/cdn-overview

Question 48:
A company wants to host an application within Microsoft Azure.

The application connects to a database in Azure.

The company would like to store the database password in a secure location.

You recommend the usage of the Azure Key Vault for storage of the password.

Would this fulfill the requirement?

- ○ Yes (Correct)
- ○ No

Explanation

A. Yes, *because Azure Key Vault is a tool for securely storing and accessing secrets. A secret is anything that you want to tightly control access to, such as API keys, passwords, or certificates. A vault is logical group of secrets.*

Here are other important terms:

Tenant: A tenant is the organization that owns and manages a specific instance of Microsoft cloud services. It's most often used to refer to the set of Azure and Office 365 services for an organization.

Vault owner: A vault owner can create a key vault and gain full access and control over it. The vault owner can also set up auditing to log who accesses secrets and keys. Administrators can control the key lifecycle. They can roll to a new version of the key, back it up, and do related tasks.

Vault consumer: A vault consumer can perform actions on the assets inside the key vault when the vault owner grants the consumer access. The available actions depend on the permissions granted.

Resource: A resource is a manageable item that's available through Azure. Common examples are virtual machine, storage account, web app, database, and virtual network. There are many more.

Resource group: A resource group is a container that holds related resources for an Azure solution. The resource group can include all the resources for the solution, or only those resources that you want to manage as a group. You decide how you want to allocate resources to resource groups, based on what makes the most sense for your organization.

Service principal: An Azure service principal is a security identity that user-created apps, services, and automation tools use to access specific Azure resources. Think of it as a "user identity" (username and password or certificate) with a specific role, and tightly controlled permissions. A service principal should only need to do specific things, unlike a general user identity. It improves security if you grant it only the minimum permission level that it needs to perform its management tasks.

Azure Active Directory (Azure AD): Azure AD is the Active Directory service for a tenant. Each directory has one or more domains. A directory can have many subscriptions associated with it, but only one tenant.

Azure tenant ID: A tenant ID is a unique way to identify an Azure AD instance within an Azure subscription.

Managed identities: Azure Key Vault provides a way to securely store credentials and other keys and secrets, but your code needs to authenticate to Key Vault to retrieve them. Using a managed identity makes solving this problem simpler by giving Azure services an automatically managed identity in Azure AD. You can use this identity to authenticate to Key Vault or any service that supports Azure AD authentication, without having any credentials in your code. For more information, see the following image and the overview of managed identities for Azure resources.

For more information, please visit:

https://docs.microsoft.com/en-us/azure/key-vault/basic-concepts

Question 49:
A company wants to host an application within Microsoft Azure.

The application connects to a database in Azure.

The company to store the database password in a secure location.

You recommend the usage of the Azure Security Center for storage of the password.

Would this fulfill the requirement?

- ○ Yes
- ○ **No** (Correct)

Explanation

B. No, *because the Azure Security Center is a unified infrastructure security management system that strengthens the security posture of your data centers, and provides advanced threat protection across your hybrid workloads in the cloud - whether they're in Azure or not - as well as on premises.*

Keeping your resources safe is a joint effort between your cloud provider, Azure, and you, the customer. You have to make sure your workloads are secure as you move to the cloud, and at the same time, when you move to IaaS (infrastructure as a service) there is more customer responsibility than there was in PaaS (platform as a service), and SaaS (software as a service). Azure Security Center provides you the tools needed to harden your network, secure your services and make sure you're on top of your security posture.

Azure Security Center addresses the three most urgent security challenges:

Rapidly changing workloads – It's both a strength and a challenge of the cloud. On the one hand, end users are empowered to do more. On the other, how do you make sure that the ever-changing services people are using and creating are up to your security standards and follow security best practices?

Increasingly sophisticated attacks - Wherever you run your workloads, the attacks keep getting more sophisticated. You have to secure your public cloud workloads, which are, in effect, an Internet facing workload that can leave you even more vulnerable if you don't follow security best practices.

Security skills are in short supply - The number of security alerts and alerting systems far outnumbers the number of administrators with the necessary background and experience to make sure your environments are protected. Staying up-to-date with the latest attacks is a constant challenge, making it impossible to stay in place while the world of security is an ever-changing front.

For more information, please visit:

https://docs.microsoft.com/en-us/azure/security-center/security-center-intro

Question 50:
A company wants to host an application within Microsoft Azure.

The application connects to a database in Azure.

The company to store the database password in a secure location.

You recommend the usage of the Azure Advisor for storage of the password.

Would this fulfill the requirement?

- ○ Yes
- ○ **No** (Correct)

Explanation

B. No, *because Azure Advisor is a personalized cloud consultant that helps you follow best practices to optimize your Azure deployments. It analyzes your resource configuration and usage telemetry and then recommends solutions that can help you improve the cost effectiveness, performance, high availability, and security of your Azure resources.*

With Advisor, you can:

-Get proactive, actionable, and personalized best practices recommendations.

-Improve the performance, security, and high availability of your resources, as you identify opportunities to reduce your overall Azure spend.

-Get recommendations with proposed actions inline.

The Advisor dashboard displays personalized recommendations for all your subscriptions. You can apply filters to display recommendations for specific subscriptions and resource types. The recommendations are divided into four categories:

- **High Availability**: To ensure and improve the continuity of your business-critical applications. For more information, see Advisor High Availability recommendations.

- **Security**: To detect threats and vulnerabilities that might lead to security breaches. For more information, see Advisor Security recommendations.

- **Performance**: To improve the speed of your applications. For more information, see Advisor Performance recommendations.

- **Cost**: To optimize and reduce your overall Azure spending. For more information, see Advisor Cost recommendations.

- **Operational Excellence**: To help you achieve process and workflow efficiency, resource manageability and deployment best practices. , For more information, see Advisor Operational Excellence recommendations.

For more information, please visit:

https://docs.microsoft.com/en-us/azure/advisor/advisor-overview

Question 51:
A company needs to connect their on-premise data center to an Azure Virtual Network using a Site-to-Site connection.

Larger image

Virtual network
Quickstart tutorial

Load Balancer
Learn more

Application Gateway
Learn more

Virtual network gateway
Learn more

Which of the following would you create as part of this implementation?

- ○ Virtual Network

- ○ Load Balancer
- ○ Application Gateway
- ○ Virtual Network Gateway (Correct)

Explanation

C. Virtual Network Gateway *because with a VPN gateway is a specific type of virtual network gateway that is used to send encrypted traffic between an Azure virtual network and an on-premises location over the public Internet. You can also use a VPN gateway to send encrypted traffic between Azure virtual networks over the Microsoft network. Each virtual network can have only one VPN gateway. However, you can create multiple connections to the same VPN gateway. When you create multiple connections to the same VPN gateway, all VPN tunnels share the available gateway bandwidth.*

Site-to-Site and Multi-Site (IPsec/IKE VPN tunnel)

Site-to-Site

A Site-to-Site (S2S) VPN gateway connection is a connection over IPsec/IKE (IKEv1 or IKEv2) VPN tunnel. S2S connections can be used for cross-premises and hybrid configurations. A S2S connection requires a VPN device located on-premises that has a public IP address assigned to it. For information about selecting a VPN device, see the VPN Gateway FAQ - VPN devices.

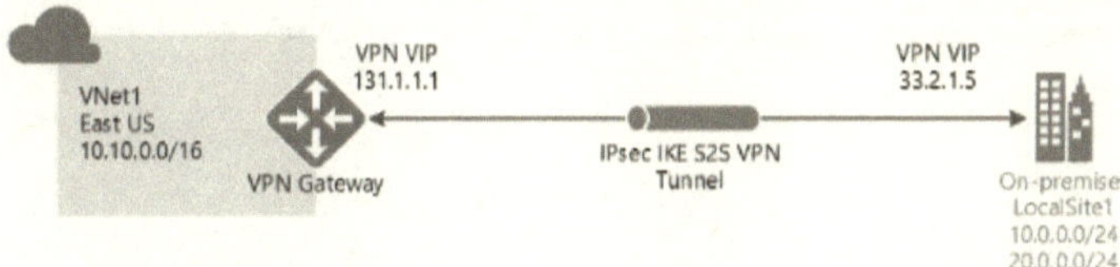

For more information, please visit:

https://docs.microsoft.com/en-us/azure/vpn-gateway/vpn-gateway-about-vpngateways

Question 52:
A company is planning on setting up a private cloud network.

Which of the following is an advantage of setting up a private cloud network?

- ○ A Private Cloud environment can only support an Infrastructure as a service model
- ○ Private Cloud environment can only support a Platform as a service model
- ○ The Private Cloud environment can be rolled out to the general public
- ○ The Private Cloud environment can be rolled out to select users (Correct)

Explanation

D. The Private Cloud environment can be rolled out to select users *is correct because a private cloud consists of computing resources used exclusively by one business or organization. The private cloud can be physically located at your organization's on-site datacenter, or it can be hosted by a third-party service provider. But in a private cloud, the services and infrastructure are always maintained on a private network and the hardware and software are dedicated* *solely to your organization. In this way, a private cloud can make it easier for an organization to customize its resources to meet specific IT requirements. Private clouds are often used by government agencies, financial institutions, any other mid- to large-size organizations with business-critical operations seeking enhanced control over their environment.*

Advantages of a private clouds:

More flexibility—your organization can customize its cloud environment to meet specific business needs.

Improved security—resources are not shared with others, so higher levels of control and security are possible.

High scalability—private clouds still afford the scalability and efficiency of a public cloud.

For more information, please visit:

https://azure.microsoft.com/en-us/overview/what-are-private-public-hybrid-clouds/

Question 53:
A company wants to setup resources within Microsoft Azure.

They want a way to manage identities within Azure.

Which of the following is used as an Identity Management solution in Azure?

- ○ **Azure AD** (Correct)
- ○ Azure Advisor
- ○ Azure Security Center
- ○ Azure Monitor

Explanation

A. Azure AD is correct because Azure Active Directory is Microsoft's cloud-based identity and access management service, which helps your employees sign in and access resources in:

External resources, such as Microsoft Office 365, the Azure portal, and thousands of other SaaS applications.

Internal resources, such as apps on your corporate network and intranet, along with any cloud apps developed by your own organization.

Who uses Azure AD?

Azure AD is intended for:

- **IT admins.** As an IT admin, you can use Azure AD to control access to your apps and your app resources, based on your business requirements. For example, you can use Azure AD to require multi-factor authentication when accessing important organizational resources. Additionally, you can use Azure AD to automate user provisioning between your existing Windows Server AD and your cloud apps, including Office 365. Finally, Azure AD gives you powerful tools to automatically help protect user identities and credentials and to meet your access governance requirements. To get started, sign up for a free 30-day Azure Active Directory Premium trial.

- **App developers.** As an app developer, you can use Azure AD as a standards-based approach for adding single sign-on (SSO) to your app, allowing it to work with a user's pre-existing credentials. Azure AD also provides APIs that can help you build personalized app experiences using existing organizational data. To get started, sign up for a free 30-day Azure Active Directory Premium trial. For more information, you can also see Azure Active Directory for developers.

- **Microsoft 365, Office 365, Azure, or Dynamics CRM Online subscribers.** As a subscriber, you're already using Azure AD. Each Microsoft 365, Office 365, Azure, and Dynamics CRM Online tenant is automatically an Azure AD tenant. You can immediately start to manage access to your integrated cloud apps.

For more information, please visit:

https://docs.microsoft.com/en-us/azure/active-directory/fundamentals/active-directory-whatis

Question 54:
You are planning on setting up a Microsoft Azure Free account.

Which of the following is not true when it comes to what is offered with an Azure Free account?

- 200 USD free credit to use for 30 days
- Free access to certain Azure products for 12 months
- Free access to all Azure products after the 12 month expiration period (Correct)
- Access to certain products that are always free

Explanation

C. Free access to all Azure products after the 12 month expiration period *because the Azure free account includes free access to Azure products for only 12 months, you don't keep access to those products unless you pay, but when you sign up, you get $200 credit to spend for the first 30 days and access to more than 25 products that are always free.*

What happens at the end of the 12 months of free products?

For 12 months after you upgrade your account, certain amounts of popular products for compute, networking, storage, and databases are free. After 12 months, any of these products you may be using will continue to run, and you'll be billed at the standard pay-as-you-go rates.

For more information, please visit:

https://azure.microsoft.com/en-us/free/free-account-faq/

Question 55:
Fill in the blank with the correct Azure service to correctly complete the statement below:

___________ is a simplified tool to build intelligent Artificial Intelligence (AI) applications.

- ○ Azure Advisor
- ○ **Azure Cognitive Services** (Correct)
- ○ **Azure DevOps**
- ○ **Azure Application Insights**

Explanation

B. Azure Cognitive Services *because Azure Cognitive Services are APIs, SDKs, and services available to help developers build intelligent applications without having direct AI or data science skills or knowledge. Azure Cognitive Services enable developers to easily add cognitive features into their applications. The goal of Azure Cognitive Services is to help developers create applications that can see, hear, speak, understand, and even begin to reason. The catalog of services within Azure Cognitive Services can be categorized into five main pillars - Vision, Speech, Language, Web Search, and Decision.*

For more information, please visit:

https://docs.microsoft.com/en-us/azure/cognitive-services/welcome